"After the war is over"

The Correspondence of Walter Hudson Pullen,

U.S. Navy Reserve, 1943-45

Edited
By
R. B. Rosenburg

After the war is over

Copyright © 2024 by Rosemont Enterprises, LLC, a cooperative agency with **BDI Publishers**.

All rights reserved. No part of this book may be reproduced or transmitted in any form by any means, electronic or mechanical, including photocopying and recording, or by any information storage and retrieval system, except as may be expressly permitted by the 1976 Copyright Act or by the publisher. Requests for permission should be made in writing via https://rosemontenterprises.com/contact/

Paperback: 978-0-9836709-9-5
Hardback: 978-0-9862965-1-2

After the war is over

For our grandchildren.

After the war is over

"It is my most earnest wish that my mom and dad can ... see this magnificent spectacle of Nature's work after the war is over...."

Walter Hudson Pullen
June 7, 1944

Walter Hudson Pullen, ca. 1949.

After the war is over

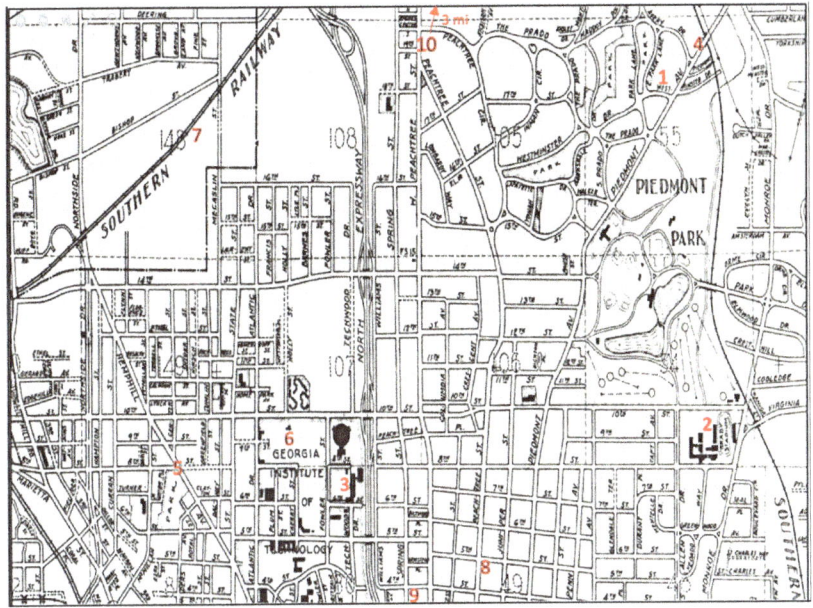

Walter Hudson Pullen's Atlanta - 1949

1. Pullen residence – 224 Westminster Drive, N.E.
2. Grady (formerly Boys') High School
3. O'Keefe Junior High School
4. Jimmye's Beauty Salon owned by Stella
5. Hemphill Avenue
6. Georgia Institute of Technology
7. Southern Railway
8. Troop #65 – St. Mark United Methodist Church
9. Sigma Chi House – 717 Spring Street
10. Second-Ponce de Leon Baptist Church

Contents

Prologue..9
Editorial method...49
Chapter 1 "I am about settled in this place."...............51
Chapter 2 "I would prefer drilling in the rain."............57
Chapter 3 "I held my first payday."............................65
Chapter 4 "I am not immune from sea-sickness."........73
Chapter 5 "I have truly a picnic."...............................87
Chapter 6 "I try to do a good job."...........................155
Chapter 7 "I cannot tell you where I am."................185
Chapter 8 "I am in the Pacific."................................221
Chapter 9 "Here I am — half way around the globe."....259
Chapter 10 "I would certainly welcome any change."....281
Chapter 11 "I should have gone into the Army."........331
Chapter 12 "I need a little money."...........................357
Epilogue..371

Index...377

PROLOGUE

Walter Hudson Pullen was born in Atlanta, Georgia, on October 28, 1919. He was the only child of Walter Stanford Pullen (1884-1957) and Stella Marie Hudson (1896-1969), who were married in Atlanta on March 1, 1918. At the time, Walter Stanford Pullen, who was from Cartersville, Georgia, was an engineer for the Southern Railway Company, working at the round house in Inman Yards. He had been with Southern Company since he was 18, and he would remain with the railroad until his death more than fifty years later. He was a dues-paying member of the Grand International Brotherhood of Locomotive Engineers, Division No. 368, Atlanta. And, according to his obituary, he attended Sandy Springs Methodist Church.

Walter Stanford's father, Thomas Jefferson Pullen (1857-1917), also was an engineer with Southern for more than thirty years, until he was struck and killed by a freight train as he attempted crossing the tracks near Marietta Street in downtown Atlanta. Walter Stanford's grandfather was Greenville Pullen (1788-1860), who was a fifer in a Georgia regiment during the War of 1812 until he broke both of his arms in a fall while building barracks in Savannah. Nevertheless, he qualified for a veteran's pension and received in 1852 a 160-acre bounty land grant in Whitfield County, Georgia, where he lived the rest of his days. Walter Stanford's mother, Anna Azar ("Allie") Stanford (1861-1897), was the daughter of a judge in Cartersville, Georgia, and a cousin to two O'Neals, father and son, who each served as governor of Alabama.

Stella's father, James Lonnie Hudson (1872-1938), worked for more than forty years for Southern Railway Company in Atlanta,

After the war is over

mostly as a locomotive engineer. Stella was the eldest of eight children, five of them girls, all born in Atlanta. Her Hudson line could be traced back to William Hudson (1571-1630), her 10th great-grandfather, who was an elder brother of Henry Hudson, the English sea explorer and navigator. Her fifth great-grandfather, Cuthbert ("Cutbird") Hudson (1732-1801), served in the American Revolution and received a bounty land grant in Franklin County, Georgia, in 1785. Stella's mother was Emma Jean Haynes (1875-1935), whose Haynes sturdy forebears had moved to Georgia from Virginia in the 1790s. She and James Lonnie Hudson married in 1895 in Atlanta, where they lived until their deaths about forty years later, by the time Walter Hudson Pullen graduated from high school.

Called by his parents, relatives, and friends "Buddy," or simply "Bud," Walter Hudson Pullen grew up in different parts of Atlanta. For the first year or so of his life, he resided on Spruce Street in Inman Park, an intown neighborhood on the east side near the round house where his father worked. By 1920 the Pullens were living with Stella's parents, some four miles northwest of Spruce, at 326 Hemphill Avenue, just west of the Georgia Institute of Technology (Georgia Tech) campus and close to the Southern Railway freight shops. In 1921, they rented a house a few doors down from the Hudsons, at 298 Hemphill. That was the same address given by an Atlanta newspaper for Walter Hudson Pullen in May 1921, when Stella entered her son in a baby show at the Atlanta Woman's Club, in which he brought home a first-place ribbon in his age group. Three years later, their address had changed to 376 Hemphill. Walter Stanford Pullen is missing in the U.S. census for 1930. But that year Stella, age 32, a telephone operator, and Bud, age 10, were listed as living with her parents and four of her siblings, at 811 Vedado Way, a two-story, 10-room home built in 1920, in the Fourth Ward. Three years later Bud indicated in his Boy Scout *Diary* that he lived at 20 11th Street, just west of Piedmont Park and three miles south of his grandmother, Emma Jean Hudson, whom he listed as his emergency contact. By 1935, according to

After the war is over

the Atlanta city directory, Walter, Stella, and Bud resided at 224 Westminster Drive in the Ansley Park neighborhood. It would be their last address together as a family.

Stella Hudson and Walter Stanford Pullen

Bud attended public schools in Atlanta, including O'Keefe Junior High School, located on Techwood Drive on the corner of 6th Street, in the heart of the Georgia Tech campus. Named for Dr. Daniel Cornelius O'Keefe, a city alderman and former Confederate surgeon during the Battle of Atlanta, who was often called the founder of the city's public school system, the school opened in 1923. When Bud was a student there a decade later, O'Keefe had an enrollment of more than 1,400 girls and boys, most of them participating in a Georgia Bicentennial costumed pageant at Georgia Tech's athletic field, the Rose Bowl, on May 5, 1933. While attending O'Keefe, he also was involved in the local Boys Scout Troop #65, sponsored by the St. Mark United Methodist Church, receiving his second-class scout badge in May 1932, earning merit badges in animal industry, swimming, and lifesaving, and marching in Armistice Day and 4th of July parades. On November 17, 1933, Bud represented Troop #65 in the annual Scout Circus at the Atlanta Municipal Auditorium, where he participated in a wheelbarrow race. His scoutmaster

After the war is over

was Dr. Frank Francisco Lamons (1900-1966), a prominent orthodontist who practiced in Atlanta for more than forty years.

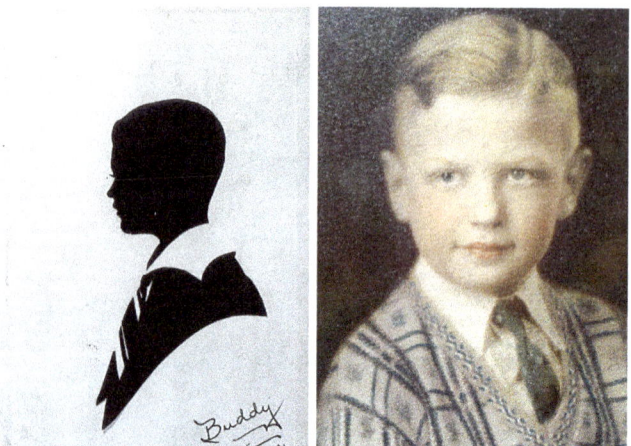

Walter H. ("Buddy") Pullen

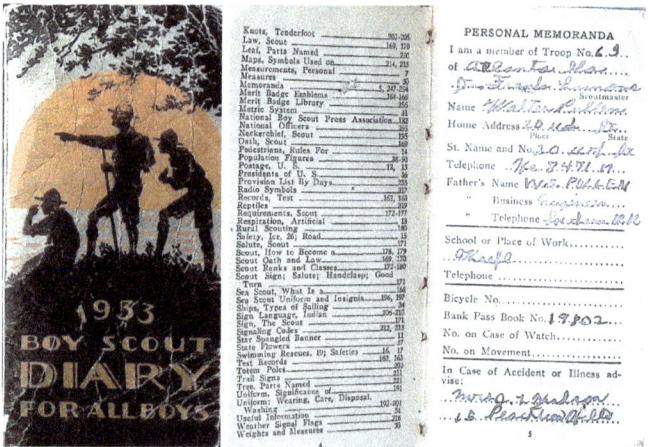

Bud's 1933 Boy Scout Diary to help keep track of "good turns," listing his grandmother as his emergency contact.

Bud also attended Boys' High School, established in 1872, which remained a school for white males until it merged with its female counterpart Girls' High, and its archrival Tech High to form Henry Grady High School in 1947. (Integrated fourteen years

After the war is over

later, Grady became Midtown High School in 2020.) The school grounds were located at Charles Allen (then Parkway) Drive and 10th Street, about a mile-long walk through Piedmont Park from the Pullen residence on Westminster Drive.

From its inception, Boys' High emphasized the classics and preparation for college and maintained demanding academic standards. Its course of studies included Latin, Greek, and German, as well as the usual modern languages, including Spanish, which Bud took. In addition, there was rhetoric, English composition, grammar and literature, and levels of physics and chemistry not usually found in Southern preparatory schools. Debates and declamations were weekly events, and every student was required to participate. During its 75 years, more than seven thousand white boys from all parts of the city enrolled in Boys' High. Far fewer graduated; barely one in ten made it through. Among its distinguished alumni was Ivan Allen, Jr. (1911-2003), Class of 1929, future mayor of Atlanta, who previously attended O'Keefe school. Two years ahead of Bud was Ernie Harwell (1918-2010), who would become a major league baseball announcer for the Detroit Tigers, and in the class behind him was Samuel Truett Cathy (1921-2014), who in 1946 would establish the fast-food chain Chick-fil-A.

Walter Pullen, Boys' High School, Alciphronian yearbook, 1938.

During his freshmen year, 1935-36, Bud joined the Boys' High School Army R.O.T.C. unit, which required cadets to wear uniforms, follow orders, and drill in formation both before and after school. Bud did not enjoy any

After the war is over

of that, so he did not return the next year. When he graduated, R.O.T.C. was the only activity listed under his name in the school's yearbook, the *Alciphronian*. Yet it does not mean that he was inactive while in high school. During those years, he was a member of the Omega chapter of Kappa Delta Kappa (K.D.K.), a social fraternity that sponsored coed dances, dinners, hayrides, swimming parties, and other events.

It was while at Boys' High School that Bud wrote a 10-page essay for 4th period entitled "History of the United States Tariff" since 1789, which is among his surviving papers. In addition, there are two of Bud's books from his Boys' High School days. One is a rare copy of the *Alciphronian* yearbook for 1938, which he signed "Walter Pullen" in black pen on the first page. There are no other signatures in it or notes or well-wishes from classmates or teachers. On page 85 of the 90-page volume in the advertisement section is one small rectangular ad for Hemlock Beauty Parlor and Barber Shop, Inc., located at Peachtree and 11th Street. Later known as Mackey's Beauty Shop, this was where his mother, Stella, worked with one of her sisters. Stella had been listed in the Atlanta city directory as a "beauty salon operator" at least since 1933. By 1940 she owned and managed Jimmye's Beauty Salon, located at 1533 Piedmont Avenue, N.E., only a 10-minute walk from their home. She continued working at Jimmye's until the early 1960s.

After the war is over

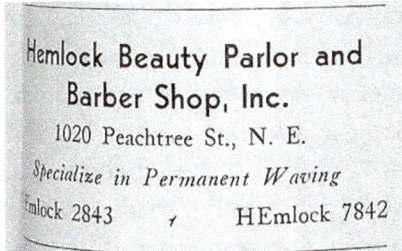

Ad in the Alciphronian yearbook (1938).

Atlanta Constitution, 1/19/1940, p. 27.

Inside front and end covers of Count Luckner, The Sea Devil (1927), presumably last checked out by Walter Pullen.

After the war is over

Bud's other book is a hardcover copy of *Count Luckner, The Sea Devil* published in 1927, authored by the internationally renowned journalist Lowell Thomas. It was last checked out from the Boys' High School library, with the due date stamped in red "JAN 22 1936." The loan card stuffed inside a sleeve affixed to the back inside cover contains the names of five other students who had borrowed the book before Bud. And there are five additional red-stamped due dates before the last one. A popular work that enticed many to go to sea, it is about an aristocratic boy who ran away from home, became an officer in the German Imperial Navy, and finally during the World War raided Allied shipping in the Atlantic and Pacific, until his ship was wrecked on the coral reef of an island in the South Seas. Given that within a few years, Bud would find himself on a ship in the middle of the South Pacific, thousands of miles from home, one wonders how often he thought about this book that he left on a shelf in his room back in Atlanta.

Atlanta Journal, 6/3/1938, p. 30.

After the war is over

Walter Pullen was one of 263 seniors who graduated from Boys' High School in June 1938. Like most of his fellow graduates, he decided to enter college; almost a third of them, including himself, chose Georgia School of Technology in Atlanta. While at Georgia Tech, he joined and served as secretary and later president of the Beta Psi chapter of the Sigma Chi fraternity. The Sigma Chi house was located at 717 Spring Street, less than half a mile from the Tech campus. He was also a member of the Industrial Management Society and the Interfraternity Council, as well as on the staff of the *Blue Print* student yearbook and Tech's student newspaper *The Technique*. During his sophomore year, 1939-40, he competed on the Georgia Tech Cross Country team, which won the Southeastern Conference championship for the fifth consecutive year, besting teams from the University of Alabama, Auburn, Georgia, and Tennessee. Although his photo appears in every *Blue Print* yearbook from 1939 through 1942, he is not listed as being a member of school's Naval R.O.T.C. program. But among his belongings today also is a copy of *Naval Terms and Definitions* (1926), Second edition, by Commander Charles C. Soule, U.S.N., that is stamped on the inside cover: "Property of Naval ROTC Unit TECH."

The Officers: KILPATRICK, BELL, MULLING, PULLEN.

Walter Pullen (far right), Sigma Chi president, Blue Print, Georgia Tech yearbook (1942).

After the war is over

Senior photo, Blue Print, Georgia Tech yearbook (1942).

Draft registration for Georgia Tech student Walter Hudson Pullen, 6' 1", 165 pounds, gray eyes, blonde hair, July 1, 1941.

On Saturday, May 16, 1942, Walter Hudson Pullen was awarded a Bachelor of Science degree in Industrial Management from Georgia Tech. Afterwards, he made his way to Saginaw, Michigan, about 75 miles northeast of Lansing, where he began working as an assistant foreman at the Saginaw Steering Gear Division plant operated by General Motors. Since 1929, the plant produced the "Hour Glass Worm and Section Gear" for GM Truck, Oldsmobile, Oakland, and Cadillac. Yet, beginning in March 1941, the plant had retooled to manufacture Browning M-1919 A4 machine guns, becoming part of the nation's "Arsenal of Democracy." In 1943, SSG began making M1 carbines as well. At the height of production, the 245,000-square-foot

After the war is over

plant had a workforce of 4,000. Since he was employed at a vital defense industry, Bud would have been classified as II-B, which exempted him from military service, if he wanted. But he chose to do his part in uniform instead.

Some two weeks after getting settled in Saginaw, on Sunday, May 31, 1942, Bud wrote his mother a brief letter by hand, which became the first in the collection of more than 150 letters transcribed and annotated for this volume. His wartime correspondence, which includes a few telegrams and several V-mails, continued through December 3, 1945.

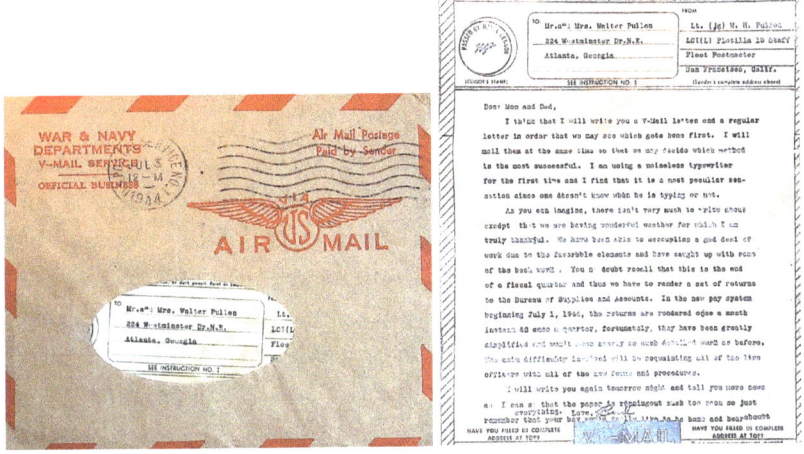

Bud's V-mail of June 24, 1944. V-mail, short for "Victory mail," involved microfilming letters cleared by military censors to reduce costs for delivery and to save space on airplanes.

Bud's letters home to his parents were but a minuscule part of a massive U.S. military mail system that flowed back and forth internationally during World War II. An unprecedented amount of mail moved about during the war from all theaters, with Army post offices, fleet post offices, and U.S. post offices flooded with mail. Each year, the number of pieces of mail increased. In 1945,

After the war is over

2.5 billion pieces went through the Army Postal Service and 8 million pieces through Navy post offices. The War Department in Washington, D.C., fully realized that frequent and rapid communication with parents, associates, and other loved ones was good for the war effort and morale. As a 1942 Annual Report to the Postmaster General stated: Receipt of mail from home "strengthen[ed] fortitude, enliven[ed] patriotism, ma[de] loneliness endurable and inspire[d] to even greater devotion the men and women who are carrying on our fight far from home and from friends."

To bring mail service to those serving worldwide, in addition to reducing costs, the military adopted the V-mail, an innovative method designed to drastically reduce the space needed to transport mail via airplanes, thus freeing up room for other valuable supplies. Although the V-mail system was only used between June 1942 and November 1945, over 1 billion items were processed through these means. Officially entitled the "Army Micro Photographic Mail Service," War Department Pamphlet No. 21-1 described V-mail as: "an expeditious mail program which provides for quick mail service to and from soldiers overseas. A special form is used that permits the letter to be photographed in microfilm. The small film is transported and then reproduced and delivered." Bud not only sent V-mails, but received them from others, including at least one that Stella mailed to him. The Navy apparently used V-Mail equipment to microfilm his pay records, as Bud indicated in his correspondence.

After the war is over

Bud and Bobby McGinty (far right), ca. 1948.

Throughout his correspondence with his parents, Bud frequently mentioned two of his closest friends who were serving in the Navy. He referenced "Hugh" nearly three dozen times and "Bobby" another two dozen. "Bobby" was Robert Franklin McGinty (1920-1994), who graduated from Marist High School a year after Bud. Born in Dalton, Georgia, McGinty was a Georgia Tech graduate, and a K.D.K. and Sigma Chi fraternity brother. When he registered for the draft on July 1, 1941, he listed his occupation as a student and his employer as Carnegie Library, 535 Luckie Street, Atlanta. He was commissioned an ensign on April 18, 1943, and served nineteen months in the Navy. Afterwards, he worked for General Motors Acceptance

After the war is over

Corporation in Atlanta and by 1950 in Chattanooga. He married Olga Marie Morris (1925-1987) on May 1, 1948, at the Cathedral of Christ the King in Atlanta. As a testimony to their friendship, Bud served as Bobby's best man. The McGintys would have five children, before retiring and relocating to the Charleston, South Carolina area.

Hugh Hawkins Howell, Jr., Boys' High School, 1938.

Rear Admiral Hugh H. Howell, Jr., ca. 1985

"Hugh" was Hugh Hawkins Howell, Jr. (1920-1990), a fellow 1938 graduate of Boys' High School and the University of Georgia. Hugh wanted Bud to be his best man, but as indicated in his letters home at the time, he was too busy. Following the war, Hugh earned his law degree from John Marshall Law School, and he practiced law in Atlanta beginning in 1946. In 1961 Georgia Governor Ernest Vandiver appointed him to the State Board of Veterans Services, which he served as chairman for more than twenty years. He was also active in the DeKalb County History Society (president), American Legion

After the war is over

(commander Post 134), Navy League (national director), Sons of the American Revolution (vice president district), Sons of Confederate Veterans (commander), Naval History Foundation, Military Order of World Wars (commander 1973-74), Old Guard of Gate City Guard (commandant), and the Ansley Golf Club. He retired from the Navy Reserve as a rear admiral. He was married twice and had three children. Hugh Howell Road, which extends from Georgia Highway 236 into Stone Mountain Park, near Atlanta, was named in the 1960s for Hugh's well-known father, who is also mentioned in Walter Hudson Pullen's correspondence.

Like Bobby and Hugh, Bud chose to serve in the Navy. He was commissioned a probationary ensign in the U.S. Navy Reserve on August 10, 1942. With a background in business and accounting and eight months on the job at General Motors, he entered active duty on January 11, 1943. Ordered to the Navy Yard in Boston, he was selected to attend Navy Supply Corps School at Harvard University's Graduate School of Business Administration in Cambridge, Massachusetts, beginning on April 19, 1943. As one of 463 student officers in the Class of August 1943, he received twenty weeks of basic training in leadership, disbursement practices, and payroll management, and the business of equipping the Navy, both afloat and ashore. Five of his letters home published as part of this collection were written while he was a student at the Navy Supply Corps School at Harvard.

Afterwards, Ensign Pullen was assigned to active duty as a disbursing (payroll) officer at the U.S. Naval Amphibious Training Base, in Solomons, lower Calvert County, Maryland, where the Patuxent River opens onto the Chesapeake Bay, some 65 miles from Washington, D.C. First established in August 1942, by war's end eventually some 68,000 sailors, Marines, coast guardsmen, and soldiers, officers and enlisted men, would learn the art of invasion by sea at Solomons, forming the major

After the war is over

components of the amphibious forces which would land at Guadalcanal, North Africa, Sicily, and D-Day. At its peak on July 22, 1944, the base housed approximately 10,150 men for training in amphibious assault procedures. "Training" might be a strong word, as essentially the early instruction at Solomons when Bud was there amounted to the crew being placed on transport ships, cruising around the Chesapeake Bay for a couple of days, and then transporting to their respective ships for shipboard duty. As a staff officer assigned to his unit's headquarters, charged with administering payrolls and submitting reports (or "returns"), Bud would spend most of his time ashore.

U.S. Navy Amphibious Training Base, Solomons, with a LST (right) and an LCI(L) in the background.

Included among those who were based at Solomons in the Fall of 1943 were members of the "Black Cat" USS LCI Flotilla 13, who with their newly launched LCI(L)s participated in mostly night maneuvers and practice landings on bay beaches and sandbars. An LCI flotilla consisted of 36 ships total, with

After the war is over

three groups of 12 ships per flotilla, two divisions per group, and 6 ships per division. Commanding the "Black Cat" Flotilla was John Henry Morrill, II (1903-1997). Born in Miller, South Dakota, he graduated from the U.S. Naval Academy in the Class of 1924. After service aboard battleships, destroyers, cruisers, even submarines, Morrill assumed in 1939 command of the minesweeper USS *Quail* (AM-15) in the Philippines at the outbreak of World War II. On December 10, 1941, in combat against enemy Japanese forces during the bombardment of Cavite Navy Yard, Corregidor, Lieutenant Commander Morrill towed several disabled surface craft alongside docks to a safe zone, thus saving the crews and vessels from serious danger. Damaged by Japanese bombs and gunfire, the *Quail* ultimately had to be scuttled in May 1942 to prevent it from being captured. Morrill's factual book, *South from Corregidor*, published by Simon and Schuster in 1943, details an escape story by him and 17 crewmembers of the *Quail* who successfully sailed the ship's 36-foot motor launch some 2,000 miles through Japanese-controlled waters from Manila Bay to Darwin, Australia. Morrill was as daring as "Count Luckner, the Sea Devil," Bud must have thought. Returning to the United States, he was eventually given command of Flotilla 13. He retired from the Navy in 1955 as a Rear Admiral and was awarded the Navy Cross and Silver Star.

Morrill photographed in Australia after escaping from Manila Bay, May-June 1942.

Among the collection of correspondence printed herein, Bud authored three letters while he was stationed at the U.S.

After the war is over

Naval Amphibious Training Base at Solomons. But he would reference his experience there several other times in subsequent letters, mostly making derogatory comments and comparisons. Solomons suffered throughout its existence from the label of being a "temporary base," which meant crowded conditions, poor facilities, and that it lacked many amenities normally afforded to other naval bases. Solomons at this time was not what Navy personnel called "good duty." Power, water, barracks, and, as Bud points out, decent officers' quarters and food, were below standard. Moreover, it was a long way from any town, and there was little transportation available. Bud ended up having to take a "long bus ride" to get to Washington, D.C., and back.

Next, from early December 1943 through early January 1944, came sea duty onboard an LCI(L), as part of the Black Cat USS LCI Flotilla 13 staff. There are five letters among his correspondence from this brief period, during which Bud's ship traveled more than 5,000 miles. LCI(L) stood for Landing Craft Infantry(Large), and despite its name, the LCI(L) was among the smallest vessels in the U.S. Navy during World War II. It was designed as a beaching craft intended to transport an infantry rifle company of approximately 188 officers and men, soldiers or Marines, to deliver them on a hostile beach once the beachhead was secured, and then to retract from the beach. The LCI(L) to which he was temporarily assigned was known by its hull number, 474, rather than a name, laid down in August 1943 at New Jersey Shipbuilding Company, Barber, New Jersey, and commissioned on October 5, 1943. It was slightly more than 158 feet long and 23 feet wide and was powered by a set of quad-mounted, General Motors diesel engines, and twin variable pitch propellers, with a maximum of 1,600 brake horsepower. It had a range of 8,000 miles at 12 knots carrying a 110-ton fuel load. Its original armament consisted of four 20-mm guns and two .50 caliber machine guns. Its original complement consisted of 4 officers and 21 enlisted men. These men had been assembled and trained at the Amphibious Training Base at Solomons.

After the war is over

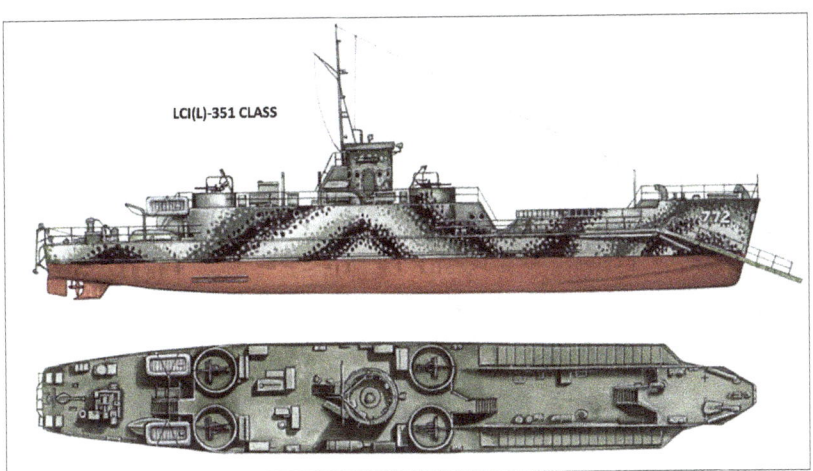

The LCI(L)-351 CLASS boats were built for hull numbers greater than 351.

But Ensign Pullen was not part of LCI(L)-474's crew. Instead, he and another staff officer, Cliff LeVee, were merely passengers, hitching a ride to their next duty assignment, along with a half dozen other Flotilla 13 enlisted members. Ensign LeVee would be Bud's constant companion or "partner" through much of the war and the subject of many of his letters home, even after the two split up. After LeVee was transferred to the States, he wrote Stella a letter, which has been included as part of Bud's wartime collection. Later he forwarded to Stella a letter that Bud had written to him, adding several comments in his own hand. Images of that letter have been reproduced below.

Cliff LeVee, Rough Roll, Navy Supply Corps School, Harvard University yearbook, August 1943.

After the war is over

A native of Aurora, Illinois, Clifford Guy LeVee (1918-2012), despite losing his father when he was seven years old, graduated from Plainfield High School (1936) and the University of Illinois (1940), with a degree in accounting. He was working as a statistician for the Chicago branch of the Washburn-Crosby Gold Medal flour milling company (General Mills) when he registered for the draft on October 16, 1940. He received a commission in the Navy in August 1942, and graduated from the Navy Supply Corps School at Harvard University in August 1943. He was in Class "H" while Bud was in Class "J," each group having about six dozen student officers. Released from active duty in November 1946, he served in the Navy Reserve the next twenty years, retiring as a lieutenant commander. In 1953 he worked as IBM department manager at U.S. Rubber Company, which he left for Caterpillar four years later. In 1961 he managed the installation and operation of the data processing system at Argonne National Laboratory, from which he retired in 1983. Active in Plainfield community affairs, LeVee served on the local school board and was involved with the Congregational Church where he met and married his wife in 1968, served as treasurer, and sang in the choir.

As Bud told his parents in his letter of December 12, 1943, written aboard LCI(L)-474, he and Cliff were "treated as guests with complete freedom to roam the ship at will." Because of security concerns, policed by Navy censors who were empowered to read personal letters and blot out or delete sensitive information before they were mailed, it was against Navy regulations to ever report any details about one's location and activities. Yet after he had arrived safely at a particular destination, he would disclose to his parents his general whereabouts and give them some idea of how he occupied his time and how he got there, which apparently was okay, since his envelopes were routinely stamped "PASSED BY NAVAL CENSOR."

After the war is over

LCI(L)-474 had sailed down the Florida coast to Key West and along Cuba and through the Caribbean Sea, past the Cayman Islands, to Panama, where Pullen and LeVee spent Christmas Eve through Christmas night. At the Balboa Naval Station on the Pacific side, LCI(L)-474 took aboard 28 Army enlisted personnel. From there the ship proceeded north and sailed along the coasts of Nicaragua, Guatemala, and Mexico, eventually arriving at the U.S. Repair Base, San Diego, California, where the 474 would be refitted with more armaments and converted into a gunboat.

On February 17, 1945, LCI(G)-474 would sink off Iwo Jima, after receiving several hits from Japanese shore batteries.

While reading nearly a dozen of Bud's letters to his parents from San Diego over the next two months, one scarcely gets the impression that there was a war going on at all. After leaving the LCI(L)-474, he and Cliff moved into the Bachelor Officers' Quarters (B.O.Q.) and rode a bicycle while on base (until their bicycle was stolen, twice). They made the most of frequent liberties, driving a car to San Diego to attend dances and to watch picture shows. He often wore his dress blues whenever he left base. He took the train to Los Angeles and back for a

After the war is over

2-day vacation. After meeting some "girls" at the Officers' Club, he and Cliff drove them by car high in the Sierra Madres, where they ended up throwing snowballs at one another. He went to Tijuana, Mexico, to buy some cheap gifts to send back home. He visited various places around San Diego County, including desolate Lake Cuyamaca, and went to dinner at a friend's house in El Cajon, some 15 miles east of the base. He flew in a Navy plane to San Pedro seeing much of the countryside by air. From time to time, he spoke to his parents in Atlanta briefly by long-distance telephone.

After he was promoted to Lieutenant (junior grade) on March 1, 1944, Bud was given a 14-day leave to visit home. When he returned to San Diego, military life did not change much for him, according to his letters. While the bulk of Flotilla 13 was on maneuvers, practicing beaching drills, engaging in gunnery exercises, and loading and unloading troops, there was not much for him and Cliff as non-combat staff officers to do, at least that is what he told his parents. He went to Chula Vista, taking a young woman he had met out to dinner and the opera. He visited the San Diego Zoo in Balboa Park. He and Cliff played golf at the Chula Vista course and the San Diego Country Club. He and another buddy went swimming in La Jolla with some "girls." And in early June 1944, he visited the Grand Canyon by train, telling his parents: "It is my most earnest wish that my mom and dad can . . . see this magnificent spectacle of Nature's work after the war is over...." From their perspective, based on the letters he wrote them, sightseeing appeared to have been his main military occupation.

But things changed on June 10, 1944, when Lieutenants Pullen and LeVee received orders and prepared to move back aboard ship. There would be no more liberty for a while. This time they were assigned to LCI(G)-729, again as "nonenlisted passengers." Laid down on December 6, 1943, at Commercial Iron Works, Portland, Oregon, launched on January 7, 1944,

After the war is over

USS LCI(L)-729 had been commissioned three weeks later. By now the ship had been reclassified from an L to a G, which stood for Gunboat, which meant that it would no longer be needed to transport troops. Its main role would be to provide fire support. At the Naval Repair Base at San Diego, it like the 474 and other LCIs in Flotilla 13 had been refitted by having ten MK7 rocket launchers, two 40-mm A.A. gun mounts, and four additional .50 caliber machine guns installed. The Navy reasoned that assault troops needed extra firepower as they went ashore. With the LCI's low draft, it could go in with the first assault wave and lay down covering fire. The gunboats would stand by at the flanks of the beach landing area and give fire support when needed. The Navy also increased the ship's complement to 5 officers and 65 enlisted men.

After taking several days to load all the supplies and ammo the ship could carry, the LCI(L)-729 and eight other ships assigned to Group 39 of the Black Cat USS LCI Flotilla 13, under the command of Commander Morrill, finally got underway on June 16. Groups 37 and 38 with 12 ships each, and three ships from Group 39, already had left port. Pulling out of the San Diego Naval shipyard, Bud's convoy headed north up the California coast and then made a big left turn. They then traveled at about 12 knots, as squadrons of planes flew overhead. At the end of his final letter from San Diego, dated June 14, 1944, Bud had warned his mother and father: "There will be a few days you don't hear from me." Ten days later, writing his next letter, LCI(L)-729 had its first General Quarters. Sonar had picked up two submarines, but nothing came of it. Up until now, the weather was fine, but the day before it had turned nasty with hurricane-like winds kicking up thirty-foot waves. Waves crashed over their LCI(L)'s bow and hit the round "castle" command bridge or conning tower, or simply "conn." Bud, Cliff, and the crew had to strap themselves in their bunks so they would not fall out. Mealtime was also a rough ride. There was a railing along the table's edges that kept their trays on the table, but there were plenty of spills and more food on the deck than on the table.

After the war is over

At daybreak on June 26, exactly ten days at sea, they finally sighted land. The next day they headed into port and tied up in a nest at the LCI docks with other amphibs. Bud still could not disclose to his parents where they were. It was not until the end of July 1944, after he sent them a series of color postcards of the place and when he was about to leave again, that they would learn that he was based at Pearl Harbor Navy Yard, Oahu, Territory of Hawaii.

Back of the postcard packet Bud sent his parents in late July 1944, leaving no doubt about his location.

Practically destroyed by the Japanese two and a half years earlier, the mangled hulls of the battleships *Arizona* and *Oklahoma* sticking up out of the water, Pearl Harbor was a busy place, with every type of ship imaginable. At nearby Hickam Field, which had been rebuilt since the attack, there remained damaged

After the war is over

planes and parts of bombed-out buildings and hangars. From the B.O.Q. at Pearl, Lieutenant Pullen would write Walter and Stella nearly a dozen letters, including one V-mail, over the course of some six weeks. He also received mail from home and from school buddies who were in the Navy. During this time, after completing routine payroll and supply duties, he was given liberty to get off base and visit Honolulu several times. He spent time at the beach, swimming in a pool, saw several movies, and he even played tennis for the first time in seven years, as well as a few rounds of golf with Cliff. He did not reveal more details about his time spent at Pearl until his letter of September 22, 1944, some six weeks after he left there.

In his letter of August 6, 1944, Bud informed his folks that he and Cliff had moved back aboard the LCI(G)-729 and were preparing to go to sea again. The scuttlebutt was that they were headed to the Marshall Islands and then on to Saipan, which was Japanese-held. But this was not true, and he did not dare tell his parents his actual destination. In fact, he apparently told them nothing at all. Nearly three weeks would pass before his next letter home. Meanwhile, LCI(G)-729 and eight other LCI gunboats from Flotilla 13 had been assigned to a task force consisting of some 50 ships, including 12 transport ships, 8 LSTs, 5 patrol craft, and 3 destroyer escorts. After taking on fuel, water, and supplies, the convoy got underway, pulling out of Pearl Harbor for the last time on the morning of August 8. Ahead of them was a vast ocean and a trip of more than 3,000 nautical miles.

Finally, on August 24, he wrote his mother, breaking his silence: "As you can imagine, there is a great paucity of things to write about for the simple reason that every day is just like the one before except for progressing a few miles through the Pacific Ocean." So, over the next ten days, he wrote five letters about the ship's officers, what certain crew members were doing, and life aboard the small craft. He said that to pass the time he was

After the war is over

reading lots of books. He took saltwater showers. He talked about his quarters and sailors playing card games in the wardroom and listening to music over the ship's record player.

His letters suddenly stopped again on September 3 and did not pick up again until September 20, when he stated: "I am extremely lucky in this war and have no complaints to make." During this period, from September 4 through 14, LCI(G)-729 was underway with a task force group for the Palau Islands. On September 15 they were maneuvering east of Babelthaup (Babeldaob) Island. On the 16th, 729 was in a retirement area south of Angaur Island. On September 21, Bud wrote two letters, telling his parents that he had been reading a lot of books lately and had enjoyed listening to news broadcasts from Armed Forces Radio based in San Francisco. His ship was so small that everyone "knows everything that is going on." On September 22, Bud informed Walter and Stella that he had crossed the equator sometime before (actually, it had been a month earlier, on August 23) and he and more than twenty others had been initiated into the "Rites of Neptune." Since enough time had transpired, after a full month at sea, he now felt he could divulge where his ship had been without violating censorship rules. After leaving Pearl his LCI had travelled to the Solomon Islands, and they were in the vicinity of the small island group known as the Florida Islands. Then, he said: "we proceeded to the invasion described in the enclosed news." "Obviously," he added, "I cannot tell you where I am so you will have to be content with the description of the action."

For the second time, Bud had written the word "invasion" in his letters. The first time he was referencing D-Day, June 6, 1944, in France. But this time was different. The enclosed "NEWS," which accompanied his letter of this date, consisted of a typed press release describing a "bombardment" that preceded the amphibious landing at Angaur Island on September 17, including "fire-spitting LCI's which raked the beach mercilessly

After the war is over

with rockets," words which Bud had underlined in blue ink, suggesting that he may have been involved with the raking.

The Battle of Angaur was a major battle (code-named STALEMATE II) of the Southwest Pacific campaign in World War II, fought from September 17 to October 22, 1944, on the island of Angaur in the southernmost part of the Palau Islands, about 500 miles from the Philippines. Units of the Black Cat USS LCI Flotilla 13 were assigned gunfire and rocket support duties for the assault landings on Angaur. Although defended by a garrison of only 1,400, Angaur would not be taken until after 36 days of fighting at a high cost of lives. Meanwhile, the 1st Marine Division, many of them veterans of Guadalcanal and Cape Gloucester campaigns, would have an even tougher time securing Peleliu, seven miles northeast of Angaur.

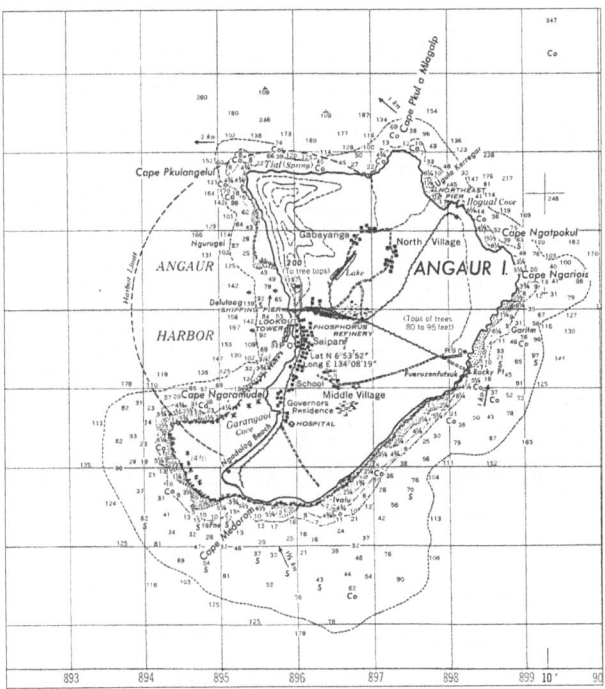

Angaur Island, U.S. Army Corps of Engineers, 1943. "Blue Beach" was between Cape Ngariois and Rocky Point.

After the war is over

The assault on Angaur began on September 17 at 5:20 a.m., when the battleship USS *Tennessee*, one heavy cruiser, three light cruisers, and five destroyers began shelling the beaches on the east and northeast sides of the island. Some ten miles from Angaur at the time, the 729 manned battle stations as the heavy warships commenced bombardment of the beaches. At a few minutes before 8 a.m., Bud's vessel was on station 400 yards inshore from its line of departure. Its mission was to guide the seven gunboats supporting Blue Beach during the assault waves by the 322nd Infantry regiment of the 81st (Wildcat) Army Division. At 8:05 a.m., USS LCI(G)-729 and its six sister crafts commenced slow firing of its 40mm AA guns on Blue Beach. At 8:17 a.m. they fired their 4.5" barrage rockets at a radar range of 1,050 yards, and three minutes later opened fire with their 20mm guns. They ceased firing after the sixth waves of assault troops had passed through their lines and the first assault wave hit Blue Beach at 8:30. Seven minutes later, 729 commenced harassing fire off Rocky Point immediately south of Blue Beach. For two hours they maintained fire on the beach, covering the shoreline. Some fire was conducted at 500 yards to observe its effect on enemy pillboxes and emplacements on the beach. Their 20mms periodically sprayed the dense foliage and treetops for possible snipers. There was no return fire, except for one rifle shot from shore that hit the water about 50 yards ahead. At 10:04 a.m. a Navy scout plane warned the 729 of a mine field close by. So, they withdrew to 1,100 yards from shore and continued methodical bombardment of enemy defenses for another thirty minutes. By 2 p.m. they had pulled back some 2,000 yards from the eastern shore of Angaur, where they remained on call until sunset.

On September 18, LCI(G)-729 took up station north of the northern shore of Angaur, where enemy planes were twice reported overhead and fired on by fleet units. The following day, standing by off the northwest corner of Angaur, Bud's ship drew mortar fire six or seven times. The Japanese evidently opened fire

After the war is over

each time they closed to 3,000 yards or less on their patrol; no splashes closer than 200 yards. On September 20, LCI(G)-459 was sunk when it hit a floating mine near the beach. No one was hurt seriously, and all crew members were picked up by nearby LCIs. From September 23 through 26, they were in an area west of Saipan Town off Angaur, acting as a mine disposal ship. Early in the morning on September 27, several shots, apparently from Japanese snipers ashore, hit the water close aboard. The next day they joined other LCI's on the eastern (lee) side of Angaur. LCI(G)-729 remained anchored near Angaur Island at least through September 30.

There is a gap of more than two weeks in Bud's correspondence that skips almost all this action, from September 4, when nine LCI gunboats of the Black Cat Flotilla 13 pulled out of the Solomon Islands to join the Palau assault convoy, through September 19. When he finally wrote home on September 20, it was the day when LCI(G)-459 was sunk, and the day after LCI(G)-729 came under mortar fire. When he penned his September 28 letter, his sixth since the 20th, it was just after enemy small arms fire nearly strafed his ship. And before the operation at Angaur was over on October 22, Lieutenant Pullen mailed another eight letters. But he mentioned nothing about guns, or mortars, or rockets, or other weapons or sounds of war in his correspondence, aside from providing the "enclosed news."

Excerpts from his letters home during this period contained mixed messages. On September 30 he noted: "As I said my sole occupation is reading and shooting the breeze." He said he and others onboard enjoyed listening to "Jap radio programs," which in addition to "Tokyo Rose" propaganda broadcasts played "popular" songs that they used to dance to before going overseas. Two days later, on October 2, there was this slight hint: "Although we are not in the slightest danger, it is brought to our attention occasionally that the Japs have not forgotten that we are getting close to their homeland." In his letter of October 10, there was

37

this disclaimer: "I cannot, of course, tell you what we are doing, yet I can assure you that it is completely devoid of any interest so that my only diversion is still reading and sleeping." On October 12 he declared: "I am in supreme health and have absolutely no worries except how long *this thing* [emphasis added] will last."

It was not until his letter of October 18 that Bud's parents would hear from him, indirectly at least, what had happened the past few weeks, even though by then the news was dated. He wrote that one of the other officers on LCI(G)-729 had received a *Time* magazine for October 2, 1944, which Bud said "had a great deal of interesting news." Then he flat out told his folks: "I heartily recommend that you be sure to buy one of that date and read it thoroughly particularly the Pacific theater of war."

It is not known if they ever did. If his parents had looked at the magazine's section, entitled "World Battlefronts: BATTLE OF THE PACIFIC: The Beach Approach," they would have learned about the U.S. amphibious landing at Angaur, a story that reported "a line of LCIs" delivering rocket fire. The article continued:

> Now the LCIs ahead start to move in slowly, just ahead and to the left of the first wave of amphibious tanks. Those LCIs are firing like coked-up gangsters in a grade-B movie. Rockets go thump, thump, thumping out of them and bursting along the shore. The big rockets, taking off with a coughing roar, scorch the beach and plow up vegetation behind them. Many 20-mm. autoguns are hammering like runaway riveters and weaving red lines of tracer shells alongshore like thin angry fingers prying and poking into every patch that might shelter an enemy.

By the time Bud's parents received his letter, the Battle of Angaur was practically over. By the end of September, the strategic

After the war is over

objectives for STALEMATE II—capturing Angaur and Peleliu for air bases and taking Kossol Passage and Ulithi Atoll as fleet anchorages—had been met. Yet some bloody fighting continued. It was not until October 23 before the infantry on Angaur pulled out. Combat casualties for the operation were 211 killed and 772 wounded. The Japanese lost more than 1,300 killed. Only a few stragglers remained, hidden in deep caves. The death toll also included large numbers of Japanese and other Asian civilians and Palauans. Peleliu was more of a blood bath than Angaur, mainly because there were 14,000 Japanese defenders there. By October 20, the 1st Marines had lost 1,750 men killed, and more than 6,000 casualties overall, and by October 22 was reinforced by the 321st Regimental Combat Team of the 81st Army Division, which also suffered staggering losses. A campaign that had been predicted to last three days actually went on for two and a half months. It was not until November 27 before the island was finally declared secure.

Meanwhile, Black Cat USS LCI Flotilla 13 gunboats were assigned patrol, picket, and harassment operations. They were ordered to head north past the big island of Babelthaup (Babeldaob), the largest island in the Palau, which was still occupied by Japanese forces, and go to Kossol Passage to be on the lookout for the enemy sending reinforcements and supplies by armed barges to Peleliu and Angaur. They patrolled for barge movement and floating mines along the entire length of the Palaus, looking for anything to shoot at and to destroy, firing into Japanese-held beaches. In addition to the floating mines, they also had to be on the lookout for Japanese suicide swimmers carrying magnetic bombs trying to destroy the ships or to board the ships and attack the crew. Running low on ammo, food, fuel, and freshwater, they were restocked by support ships and tankers in the Kossol anchorage area. Kossol was enclosed by a ringing coral reef in northern Palau. The area had about 300 repair ships, supply ships, tankers, and support ships of all kinds and was about five miles from shore. In fact, LCI(G)-729, according to

After the war is over

its War Diary, spent most of October, from the 3rd through the 24th, anchored in Kossol alongside the USS *Prometheus* (AR 3) for "repairs, fuel, water, and provisions." It was not until the 25th before 729 was on picket duty off the northwest side of Babeldaob, between Kossol Passage and Konrei Point.

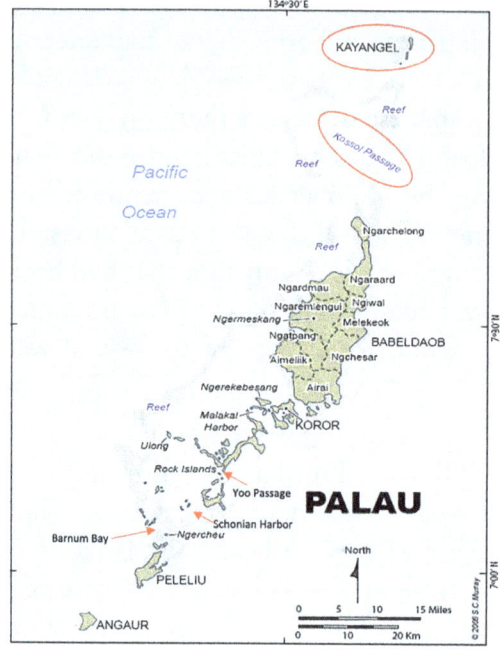

The Palau Islands

As Bud explained to his parents in his letter of November 3: "We (the LCI (G) 729) move around a good deal, but we never go very far and are anchored most of the time." On this day, his LCI was anchored in Barnum Bay, north of Peleliu. On November 7-8 they were anchored in Schonian Harbor (Sebeseb), south of the Rock Islands, "riding out [a] storm." On November 15 they encountered an "empty 75-foot Jap coal barge" and, "after shelling it," they "towed" the barge back to Barnum Bay and anchored there. Although "not much more than a heavy wooden box pointed at either end," Bud wrote, "nevertheless, we are extremely proud of our prize." From November 20 through 22, while on picket station in Schonian Harbor, LCI(G)-729 shelled

After the war is over

Eomogan Island. A week later 729 was one of three LCIs that took part in a joint operation with a company of Army cavalry troops, a reconnaissance unit of the 81st Infantry Division, in the seizure of Kayangel Atoll. From December 5 to 8, 1944, Bud's LCI was anchored on a picket station one-half mile south of Urukthapel Island, in the center of Palau, and west of Yoo Passage. On December 12 Bud wrote that they "discovered an old Jap wreck piled up on a reef several miles off" of Eil Malk (Mecherechar) Island.

Yet few of these actions received more than a passing reference in Bud's letters to his parents. Instead, his correspondence related mostly to other, more mundane matters. His life aboard the LCI, which he repeatedly described as monotonous, his cramped living quarters, the quality of the food he ate, how he and the crew spent their free time, and the personal tragedy of one of his fellow officers, all received some attention. He complained about intrusive Navy censors and life at sea, though he said it was preferable to being stationed on some uninhabitable and inhospitable jungle island. He occasionally mentioned fraternity brothers at Tech, high school classmates, former K.D.K. dance dates, and friends from Navy Supply Corps School whom he bumped into or had heard from. But uppermost was his need to hear from home, beginning almost every letter with some comment about mail he had received or more often not. He craved news about Georgia politics and Georgia Tech football, provided the Yellow Jackets won. He offered advice relating to Stella's problems with finding reliable help in her beauty shop. He worried when he learned that his father had been accidently injured on the job, falling off of his diesel engine. He frequently asked his parents to pass on some information to their maid, Belle, mentioning her and her cooking nearly three dozen times. He missed his dog "Susie," too, and the "Pups."

After the war is over

Bud, Stella, Susie, and the "Pups," ca. 1950.

An ongoing subject in his correspondence home was his parents possibly buying a "country place," which Stella would name "The Hitching Post," or as Bud once described their obsession: "farm fever." "The whole family is engrossed in a mad scramble to find a little farm," Bud once wrote. The prospect was discussed so often that it became a theme throughout his letters home, reflected in the title of this work. Bud was looking forward to the time when the war was over. He used the phrase "after the war" nearly a dozen times, most of which referenced what he planned to do when he returned home. More than anything else, he wanted to own some land and live on it, after the war.

Stuck in the middle of the vast Pacific, confined to a tiny boat thousands of miles from home, the idea of living on a piece of land far from a war zone was about all he could think about. "That is where I want to build a little shack to hide from the next war," he once told his parents. Among the books he was reading at the time was about a guy in rural Ohio who retreated to "a little farm" he inherited "to make a living out of it." The place

After the war is over

had no electricity or plumbing, and that was exactly the kind of place Bud imagined, even though the man in the book resorted to sheep raising, which, Bud confessed, "holds no charm for me." He wanted a place where he could reside in solitude, or perhaps escape to remote Brazil where some relatives lived, and maybe not even work at all. After his parents finally bought such a place in July 1944, he wrote: "I derive an intense feeling of satisfaction from knowing that there is some place I can go — take off my shoes, prop my feet up on the railing of the porch and watch everybody go by in a big hurry to do nothing while I just sit there and reflect on the futility of haste and quest after money." But first, he had to survive the war.

Early in the morning of January 8, 1945, a group of suicide Japanese swimmers, "under cover of heavy rain and low visibility," placed a magnetic bomb under the stern of LCI(G)-404 which was anchored in the Yoo Passage. Bud's 729 was anchored about 300 yards west of the 404. The blast severely damaged the craft's propellers and rudders and knocked out its engines, though there were no injuries among the crew. A dozen Japanese were found dead floating in the water after the explosion. At dawn, the 729 went along the port side of LCI(G)-404 and towed them to Schonian Harbor. Another LCI pulled the 404 to Kossol Passage, where it entered into a dry-dock for major repairs. On January 13, LCI(G)-732 was attacked by two torpedo boats. The 732 blew them both away with no survivors. Five days later, LCI(G)-396 struck a floating mine off Urukthapel Island while heading out of Yoo Passage. The blast pealed back the entire front section of the ship, but it was able to stay afloat. Four of her crew were killed, three missing and presumed dead, and a number were wounded, five seriously. Patrolling the inner lagoons of northern Eil Malk, about eight miles southwest of the 396, Bud's vessel was among those that arrived on the scene to assist, making a smokescreen and returning fire on enemy shore batteries, while the 396 was being towed away by another LCI to Schonian Harbor. The wounded were taken to a hospital on Peleliu.

After the war is over

Although undoubtedly in the back of his mind, Lieutenant Pullen does not mention any one of these incidents in his correspondence, as there is another gap in his letters between January 8 and 21. During that period he flew in a transport plane to Guam on official business. While waiting for the Navy to microfilm his payroll records, he spent several days with his friend Bobby McGinty. We learn indirectly about Bud's "vacation" on Guam, which included beer parties, through a letter that he wrote to Cliff LeVee, who forwarded it with written comments of his own to Stella, who despite not approving of her son's drinking, decided to keep the letter among his correspondence anyway. In his letter of January 26, 1945, Bud indicated his intention not to discuss the nastier aspects of the war. He told his mother: "We have had several exciting events to happen lately, but the security regulations prevent me from telling you all any of the particulars." Perhaps he was referencing the two explosions and attack earlier that month.

LCI(G)-396 at anchor in Schonian Harbor after striking a mine on January 18, 1945.

Bud remained with the LCI(G)-729 until sometime in April 1945, when he was assigned to LCI(L)-737. By then Commander Morrill of the Black Cat LCI Flotilla 13 had been relieved, as well

After the war is over

as other officers and sailors who had served with him during the Palau invasion, including the skipper of 729. There are seventeen letters from the period from February through April 24, when Bud first mentioned his new ship. Following V-E Day, May 8, he learned that he too would be leaving the war zone for Pearl Harbor and ordered back to the States for a rehabilitation leave of 30 days. On May 12 he wrote his parents: "It looks as though I may have to make a trip in the next few days so I will forewarn you, perhaps unnecessarily, that there will be [some] time when you won't hear from me." He added: "Don't worry (if you did you would already be a nervous wreck) if you don't get a letter from me for a week maybe two."

It is not known if he wrote or contacted Walter and Stella by mail or telephone before then. It is known that Bud eventually made it back to Atlanta to spend time with his folks, Belle, Susie, and the Pups. The next letter published here is dated June 17, 1945, when he already had arrived at his next duty assignment as chief disbursing officer for the U.S. Naval Hospital north of Memphis, Tennessee, following his promotion to full lieutenant. Ten letters concern his time there before he was transferred again in October 1945. As he explained to his parents, he did not have enough "points" to be discharged from the Navy. So, he was given another assignment, this time at the U.S. Naval Repair Base in New Orleans. He wrote seven letters from there.

Most of Walter Hudson Pullen's wartime letters are in their original envelopes with canceled postage stamps still attached. As illustrated throughout, he used various stationery, sometimes with an official U.S. Navy embossed golden crest at the top, other times with a Flotilla 13 or U.S. Navy Hospital imprint, though mostly just plain paper. He typed some letters, but wrote most of them by hand using a pen or sometimes a pencil. Since his letters were addressed to his parents, they were obviously retained by them, and probably Stella, for some unknown reason. At some point, perhaps after his father died in 1957, they were given

After the war is over

back to him. They remained for over sixty years in a cardboard box placed on a shelf of a closet at his home, until they were rediscovered recently.

Bud's World War II letters home.

Along with his correspondence were three yellowed Atlanta newspapers, now brittle and prone to flaking. One was a partial copy of the *Atlanta Journal*, dated September 6, 1939, including a full-page map of Europe at war following Germany's invasion of Poland. The other two were complete issues of the *Atlanta Constitution*, for May 8 and 10, 1945, both with headlines dealing with Germany's surrender.

Walter Hudson Pullen's letters home provide a narrow window through which to view selected events and people from May 1942 through December 1945. We learn mostly about other Atlantans, all young white Southerners in their early to mid-

After the war is over

twenties, who like Bud served in the military and helped in their own way to win the war. We also glean information about Bud's parents and some wartime challenges that they faced back home, such as coal and cigarette shortages, and tire and gasoline rationing. We are offered glimpses of life both inside and outside of naval bases near Key West, San Diego, Los Angeles, Pearl Harbor, and New Orleans. Bud provides detailed observations about his time aboard various amphibious crafts in the Pacific, their officers and crew, their diversions and activities. He occasionally criticizes military censors and downplays his role as disbursing officer and paymaster. He discusses both Georgia and national politics, claiming that Dewey supporters outnumbered FDR's 2-1 in the Navy. He also comments on news he had read or heard on Armed Forces Radio, including the Iwo Jima and Okinawa invasions, the deaths of FDR, Wendell Wilkie, Adolf Hitler, and Ernie Pyle, as well as Germany's surrender, V-E Day and V-J Day celebrations, the establishment of the United Nations, and Truman as commander-in-chief.

Aside from these noteworthy subjects, much of what Bud divulges appears to be pedestrian and of limited historical value. He was largely hesitant to relay any information that would have caused his parents or other family members to worry or that violated security guidelines, instead choosing to discuss lighter topics. He once explained that he could not reply to one of his uncles who had written him because his letter would be "rather devoid of news," adding: "It is so difficult to conjure up anything to say when one is prohibited from telling where, what, how much, or anything about [one's] activities." He later told his parents: "I have seen a lot of interesting things and could write quite a letter— if I were permitted to."

Yet, from today's perspective, some eighty years after he wrote those words, he does have some interesting things worth reading. His letters were personal in nature, which enhances their appeal. To his family, his grandchildren, and now his great-grandchildren,

After the war is over

Walter Hudson Pullen's surviving correspondence, however routine, serves as their most tangible and enduring link to World War II, the most significant and influential event of the twentieth century. In response to the age-old question — "And what did you do in the war, Grandpa?"— we know, at least part of the story.

Editorial Method

In transcribing Walter Hudson Pullen's wartime correspondence, a genuine effort has been made to remain faithful to the original text with consideration for the reader. Bud's spelling has been reproduced without alteration, except where confusion might occur. In such cases, bracketing of letters or words and occasional [*sic*]s have been employed. Punctuation and capitalization have been standardized, but abbreviations and double words have been left undisturbed. The dates of his letters have been moved flush left, regardless of where he placed them. His salutations and closings are unchanged from the originals. In most cases, he signed his letters "Bud," as indicated below each letter, whether they were typed or handwritten, or both. Footnotes have been included to provide brief information about individuals and to explain certain events he referenced. Where possible, maps and images have also been added. To illustrate the stationery he used, censorship stamps, and postal cancellations, several of his letters, as well as envelopes which he addressed, have been copied and reproduced in part or whole. Notations of whether a letter was written by hand or typed, signed or unsigned, is still or not in an envelope, with or without postage affixed, or if there are any enclosures, have been provided at the end of each letter. Of course, there are no chapters among Bud's letters. They have been added based on what he was doing or where he was located at the time, titled using his own words.

After the war is over

Chapter 1

"I am about settled in this place."

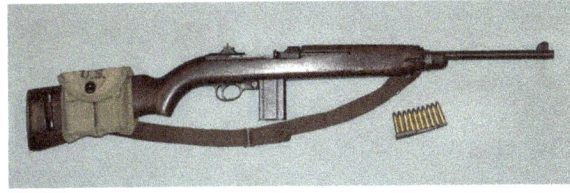

Saginaw Steering Gear (SSG) Division Plant No. 2 was the 4th largest maker of the .30-caliber semi-automatic M1 Carbine.

2302 S. Niagara St.
Saginaw, Michigan
May 31 [1942], Sunday

Dear Maw,

Please forgive me for not writing sooner, but I wanted to get my final address to send you. It is at the top of the page. I am going

After the war is over

to eat three meals a day here at this place.[1]

Although there is no alumni association of Sigma Chi here, I have bumped into two of the brothers at my plant,[2] and also, I have met several boys to run around with.

Mom, I didn't get to church today because I had to move and was to[o] lazy to do it early; however, I will try to go soon.

How did your X-rays turn out? I hope that Dr. Garret[3] can find something, or do something to help you lose that trouble. Is Susie losing any weight from her exercise? I doubt it.

I am rooming with a fellow who works in the same office as I, but he is going to be married in about three weeks and will leave.

Tell Paw that everybody around here is pro-labor so I don't have to do so much arguing.

I will write soon; please write me.

Love,

Bud

Autograph Letter Signed (ALS), no envelope.

---

1. Bud was staying at a boardinghouse owned by Phebe Della Allen Near (1872-1959), whose late husband, a former iron foundry worker, was a native of Walpole, Canada. A few years earlier, Mrs. Della Near of 2302 S. Niagara Street, Saginaw, had provided a testimonial for Indo-Vin tonic, an anti-gas and indigestion medication, whose inventor earned a fortune because of the elixir's high alcohol content. A few years later, the Food & Drug Administration banned Indo-Vin, asserting that the mixture of water, glycerin, caramel coloring and some miscellaneous herbs, advertised as "ethyl fuel for the human motor," had no medicinal effects.
2. Bud worked at the Delphi Saginaw Division Plant 2, located at 1400 Holmes Street, less than a quarter mile from Mrs. Near's boardinghouse.
3. Possibly Steve Arthur Garrett (1891-1968), a long-time Atlanta dentist.

After the war is over

Indigestion and Stomach Pains Left This Lady

MICHIGAN RESIDENT TELLS HOW INDO-VIN RELIEVED A LONG PERIOD OF SUFFERING.

MRS. DELLA NEAR, of 2302 S. Niagara St., Saginaw, Mich., says: "As long as I can remember, I had suffered from indigestion. Gas pains kept me in such misery that I could hardly do my housework, and I was subject to severe headaches. I heard about Indo-Vin and tried it. This medicine has done me more good than anything I ever tried. I can eat anything now and my food digests well. The gas pains are all gone. I never have those headaches any more, and I have more energy. It certainly is a relief to be free of my suffering, and I am glad to endorse Indo-Vin."

Indo-Vin is now being sold here in Homer at Parker's Pharmacy, and by all leading druggists throughout this whole section.

MRS. NEAR

The Homer (Michigan) Index, 12/26/1935, p. 7.

2302 S. Niag[a]ra
Saginaw, Mich.
Tuesday night
[June 2, 1942]

Dear Maw,

Well, I am about settled in this place — it really is a good homey place even though it's not particularly fancy.

I have a swell fellow for a roommate — he went to college in Ohio; however, he is getting married in 3 weeks or have I already told you?

Although I haven't cashed that check yet, I may have [to] this week; if I do cash it, I'll send you the money in about a month.

After the war is over

Today, I had to buy a shirt, since I don't get my laundry until tomorrow — it's possible that we may get a washwoman.

Mom, if it wouldn't be too much trouble, I would like to take the Sunday [Atlanta] Journal — the daily won't be necessary. I believe that they can send it much cheaper than you can.

How did your x-rays turn out — I really want to know because someone will find [out] what your trouble is I know.

Well, really there isn't so much to tell you except that I shure [*sic*] miss you and Paw and Susie and ole Belle, and I send you all my love.

Bud

Autograph Letter Signed (ALS), no envelope.

After the war is over

Wednesday
[July 22, 1942]

Dear Maw and Paw,

How was the trip? I'll bet those mountains were really pretty— I miss seeing that hilly country down there.

Last Monday I drove my car down to Detroit[4] and back without any trouble which greatly surprised me.

I think that I will be home in about 3 or 4 weeks—maybe a little longer, but not much. I will really be glad to see ya'll and Susie. By the way, did you have much trouble with her on the trip? Did she go swimming?

We finally got some hot weather up here,[5] and boy, you can really feel it because the Saginaw Valley is so humid.

I sure enjoyed talking to Mom last Sunday, but I would really hate to have to pay the phone bill at home.

I hope Dad's tomatoes are ripe when I get home — they don't seem to have much of any vegetables up here that are as pretty as those at home.

Did the car run all right on the trip? I guess those old tires are about to give up and go. It might be better to put on the good tires than to risk a blowout which might ruin one of those precious tubes.

Love,

Bud

Autograph Letter Signed (ALS), stamped envelope.

4. About a hundred miles from Saginaw.
5. The high this day in Saginaw was 89 degrees.

Chapter 2

"I would prefer drilling in the rain."

Still from a motion picture depicting students at the Navy Supply Corps School at Harvard marching to classes.

Thursday
[May 6, 1943][6]

Dear Mom & Dad,

This place hasn't improved a bit, in fact, the work has become more obnoxious if possible; however, it is a great deal better than some things such as the sacrifices some of the boys are making.

---
6. Bud is writing from Navy Supply Corps School, Harvard University. Back of envelope reads: "Ens. W H. Pullen Norris Hall D-42, Soldiers Field, Boston, Mass."

After the war is over

A review by the Admiral[7] is scheduled for this afternoon and it is beginning to drizzle so I doubt if they have it, but I think I would prefer drilling in the rain to sitting in class.

My roommate's name is Glenn Putnam[8] who hails from Seattle, Wash. And he is a very agreeable fellow which helps a great deal in a little place like this room.

I still haven't received my [Atlanta] "Journal" here — it is probably being delivered to the Beacon Street address, but maybe I'll get next Sunday's issue.

As you-all realize I really have to scratch for news here at this place and can find little to talk about except to growse [*sic*] about the work so please overlook any seeming hate of the school; it's just natural to gripe about it.

Tell Belle "hello" for me and tell her I'll be home in September for some home cooking.

Love to everybody,

Bud

Autograph Letter Signed (ALS), stamped envelope.

---

7. Rear Admiral William Brent Young (1888-1959), Chief of the Bureau of Supplies and Accounts and Paymaster General of the Navy.
8. Glenn Richard Putnam (1916-2001) was a graduate of the University of Washington (1940) and had worked for two years as an assistant traffic agent for North Coast Transportation Company of Seattle prior to attending the Navy Supply Corps School at Harvard.

After the war is over

22 The Atlanta Journal FRIDAY, SEPTEMBER 3, 1943

WITH THE COLORS

... Walter H. Pullen, 224 Westminster Drive, N. E., Ernest D. Woods, 11 The Prado, N. E., and G. Dean Garner Jr., Atlanta, from Navy Supply Corps School, Harvard University, Soldier Field, Mass. . .

Atlanta Journal, 9/3/1943, p. 22.

NAVY SUPPLY CORPS SCHOOL
HARVARD UNIVERSITY

Sunday

Dear Mom,

I tried to call you today several times, but there wasn't a chance — I think everybody in the country wanted to make a long-distance call today. I just wanted to wish you a happy Mother's-Day and tell you that you are undoubtedly the best mother anyone ever had. It truly is a wonderful feeling to know

After the war is over

Sunday
[May 9, 1943]

Dear Mom,

I tried to call you today several times, but there wasn't a chance—I think everybody in the country wanted to make a long-distance call today. I just wanted to wish you a happy Mother's Day and tell you that you are undoubtedly the best mother anyone ever had. It truly is a wonderful feeling to know I have such a wonderful mother at home who would do and does everything in the world for me. Many people aren't so fortunate as I [am] in having parents like you and Dad.

Yesterday afternoon several of us got some of those long thin one-man boats (wherrys) and went rowing on the Charles River — we thoroughly enjoyed it and also discovered that it (rowing) is much more difficult than appears at first glance.

Spring, beautiful Spring, has finally come to Boston & Cambridge and the river is a beautiful sight lined with green grass and budding trees.

Last evening we saw "Candida" a play by GBS which starred Elissa Landi.[9]

All my love, Mom.

Bud

Autograph Letter Signed (ALS), no envelope.

---

9. The comedy by George Bernard Shaw was at the Copley Theater in Boston. The Austrian-American former film star Landi (1904-1948) played the title role.

After the war is over

Wednesday
[June 2, 1943]

Dear Mom & Dad,

Boy, it is <u>hot</u> here today and I can no longer complain of the cold weather — it will doubtless rain tomorrow, however.

I got the pictures of Little Sue and was surprised to see how much she has grown — also she looks a lot like old Susie when she was young. It's just as well that she doesn't like to ride in an automobile these days.

I went up to the [Hotel] Statler Monday and met Bobby[10] and brought him out here for a while; he is in the communications branch of the Navy over across the river and I guess he hasn't had a chance to get away for the last two days because he hasn't been over to see me.

Our big final exam is coming up [on] Friday week and I am beginning to worry about it — there are so many little details to remember and you know the kind of memory I have.

On January [June] 11, Fred Waring[11] is going to salute the Navy Supply Corps School on his program so you might listen if you don't have anything else to do, but we won't have anything to do with it except to select the songs.

Well, hope to hear from you-all tomorrow.

Love

Bud

Autograph Letter Signed (ALS), no envelope.

10. One of Bud's closest boyhood friends, Robert (Bobby) McGinty, who was enrolled in the Naval Training School (Communications) on a different part of Harvard's campus across the Charles River.
11. Fredrick Malcolm Waring, Sr. (1900-1984) was an American musician, bandleader, and radio personality, sometimes referred to as "America's Singing Master." The Fred Waring Show was an old-time radio musical variety program, a regular Coast-to-Coast feature, broadcast at the time on weekday evenings over the entire National Broadcasting Network, sponsored by Chesterfield cigarettes.

After the war is over

Ensign Walter H. Pullen, Navy Supply Corps School, Harvard, ca. August 1943.

Thursday
[June 3, 1943]

Dear Dad,

I was very happy to get your letter and wish I could have been home to help you eat that watermelon — so far, I haven't seen any around here.

We are having very moderate weather now — it seems to stay around 70° to 80° most of the time.

Last night we had a little poker game downstairs in one of the boys' rooms, but evidently you didn't teach me enough in the old days because the fellows put the bite on me for a couple of bucks.

After the war is over

They just brought in a new bunch of sailors here at Harvard[12] so now there is a total of about 6000 men in the armed forces here studying special subjects. There are approximately 1000 studying supply.

Ole McGinty was over today and we shot the bull for a while; I believe that they get better food over where he is than we do. We didn't have any meat for breakfast or lunch and had some lean spare ribs for dinner tonight — guess I'll go over at 10:00 tonight and have a hamburger at the Students Club.

Well, write sooner next time.

Your boy,

Bud

Autograph Letter Signed (ALS), no envelope.

Friday
[July 1943]

Dear Mom,

Another week-end is here and that is the only thing that makes life seem livable at this place.

Yesterday the temperature went up to 96° and our room is

---

12. These probably were students enrolled in Navy Supply Corps Midshipmen Officers' School that began on June 1, 1943. The Navy Supply Corps School was but one of six military schools (three Navy, three Army) that would comprise the wartime schools at Harvard. In addition, there were programs for Naval Reserve Officer Training, Naval Aviation Cadets, Army Quartermaster Corps, Electronics and Radar courses, as well as a Chaplain Training Course. Also the Navy Supply Corps School for Women Accepted for Volunteer Emergency Service (WAVES) was held at Radcliff College in Cambridge.

undoubtedly the hottest spot in Boston, but I can stand the heat all right much better than my roommate who isn't used to such weather. I really can't complain [about] the weather here now — we have taken off our coats and are required to wear only pants & shirt [at] the station which is truly a blessing for me particularly as you know.

Bobby hasn't been over since he first arrived probably because he is too busy; however, I expect I'll see him this week-end sometime. We have only one more week of this Disbursing and then a big exam over everything; former students say that the Supply part of the course is more interesting so I have hope that the remainder of the course for the next two or three months may be happier than this present course.

My [Atlanta] *Journal* comes, but at intermittent periods in bunches of two or three; I really don't need it because I read two Boston papers every day.

Love to the whole family

Bud

Autograph Letter Signed (ALS), no envelope.

After the war is over

Chapter 3

"I held my first payday."

Aerial view and map of the 115-acre U.S. Navy Amphibious Training Base, Solomons, Maryland.

Oct 17, 1943

Dear Mom & Dad,

I got the package today and certainly appreciate your trouble in sending it. Unfortunately, the mothballs sort of flavored the candy and I had to pass it out to my friends who didn't care for my little joke. I just this minute discovered the fellow in the bunk next to mine is from Georgia and went to the university at Athens — he is Vassar Cate[13] who was famous as a football

---
13. From Brunswick, Georgia, Gustavus Vassa Cate, Jr. (1917-1999) was starting halfback and captain of the UGA football team during the 1939 season under first-year coach Wally Butts, during which the Bulldogs went 1-3 in the SEC and 5-6 overall. At the Southeastern Conference track championship meet in Birmingham in May 1940, Cate won the 220-low hurdles and came in 2nd in the 100-yard dash and 120-high hurdles, leading UGA to a surprising 2nd place overall finish to LSU. After graduation, he served as assistant football coach and head track coach at Riverside Military School in Gainesville (1940-41), his trackmen winning the state championship. He took over as head football and track coach at Waycross High the following year, before enlisting in the Navy on October 5, 1942, and serving until his discharge on January 22, 1946. He retired in 1956 with the rank of commander in the Navy Reserve. Cate was elected to the Georgia Sports Hall of Fame in 1962.

After the war is over

player back in 1938-40; he is also a great track star you probably remember seeing his name in the papers.

University of Georgia football player Vassa Cate (1940).

It may be possible for me to get to Baltimore this week-end to see Georgia Tech play Navy and I sure hope Tech wins because I have a few bucks bet on my team.[14] Is Dad keeping up with the Georgia football teams this year even if Castleberry[15] and Sinkwich[16] aren't playing? Sinkwich is playing with a professional team.

Boys' High stand-out Clint Castleberry would be killed in World War II after an All-America season at Georgia Tech.

---

14. Tech lost to #3 Navy 14-28 at Municipal Stadium in Baltimore on October 23, 1943.
15. A graduate of Boys' High School in Atlanta, Clinton Dillard Castleberry, Jr. (1923-1944) played halfback for the Georgia Tech Yellow Jackets in 1942-43, leading his team to a 9-3 record despite injuries. On November 23, 1944, Lt. Castleberry of the U.S. Army Air Corps, co-piloting a B-26 Marauder, failed to return from a mission.
16. Born in Croatia, Frank Francis Sinkwich, Sr. (1920-1990) won the Heisman Trophy in 1942 as a halfback playing for the University of Georgia, which went 11-1 that year and beat UCLA in the 1943 Rose Bowl. After his collegiate career, Sinkwich played with the Detroit Lions for two seasons and the Baltimore Colts.

After the war is over

Last night I saw Bob Hope in "Let's Face It"[17] here at the base and it is undoubtedly an all-time high in crazy [antics] movie — I recommend [you see] it if you want some good laughs, however.

Well, yesterday, I held my first payday; I paid out over $2000 and my books balanced out last night O'K so I can rest easy again. There is nothing at all difficult about this work except at the end of the quarter when returns go in —the next time will be December 31 so I have quite a while to study up on how to render the returns; also, I have a Chief Petty Officer who knows a good deal more about disbursing than I —there's not much to worry about right now.

I had no trouble at all getting the call [through] from Washington Sunday night and sure enjoyed talking to you. One thing I said and would like to repeat is that I don't want my Maw to work anymore than absolutely necessary and it would be a good idea to hire another operator even if she does require a guarantee especially when you have to turn the work away. Also, you might be looking around to see if we could use the rest of our money anywhere if there is no need for it in your own shop. I could certainly stand to send $75 a month home to take care of any payments we would have to make.

It has turned rather chilly here and I believe that winter is not far off. The leaves are beautiful here in Maryland and the trip to Washington is on a road that is sparsely settled thus the autumn colors run riot making the trip quite pleasant.

Hope the whole family is getting along all right and Belle's cooking is the same as usual.

All my love,

Bud

---

17. A musical military comedy released on August 5, 1943, by Paramount Pictures.

After the war is over

Address my mail from now on:
Ensign W. H. Pullen
LCI Flotilla Office
USNATB
Solomons branch
Wash, D.C.

Autograph Letter Signed (ALS), stamped envelope.

Thursday

Dear Mom & Dad,

It seems I am guilty again of a delay in writing, but the few hours leisure I have at night have been taken by riding the long bus ride to Washington. Bobby and I went in together last night and went out with Emmit and really had a good reunion.

I received two letters from you today — one was dated a few days ago and the other was dated Oct. 23 which was before I got home.

Yesterday, I received a letter from you which had been sent to Oakland, California by mistake; it had also been opened by mistake. I think

After the war is over

Thursday
[November 18, 1943]

Dear Mom & Dad,

It seems I am guilty again of a delay in writing, but the few hours [of] leisure I have at night have been taken by riding the long bus ride to Washington. Bobby and I went in together last night and went out with Emmit and really had a good reunion.

I received two letters from you today — one was dated a few days ago and the other was dated Oct. 23 which was before I got home.

Yesterday, I received a letter from you which had been sent to Oakland, California by mistake; it had also been opened by mistake. I think the confusion was caused because there was a fellow here at Solomons named Earl W. Pullen;[18] once before, I experienced some trouble because of a mix-up in our names.

Imogene[19] wrote me a very nice letter inviting me to come out to Akron and see her, but I'm afraid that would be impossible now. John[20] also wrote me a fine letter thanking me for sending

---

18. Probably Earl Winfield Pullen (1914-2001) a former teacher from Morris Plains, N.J., who served as a lieutenant commander in LCT Flotilla 6 during the war.
19. Stella's sister, Mary Imogene Hudson Blackstock (1907-1966). (See letter of April 11, 1944.)
20. Stella's youngest brother, John Wesley Hudson (1915-1988). A graduate of Tech High School (1933), John attended Georgia Tech evening school and worked as an engineer/repairman for Southern Bell Telephone Company in Atlanta. In 1937, he married Elizabeth Louise Anderson (1917-1998), a graduate of Girls' High School, in a ceremony that Bud and his parents undoubtedly attended. In October 1940, when John registered for the draft, he and Elizabeth were living with Elizabeth's parents at 738 Argonne Avenue, N.E., less than two miles south of the Pullen residence. John and Elizabeth Hudson were long-time members of Second-Ponce de Leon Baptist Church.

After the war is over

him some "Hindy." He says that Bill Anderson[21] is an executive officer in his outfit — that is quite a big job and must require an awful lot of responsibility.

Bud's uncles, John Wesley and Halbert Austin Hudson.

As to the time we are leaving, I can't say any more except that we won't be here for Christmas. The best of the present[ly] available data indicates that we are going to shove off somewhere near the end of the month — probably a few days later. Perhaps you had better start writing to the new address listed below so there will be no chance of my losing any mail.

Ens. Walter H. Pullen
Disbursing Officer
LCI (L) Flotilla 13
c/o Fleet Postmaster, New York, N.Y.

---

21. Elizabeth's brother, William Knoll Anderson, Jr. (1920-1999), a graduate of Boys' High School, who attended Emory University and was employed by Delta Air Lines at Candler Field in Atlanta when he registered for the draft in 1940. He enlisted in the Army Air Corps in March 1942 and was commissioned a second lieutenant and earned his wings at Craig Field, Selma, Alabama, a year later. During the war he piloted a B-25 Mitchell bomber and was an assistant operations officer in the China, Burma, and India (CBI) Theater, with headquarters at Karachi Air Base (Pakistan) and Calcutta (Kolkata). Returning to Atlanta after the war, he went back to his old job in the reservations division of Delta Air Lines, before becoming traffic manager at Jacksonville, Florida. Afterwards, he was a sales representative for 3M Company for more than twenty years.

It is up to you whether you try to come up and see me, but it really doesn't seem practical; however, I would be delighted to meet either or both of you in Washington should you want to come up. I shall call sometime in the next day or so to talk with you about such a possibility.

Your loving and grateful son,

Bud

Autograph Letter Signed (ALS), stamped envelope.

Wednesday, Nov. 24 [1943]

Dear Mom & Dad,

Well, the time for leaving is drawing nearer and nearer, and it now looks as though we will leave in about ten days; I'm sure that it will be somewhere around that date.

I haven't received any mail from you lately so I guess the Fleet Post Office address takes longer to get here — if possible, I will try to call home tonight to see what Dad has decided about coming up to see me before we shove off. It does seem sort of impractical to make such a long trip, especially during the holiday rush, and unless he wants to come very much, I wouldn't recommend his making the trip.

We are having a great time getting all our equipment together even if it is a seemingly endless task; we're requisitioning everything that we can think of for our comfort such as a coffee pot, electric toaster, electric iron, mosquito netting, and many, many, other items. We are trying to decide whether or not to buy a bicycle to use when we get to our destination and we will doubtless decide in the affirmative because there will be many times when quick transportation will be necessary.

After the war is over

My Thanksgiving box is sitting right beside my desk on top of the safe so apples, lemons, tangerines, etc are easily within reach.

It turned off a little cold here yesterday, but today is much warmer — the climate here is fortunately trying to stave off the bitter weather until we leave.

Imogene lived up to her usual wonderful self by writing such a flattering letter to you concerning the tiny little help I gave. The world is lucky that there are people on earth like her.

Mom, I hope I can get a call through sometime tonight or in the next few nights so I can get the news.

Your loving son,

Bud

Autograph Letter Signed (ALS), no envelope.

After the war is over

Chapter 4

"I am not immune from sea-sickness."

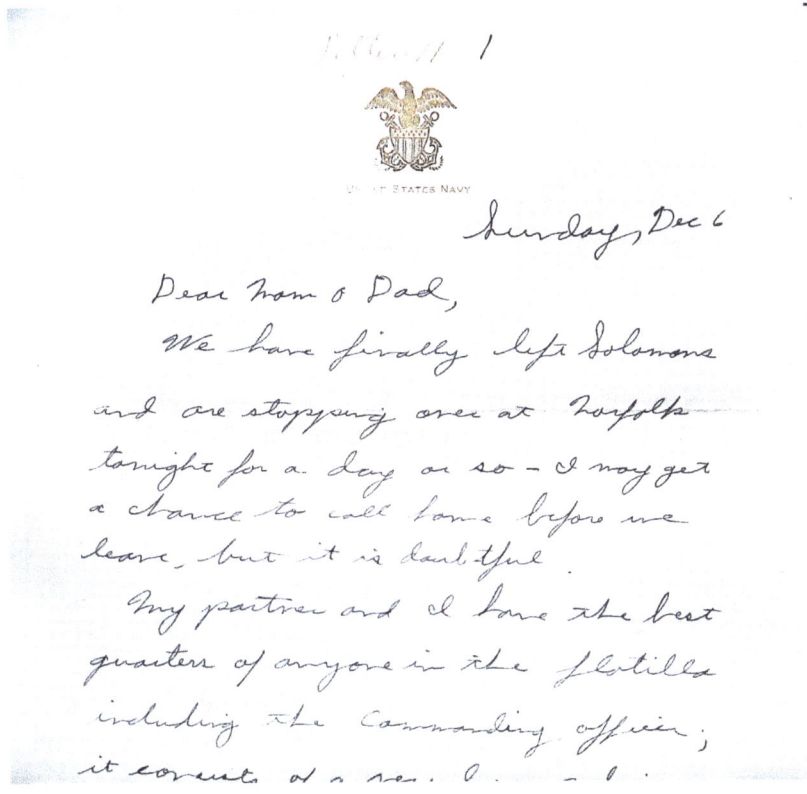

Letter #1
Sunday, Dec 6 [1943]

Dear Mom & Dad,

We have finally left Solomons and are stopping over at Norfolk tonight for a day or so— I may get a chance to call home before we leave, but it is doubtful.

After the war is over

My partner and I have the best quarters of anyone in the flotilla including the commanding officer; it consists of a very large cabin originally designed for seven or nine men so you can see that we have plenty of room. We have extremely comfortable bunks and furniture just like an office. We are equipped with fans, a heater, desk lamps, a porthole, in fact — all the comforts of home.

I really didn't get a chance to tell you how much I deeply appreciate your coming up to see me. It was a hard trip I know — no matter what you say and I'm afraid I didn't show all my love and happiness at seeing my folks; you were wonderful to do so much for me and I feel very humble to have such parents.

It is very likely that the next letter I write will be censored so you will understand if the news appears very meager concerning our whereabouts. I <u>can</u> say that it looks as though this winter will be a mild one for me — I could probably go swimming [on] Christmas day with no ill effects.

Bobby was getting along fine last night when I left him, but of course, he was extremely jealous of our good luck in having such capacious quarters.

We have a sort of office set-up on the ship, but I don't know how successful it will prove to be in rough weather because there is an ugly rumor to the effect that these LCI's are somewhat prone to roll and pitch in rough weather. However, we must accomplish some work <u>now</u> since my returns are due after the end of December and that is the worst part of the job; I am convinced that there are many other places I could be which are worse than this job and on the whole, I consider myself very fortunate particularly when I compare my lot with that of the enlisted men. There are plenty of fellows who probably would like to trade jobs with me and so don't feel sorry for me because I'm not doing exactly what I prefer.

After the war is over

Well, Mom & Dad, I will write again soon and call you sometime in the next month or so. My address now is:

Ens W. H. Pullen
LCI (L) Flotilla 13 Staff
c/o Fleet Postmaster, San Francisco

All my love

Bud

Autograph Letter Signed (ALS), no envelope.

Walter Pullen: "These LCI's are somewhat prone to roll and pitch in rough weather." December 6, 1943.

After the war is over

Letter #2

Sunday
Dec. 12, 1943

Dear Mom & Dad,

We have just completed a very uneventful trip, and there is very little I can tell you except that when the sea gets a little choppy, these LCI's act like a bucking mule. Several of my boys got a little seasick, and my partner Cliff LeVee was in pretty bad shape for the first two or three days; however, he has now recovered and blames his state on a candy bar that he ate just after we left. Fortunately, I have escaped all but the most common symptoms of seasickness which are headaches and sensations of dizziness; of course, we are yet to encounter any really rough weather, and until we do I cannot claim immunity as an old salt.

The food here aboard ship is excellent—it is a great improvement over Solomons and strangely enough, we have more fresh fruit and vegetables than when ashore. Obviously, on a long trip the majority of the food will be canned or preserved, but the meat (frozen) can be kept indefinitely — it is possible also to keep vegetables in the cold locker.

The four officers of the ship are all ensigns and are a very congenial bunch; Cliff LeVee and I are treated as guests with complete freedom to roam the ship at will. If you remember those pictures in "Life" and newspapers, however, you can imagine the time required to complete a circuit of the ship. We spend a good part of the time when we are not working in the "conn" which is the place from which the ship is directed. It is an experience to be right at the nerve center of the ship when things are happening.

After the war is over

In the "conn" of the LCI(L)-474.

As you probably remember now is the time for my quarterly returns which is undoubtedly the most exacting part of my job. We have been able to get quite a bit of work done during the periods when the sea was calm, but it is rather discouraging to work in such confined spaces especially when a good part of my records are packed away or misplaced. I am willing to bet that this will be the first set of disbursing returns rendered from an LCI. We type on wood boxes and chairs due to the paucity of desks and the poor supply officer has to stand up to do his work which has started since we left Solomons.

Much to my pleasure and delight I haven't worn a tie since we left, and I doubt whether I will get into blues again for a long time. The uniform for enlisted men is white so you know that we are in a comparatively warm climate.

After the war is over

You can understand the necessity for the lack of specific information as to our whereabouts or destination and also the reticence with which I express my feelings since this is the first letter I have ever written under censorship and I am not yet used to the idea (or reconciled I might add).

Hope the shop is coming along fine and the whole family is O.K. Don't worry if my next letter is quite a few days in arriving.

Bud

Autograph Letter Signed (ALS), stamped envelope.

Thursday
Dec 16, 1943

Dear Mom & Dad,

Well, now you know where I am so there's no use being so secretive about my location — by the way, don't spread the news around about my calling home the other day because there were very definite orders prohibiting long distance calls.

Key West is a pretty little town which like many others is now swollen to many times its former size with war workers and members of the armed forces with their families. The town is a good deal like most Florida localities except for the fact that there are quite a few Cubans here which gives the place a somewhat Spanish aspect.

The weather has been very warm up until yesterday when the temperature dropped to 60°; at the present time it is drizzling outside. I felt very sorry for you when I read of the cold wave

After the war is over

which swept the country and the paper says that snow fell in Pensacola, Fla., for the first time in 18 years so I know it must be a little chilly in Atlanta.

The Casa Marina Hotel, on Flagler Avenue, Key West, opened in 1920.

A couple of days ago we went swimming over at the Casa Marina which is a beautiful hotel taken over by the Navy for the housing of officers and their families. The water was fine, but much to my surprise, there was practically no surf and the beach was only a few feet wide with very little of the famous Florida sand that you are familiar with. The base here boasts a swimming pool which I plan to visit if the temperature ever gets back to the normal 75° or 80°.

Last evening we attended a supply corps banquet at the Casa Marina which was attended by all the supply officers in the area; I was amazed by the number (45) who attended because the base here is small and one would never think that there would be a need for so many.

After the war is over

My partner and I consider ourselves old salts by now and look with condescension [at] the shore-based supply officers, and they are a little jealous of us because we are afloat. However, all of them have been very helpful to us and have answered many of my questions about my returns which we are starting on soon.

From the few scraps of information garnered from many sources, I gather that it will be a long, long time before we actually get where we are going.

My address is still c/o Fleet Postmaster, New York, regardless of what I told you any other time and mail so addressed will be delivered just as promptly as the other address. Please forward any mail which I might receive to that address.

I'm afraid that I did most of the talking over the phone the other morning and I didn't get to hear much about you-all and the rest of the family, but maybe the next time I call you can talk and I will listen.

Give Belle my love
Your loving son,

Bud

Ens. W. H. Pullen
LCI (L) Flotilla 13 Staff
c/o F.P.O. New York, N.Y.

Autograph Letter Signed (ALS), stamped envelope.

After the war is over

Letter # 4

Thursday
Dec. 23, 1943

Dear Mom & Dad,

If the writing seems a bit shaky, blame it on the ocean — this ship would roll and pitch in a millpond so you can imagine what it does here on the Atlantic; I only hope that the next ocean I see will be smoother — of course, we haven't seen any storms or even rough weather, but the way this ship acts on a normal day is enough to make a landlubber out of anyone. I have not been really sick as have some of the boys, but I do stay slightly dizzy when I go below and try to do much work. Fortunately, two of my three disbursing storekeepers are not affected by seasickness so we have been able to get quite a bit done in spite of the difficulties. I don't remember whether or not I told you, but my chief storekeeper got sick at Norfolk and was sent to the hospital so I really had to work fast in order to get another man before we sailed which was the same day. My new man, Perry,[22] storekeeper 1st class, is a hard worker and [a] much more likable fellow than the chief so we are very well pleased that the swap occurred.

Our treatment aboard ship has been wonderful and yet, I don't see how anyone could ever choose the Navy for a lifetime job. The life is monotonous, particularly for the enlisted men, and one longs for a place to sit where he would be perfectly still if only for an hour or so.

As you can no doubt imagine it is rather warm here, and today I put on my shorts to take a sun bath — I'm afraid I somewhat resemble a tomatoe [*sic*] right now because the sun down here is plenty hot. Naturally, since the ship is moving, there is a nice breeze always and the heat, so far, hasn't been bad at all.

---
22. Lynn Dennis Perry (1915-2007), a former truck driver from West Point, Virginia.

After the war is over

I heard about the cold wave which swept the country just before we left our last stop so please accept my sympathy, and send me a little bit of the snow to rub on my sunburn.

The fact that [the] day after tomorrow is Christmas seems almost inconceivable, especially in view of the weather we are having right now. Obviously, the real reason that it doesn't seem right is because I am not home for the first time in my life and I sure do miss seeing my Mom & Dad and all the rest of the family. However, please don't feel sorry for me as far as Christmas dinner is concerned because we are having a real Turkey dinner with all the trimmings. My only hope is that we are in port so I will have no doubt about the quantity I should eat with safety.

I doubt that I have received any personal mail, but if I have, please forward it to me even though I won't get it for quite a while. It was wonderful talking to you from the last stop and I hope it won't be too long before I can call you again.

Give my love to Belle and her chillen and remember that I wish I could be with you this Christmas.

Your loving son,

Bud

Autograph Letter Signed (ALS), stamped envelope.

After the war is over

Ensigns Pullen and LeVee listed as "nonenlisted passengers" on this December 27, 1943, muster roll for USS LCI(L)-474.

Saturday
Jan 9, 1943 [1944]

Dear Mom and Dad

We are arriving at a west coast port tomorrow and I shall try to call you as soon as I can; I expect there will be some difficulty involved in getting a call through all the way across [the] country, but I will manage it somehow.

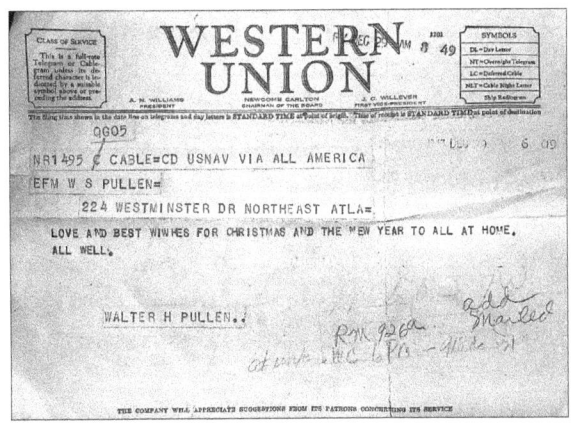

After the war is over

I sent you a telegram from Panama on Christmas Eve about fifteen minutes after we arrived at Cristobal—of course, it was one of those regulation messages, but I thought it was extremely fortunate that we arrived in time for me to send you Christmas greetings.[23] As I said, we were very lucky to get to Panama in time to celebrate Christmas with a wonderful turkey dinner with everything even including dressing and ambrosia just like but not quite as good as Belle's cooking.

The trip down from Key West was pretty rough and I am forced to admit that I am not immune from seasickness— I don't get nauseated, yet I feel kind of dizzy and uncertain as to whether I should eat or not upon occasions.

Fortunately, several of my storekeepers are unaffected by the rough weather and have continued to work diligently on the quarterly returns so that except for a few details, the returns are complete and ready for mailing. I am really relieved now that the returns are _over_ with, but, of course, they must be audited by the Federal government and I won't know for a long time whether they were completely in order. All disbursing officers make mistakes so I expect the auditors to find a few mistakes; however, I don't believe that they will find anything serious and on the whole, I am well satisfied with them.

We spent Christmas day and night in Panama, and as usual, the supply officers (my partner and I) were the first ones off the ship to see the sights. Cristobal and Colon which are on the Atlantic side of the Canal are right together, and as far as I can tell, no one seems to know which is which. The streets were filled with jabbering natives and American sailors doing their Christmas shopping. The natives vary in color from white to coal black and I defy anyone to tell the dark ones from a regular Georgia nigger until he opens up with a flow of excited Spanish.

---

23. See telegram on page 83.

After the war is over

Some one told me that the negroes came from Jamaica, but if they did, they sure came in droves because they appear to predominate in color.

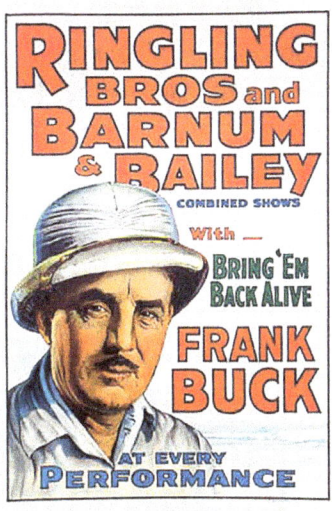

Frank Buck-Ringling Bros. and Barnum & Bailey Circus poster ca. 1938.

My partner and I purchased those jungle helmets of the type worn by Frank Buck[24] which are worn by many of the officers down here though as yet, we haven't worn them much.

I found my knowledge of Spanish of some use in reading the newspaper (which was also printed in English) but of little use in talking, since the natives speak so rapidly that I can't make any sense out of their conversation. However, we did have quite a bit of fun trying out the meager knowledge we do own and employed it at every opportunity.

We were amazed at the abundance of goods which are practically non-existent in the States now such as alarm clocks, razors, and

---

24. Frank Howard Buck (1884-1950) was an American big game hunter, exotic animal collector, global adventurer, circus performer, and author of seven books chronicling or based on his expeditions, beginning with *Bring 'Em Back Alive* (1930), which became a bestseller. He also starred in seven adventure films based on his exploits. The pith style helmet that he wore was common civilian headgear for Westerners in the tropics.

After the war is over

many others. I bought Mom a couple of little presents which aren't very much of anything, but are something you couldn't get at home. I think the bracelet is handmade by somebody or other out of silver.

There is no news as yet what we will do now, but it seems fairly certain that we will be here on the coast for some time. I will write again in a day or so.

Sure hope I have some mail tomorrow when we arrive at port.

Love to Belle and the Pups and I will hear the news from home soon, I hope.

Your son,

Bud

Autograph Letter Signed (ALS), no envelope.

Chapter 5

"I have truly a picnic."

Tuesday[25]
[January 1944]

Dear Mom & Dad,

My address has reverted back to the original one, that is, Flotilla 13 Staff so you will no longer need to put No 474 on the envelope.

---

25. Bud is now stationed at the U.S. Repair Base, San Diego, California, across the bay from the Amphibious Training Camp on Coronado Island.

After the war is over

Be sure to observe the change because I am no longer on the 474 and won't be with the ship.

I was very surprised today when a fellow who was working with me at Solomons, Md., came walking out of a clear sky. He and another fellow came across [the] country and are to be assigned here, but in what capacity nobody seems to know. If you remember my telling you, he was in the class following me at Harvard Supply School and was working as my assistant on the East Coast.

Well, an order came through several days ago which very definitely changed our organizational setup and at the same time postponed our time of leaving a month or so — maybe more. The future of this organization is always shrouded in doubt and our plans change almost daily. As the situation now stands, I don't know when or where we are going.

Thanks awfully for the clipping about the Atlanta boys in the service. Every one of the fellows was quite a good friend of mine except one whom I did not know. I was particularly glad to hear about Hugh Howell even though the news was most meager.

Our business is still rushing and according to the latest information obtainable, we expect to continue at the same tempo or at an increased rate.

Last night my partner and I with a couple of local girls attended the Ballet at the auditorium. It was our first exposure to such [an] aesthetic culture, we didn't know too much about what they were doing or how to interpret the choreography as it is called, yet even the most ignorant persons (about ballet) which we certainly are could not but appreciate the wonderful grace and fluid motions of the dancers both male and female. Some of the dances are a good deal like pantomime and are readily interpreted. Surprisingly

After the war is over

enough, a good part of the program was devoted to farcical dancing with some really good comedy scenes.

The stocking and snapshots haven't been mailed yet so don't worry about getting them—I will mail them in a day or so and write on the reverse of the pictures where they were taken.

Yesterday, I got a letter from both of you so I am very happy today.

Your son,

Bud

Autograph Letter Signed (ALS), no envelope.

Sunday

Dear Mom & Dad

It was certainly great talking to you last Friday night despite the trouble I encountered getting a call though – the tariff was a little high, but talking to my family is about the most enjoyable way I can imagine to spend my money.

My box arrived a couple of days ago – if there is anything omitted from it, I haven't discovered it

After the war is over

Sunday
[January 16, 1944]

Dear Mom & Dad

It was certainly great talking to you last Friday night despite the trouble I encountered getting a call through — the tariff was a little high, but talking to my family is about the most enjoyable way I can imagine to spend my money.

My box arrived a couple of days ago — if there is anything omitted from it, I haven't discovered it yet — you all were wonderful to go to so much trouble for me. The fruit cake is extremely popular with my boys and I have to ration it to the staff or else it would last only about fifteen minutes. I haven't opened some of the boxes yet and so I can't thank you for everything yet.

You will have to make up another list of those questions for me to answer because I remember only a few; one in particular regarding the vitamin pills. I answer in the affirmative — the rest I beg you to repeat just once more and I promise not to forget them.

The weather here is still very pleasant and the only time a top coat is necessary is in the early morning (by early morning I mean 6:00 which is _too_ early). We haven't had a real rain or cold snap yet and it looks as though we will be gone before the cold weather arrives. It is very likely that we will entirely miss this coming winter, but then that is only a guess. Such a possibility doesn't sound bad to me because you know how I like cold weather.

I wish you wouldn't worry about sending me anything for Christmas except maybe something very small and inexpensive — you see, I can't think of anything that I need and have no place to put anything of any value here at the base or on the ship when we do sail.

As a good supply officer, I have secured myself a complete set of winter clothing. So please don't worry about me getting cold either.

Bobby and I are going to the picture show tonight to see "Flesh and Fantasy."[26] Would you recommend our seeing it? Bobby has been assigned to a flotilla of LCT's which I showed you in the magazines when I was home.

Give my love to the whole family and tell Belle to take good care of my sisters.

Your son

Bud

P.S. Certainly appreciate your finding out what I must do to vote in the next elections.

Autograph Letter Signed (ALS), no envelope.

Monday
Jan 17, 1944

Dear Mom & Dad,

Somewhere back there I forgot the number of the letter, and so now I don't know what number to give this one. There isn't so much likelihood of my letter getting lost as there is of yours. We

26. An American anthology film starring Edward G. Robinson, Charles Boyer, and Barbara Stanwyck, partially written by Oscar Wilde, released on October 29, 1943, was one of Universal's top-grossing movies for that year.

After the war is over

still have received no mail at all, and, of course, I am dejected at the poor mail service. It seems that the mail addressed to the staff has gone somewhere else by mistake; therefore, I told you to send my mail to the LCI 474 because the fellows on the ship are getting their mail with little trouble.

My partner and I went to see the commandant of the yard, a Commodore[27], and asked him to provide us with an office ashore — he was very accommodating and placed us [in] a very commodious hut right down at the dock by the ships. We have secured a room in the Bachelor Officers' Quarters which is most convenient to our work — we can ride our bicycles to and from our office and are completely free since our boss, the flotilla commander,[28] is out on the bay and there isn't anyone else we have to answer to about anything.

From all I can gather we will be here about a month to six weeks before leaving for Pearl Harbor, and no one knows where we go from there. It is possible that I may be stationed in Honolulu.

Ralph Willis, Georgia Tech.

---

27. Byron McCandless (1881-1967), U.S. Naval Academy graduate (1905) who was awarded the Navy Cross during World War I. Although officially transferred to the retired list in 1940, he remained on active duty and in command of Repair Base San Diego until the end of the war.
28. John Henry Morrill, II. (See letter of February 7, 1944.)

After the war is over

Day before yesterday I bumped into Ralph Willis[29] who was a fraternity brother at Tech — you remember his father worked for the Southern Railroad. He is a Lt. (j.g.) and is stationed here at the base in the engineering department. Strangely enough, he was getting married at 4:00 o'clock the afternoon which I ran into him, but I was unable to get to his wedding which was quite a ways out from the city proper. He is now on a five-day honeymoon [in] Palm Springs.

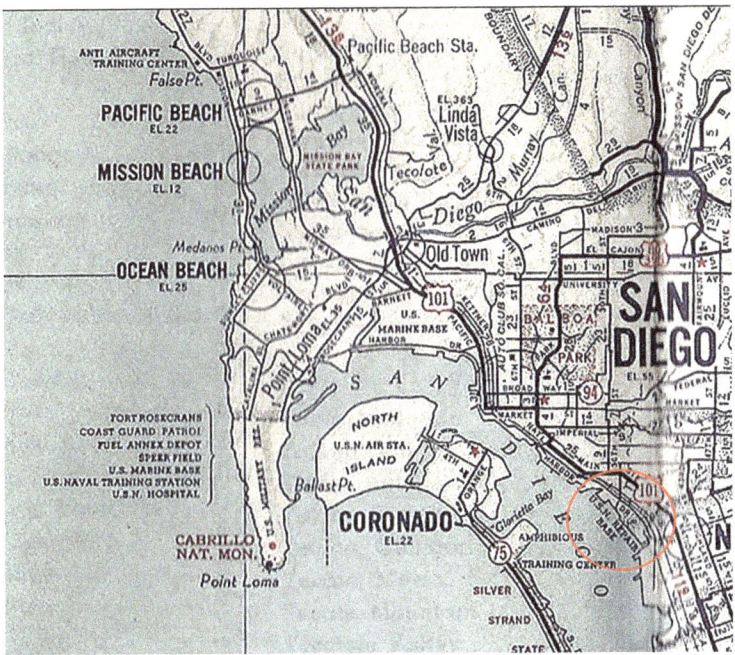

Military version of Auto Club map 1944 for San Diego, showing the location of the U.S. Navy Repair Base and other facilities.

---

29. Ralph Holland Willis (1919-2000), a son of locomotive engineer Charles Henry Willis (1881-1969), graduated in mechanical engineering from Georgia Tech in 1941. After joining the Navy, he entered Naval Training School at Dartmouth University. On January 14, 1944, at the Episcopal Chapel, St. James-by-the-Sea, in La Jolla, he married Nancy Alice Booth (1923-2006), a native of Grand Rapids, Michigan, who attended San Diego High School and Scripps College in Claremont, California.

After the war is over

Since I have received no letters, I don't have any idea of what you-all have been doing other than the brief news over the telephone — have you found a house anywhere that looks like a good deal? I still think it would be wise to make a down payment on a house even if you aren't particularly desirous of getting it all paid for; of course, it's only a suggestion, but I remember that we talked about such a possibility many times before but never actually progressed any further than looking at a house.

Also, you haven't told me (I know you have) whether you have seen any other beauty shops which are for sale and look like a good buy.

As yet we haven't had the opportunity of going up to Los Angeles, but we expect to next weeks perhaps for a couple of days. Maybe I will get up to the mountains and go skiing (don't worry about that too much).

Well, that is about all the news from here except that I miss everyone so much and certainly would like to get home to see everybody and the pups. Don't forget to write to my new address—

Your boy,

Bud

Autograph Letter Signed (ALS), no envelope.

After the war is over

LCIs moored in a nest in San Diego Bay.

Jan 22 [1944]
Saturday

Dear Mom & Dad,

I know it is unforgivable to go so long without writing because no one is ever so busy that he can't sit down a few minutes and write a few words, but I just didn't seem to have a chance the last few days.

On the spur of the moment, a friend on one of the ships and I caught the train to Los Angeles which is only a three-hour train ride by the streamline. That was on Thursday, and we returned this morning before work hours. Today was payday — the busiest time of all for me — particularly when it is difficult to balance such as tonight so you see I really haven't had too much time to write.

In the last three days, I received the first fourteen of your letters along with the wonderful fruit cake. After arranging the letters in chronological order, I alternated between reading letters and eating Christmas cake both of which were delightful and most welcome, especially since it had been so long since I received any mail. The clippings were also a happy thought because I always

After the war is over

like to be up to date on my Georgia politics and other sundry news which doesn't make the national scene.

Of all the cities on my travels, that is, since we began this cruise, Los Angeles is far and away the best. What was most surprising to me was the predominance of civilians — a condition unique among the other cities which are simply flooded with servicemen. We took a bus ride to Santa Monica and Wilshire Boulevard, and the shops and apparent unbroken stream of prosperous- looking establishments are rivaled only by New York in my estimation.

In sort of a whirlwind tour we took in the village of Hollywood where I did pass a male movie star on the street — I can't think of his name, but I have seen him in several minor roles on the screen. As expected, we were unable to get in[to] any of the the [sic] studios without passes which were unobtainable for that particular day.

There is the possibility that we might in a few days slip away and go to the Yosemite National Park about 300 miles above Los Angeles. The California scenery is fabulous and unlike anything we are familiar with at home. The mountains (in this area) are smooth, rolling and absolutely devoid of trees. Covered only with grass they are spotted with cattle grazing in huge numbers.

We are also considering the possibility of going up to some of the snow covered mountains in Southern California if only to watch the skiing.

> **Georgia 'Flu' Epidemic Is Reported Breaking**
>
> Georgia's epidemic of mild influenza is breaking, with a decline of 3,456 cases shown during the week ending January 8.
>
> Dr. Dan Bowdoin of the state health department reported a total of 3,054 cases in Georgia on January 8, as compared with 6,510 cases on January 1.
>
> Prior to last week the number of influenza cases had risen sharply for the past month, the report showed. On December 18 there were 1,218, on December 25 this figure had risen to 1,405, and on January 1 there were 6,510.

Atlanta Constitution, 1/14/1944, p. 2.

I'm so sorry to hear that flu is prevalent at home — hope your sore throat is nothing serious and the whole family can avoid the epidemic.

With my other mail I received a letter from Hugh who, as usual, didn't give the slightest indication of what he is doing or where he is. I sure appreciate your keeping me informed on the whereabouts of my friends and obtaining their addresses. I intend to write them just as soon as I get a chance.

Tell Belle that I can get her a job as [a] cook on any of these ships. The cook on the 474 would rather be a machinist's mate so the Quartermaster cooks most of the meals with surprisingly good results.

I sure miss my folks!

Bud

Autograph Letter Signed (ALS), no envelope.

After the war is over

Tuesday
Jan 25, 194[4]

Dear Mom & Dad,

My mail seems to be coming through O'K now both official and personal so maybe we are in better contact. I am all dressed up (if wearing blues is dressing up) and after paying one ship, I expect to catch a train for Los Angeles. You remember that when the flotilla goes out I am completely free to do as I please. We have a very nice little room here at the base in the Bachelor Officers' Quarters which is a great improvement on Solomons. Right now we have an automobile at our disposal for business purposes, but of course, we consider riding to and from work as well as other small trips as being in the line of business although it might be frowned on by some navy people, <u>particularly</u> those who have to walk.

I have had a run of luck both good and bad: first, my bicycle was stolen; I had about given it up after ten days when one of the storekeepers caught a boy riding it and repossessed it. However, I have not been so lucky in another respect. Last payday I paid out about $20,000 and upon checking up I discovered that I must have paid someone $20.00 too much and as yet I haven't recovered it. Losing money is a curse that sooner or later happens to all disbursing officers so I expected it and am not too chagrinned at reaching in my pocket for said $20.00; hope it doesn't happen too often.

Yesterday was very stormy here with [heavy?] rain and hail if not cold so I no longer harbor any illusions of sunny California; it really is a wonderful climate, however, except for the chilly nights.

The flotilla was in for the last three days, consequently our office has been like a madhouse and the quiet now is quite a rest. Three

After the war is over

or four weeks more is apparently the best estimate now before we leave; but I will call you again before we leave.

This letter has been all about me so please forgive it. I had a very nice letter from Imogene, and also one from Hugh and surely love getting your letters.

Your loving son,

Bud

P.S. Not censored so no return address on envelope. Use same address.

Autograph Letter Signed (ALS), no envelope.

Friday
January 28, 1944

Dear Mom & Dad,

The letter I got from home today was mailed on Jan 21 so evidently it takes about a week for even airmail to get here.

We got back from Los Angeles late last night after taking a two-day vacation from our duties here [in] San Diego and thoroughly enjoyed the trip.

A little bit of conscience-stricken, we rented an automobile and with two very nice girls that we met the night before at the Officers' Club, we took the whole day for a ride up in the California mountains (Sierra Madres). As is usually my luck it was so cloudy

After the war is over

after we got up above the cloud line that it was impossible to see more than 100 yards. It was just as though one were enveloped in a fog. However, the skies cleared for a few minutes occasionally and disclosed the magnificence of the California mountains which [are]quite different from the familiar Blue Ridge smokies. The beauty of these mountains is beyond description with human words. In the small time interval of one hour, we were debating whether to climb a fence and pick oranges off the heavily laden trees, and in the same hour we were throwing snowballs at each other. All this is within 40 or 50 miles of Los Angeles — I guess I forgot to mention that our trip was up to the Mount Wilson observatory which is about 5,000 ft elevation — not so high when compared with the San Jacinto and other surrounding peaks which go up to 8,000 and 10,000 ft. Because of the cloudy weather, the observatory was completely closed and we didn't get to look at the telescope, but even so, the view of the San Gabriel Valley was awe-inspiring when the curtain of mist lifted momentarily. I am enclosing some postcards of the snow-covered peaks in the Mt. Wilson area. Since we had only a few hours and were somewhat restrained by the bad weather not to mention the eleven cents a mile that the car was costing us, we didn't attempt to drive up to the ski fields so I have yet to see real live skiers except in the newsreels; maybe we can see them when this war is over and the world becomes sane again.

Another experience I would like for my folks to have is having a deer eat from your hand as he did mine. They sell crushed peanuts to feed the deer who are always hungry it seems. Though they like to be fed, it is very difficult to pet one and they are easily frightened; nevertheless, it was a novel experience to see the graceful creature at such close range.

Well, the ships are due back in tomorrow so we will have our usual busy weekend, and I have a little work to do before we walk down to the show to see "Madame Curie."[30]

---

30. The MGM-produced biopic, starring Greer Garson in the title role, was released on December 15, 1943. (See letter of February 7, 1944.)

After the war is over

I sure wish you all could have gone with me to see Mt. Wilson and hope that it will be possible someday.

Your boy,

Bud

Autograph Letter Signed (ALS), stamped envelope.

Monday
Jan 31, 1944

Dear Mom & Dad,

What fun it was talking to you early this morning — seems as though I am right there with you with the dogs hollering at the phone and Dad offering me razor blades. Please, please take the cost of the phone call out of my money because it is most unreasonable for you to pay for it merely because I couldn't possibly get enough change to suffice.

While riding uptown today in that automobile that I previously told you about, I saw John Beall's brother, Lamar,[31] but I didn't get a chance to do more than wave and yell at him.

Just to make certain that I didn't have sinus trouble, I had X-rays taken last Friday, and today I received the result which was negative. It must be that I am allergic to something which causes my nose to fill up — these symptoms are annoying in a small way yet there doesn't appear to be anything tangible causing them so I guess there's nothing I can do—

---

31. Madison Lamar Beall (1912-1979), a UGA graduate, whose younger brother was John Andrew Beall, Jr. (1919-1979), who went to Boys' High School and was a member of K.D.K. fraternity with Bud. John was at the time serving in the Army Air Corps, having enlisted at Fort McPherson near Atlanta on January 20, 1942. Lamar enlisted in the Navy on December 12, 1939, and was commissioned an ensign. He was discharged in 1961 as a commander.

After the war is over

I'm afraid that you have had a rather serious attack of the flu, and minimized it in order not to worry me — hope that your throat has returned to normal and the weakness disappears quickly. Please let me know if anything serious occurs. Also, tell me how Dad's health is — tell me whether he has had to work those extra long hours which he was afraid he might.

For the first time, several of us are planning to go down to Tia Juana [*sic*] tonight if for no other reason than to be able to boast to the home folks that we have been to Mexico. If there are any nylon stockings available, I shall certainly buy them for you. I'm afraid that those stockings from Panama weren't of the best material or workmanship, but I hope you liked the silver bracelet.

Since this is the last week that the ships are going out in the bay and leaving us on the beach, I think that we'll probably drop up to L.A. for a day or so because after this week we will be very busy taking care of all the ships various supply and dispersing needs.

Your letter #10 arrived yesterday quite a while after it was mailed on Jan 3 so I think that just about all of them have arrived now. I now have received up to #16.

Although the weather gets a little nippy here at night, one couldn't ask for more beautiful weather than we have —the temperature ranges around 60°-70° with the sun shining most of the day. It really is a paradise compared to the bitter cold of Boston and the varying temperature of Atlanta.

My bicycle was stolen again so I immediately made a canvass of the flotilla with good results for I recovered it in less than four hours.

I sure enjoyed hearing my family over the phone and miss them much—

Your boy,

Bud

Autograph Letter Signed (ALS), no envelope.

After the war is over

Wednesday
Feb. 2, 1944

Dear Mom & Dad,

Our beautiful weather is still prevailing here, and it is almost warm enough to go swimming — in fact, Ralph Willis suggested that we go to the beach next Sunday, but I demurred because it just doesn't seem quite hot enough.

My office is just about deserted since we gave all the boys liberty for 65 hours and they deserve it— that is — some of them; we are negotiating with the personnel division to obtain two more storekeepers for whom we want to trade two of our present men. If we are successful, it will certainly be a blessing because two of our men are definitely unsatisfactory. One, a college graduate, is a chronic loafer and complains about any work assigned to him. The other, is possessed of a most disagreeable disposition and you all know how it is to work around such a person. Maybe we'll get a couple of fellows who believe in more work and less griping.

According to the best information available which is of dubious character, we will be here about two weeks from next Saturday. Of course, that is only guesswork and it may be much longer— at least so we hope.

As I told you in the last letter, we went down to Tia Juana the other night. The entertainment there is miserable — evidently that is a secondary consideration. The prime attraction is the sale of articles which are rationed or non-existent in the United States.

Unfortunately, one is permitted to bring duty free only $7.50 worth of merchandise — over that amount the duty is very high

After the war is over

and applies to the whole amount of goods bought including the $7.50 worth so it is very advisable and economical to stay under the limitation. We derived a good deal of amusement from the precautions taken by the customs authorities. They asked one of our party to remove his hat so they could look into it.

One is not permitted to take any American money into Mexico except two dollar bills and silver; apparently, the Axis agents have American currency and would like to put it into circulation hence, the regulations against the use of American money.

> **MEXICO, U. S. CURB FLOW OF DOLLARS**
>
> Move to Stop Axis Agents From Use of Republic as Dump for Looted Currency
>
> COINS, $2 BILLS EXCEPTED
>
> Other American Money There Must Be Exchanged at Banks for Pesos and Imports Ended
>
> *Special to The New York Times.*
> WASHINGTON, Aug. 13 — To prevent the use of Mexico by Axis agents as a place to dump dollar currency loot from Europe, the Mexican Government has restricted the importation and use of American currency in Mexico and the United States Government has taken confirmatory measures.
> Mexico has prohibited the importation of all United States currency except $2 bills and coins. All United States currency now within Mexico must be turned over to the Bank of Mexico and associated banks, where its peso equivalent will be given to those who can prove that the dollars were legitimately acquired and free from Axis taint.
> Those who fail to turn in United States currency will be treated as enemies of Mexico under the laws prohibiting trading with the enemy.
> To supplement these measures the United States Treasury has made it illegal to export to Mexico after tomorrow any United States currency, other than coins or $2 bills. All other kinds of United States currency brought into this country from Mexico after tomorrow must be surrendered to the United States customs authorities at the border, who will turn it over to the Federal reserve banks for checking.
> The Treasury said that for the benefit of residents on either side of the border who have long been accustomed to use pesos and dollars without distinction the exemptions provided in the Mexican and United States rulings would allow pesos to enter and leave the United States and American two dollar bills and coins to enter and leave Mexico.
> The regulations will not affect the free passage across the border of checks, drafts, travelers checks and other credit instruments or prevent Americans or Mexicans from maintaining bank accounts in either or both countries. Such existing accounts will also be exempted.
> Tourists may avoid all inconvenience in going from the United States to Mexico by changing their money into credit instruments or $2 bills and coins. The $2 bill was excepted because very few such bills have fallen into Axis hands, although large amounts of United States currency of other denominations have. The total amount of $2 bills outstanding on June 1 was $54,000,000.
> The Treasury states that any person going through Mexico from the United States on the way to some other country would be allowed to take up to $250 of United States currency, plus $250 for each accompanying dependent.

New York Times, 8/14/1942, p. 27.

I purchased a little over the $7.50 limitation, but got by all right — the package was mailed to you yesterday. I was unable to find any nylon stockings, but I did buy a couple of pairs of silk stockings — they probably aren't of very good quality. Also, I bought a few other things: a tablecloth with napkins, a set of salt and pepper shakers, a Serape (I'm not sure what it's for), a bunch of Mexican coins both silver and copper, and a trick which I will try to explain. Hold the series of wood blocks at the end upon which is printed "Mexico"— bend it over until it is exactly upside down; if nothing happens, bend it the other way. Hope you can work it. Wish you could have gone with me, and if you decide you think the silk stockings are worthwhile I'll get more.

Your son,

Bud

Autograph Letter Signed (ALS), no envelope.

Monday
Feb 7, 1944

Dear Mom & Dad,

The last three days have been as hectic as always when the ships are in — thank goodness they are going out tomorrow again for a few days.

We are planning on taking a little trip in our Navy automobile just as soon as the ships pull away from the dock, but may be held up for a day or so by business.

A delay of maybe a couple of weeks before sailing is the dope now so it will probably be quite a while before we leave.

I have been very worried about Mom's health because I'm afraid you-all didn't tell me how serious the throat trouble is. I hope sincerely that the infection has cleared up by now and there are no ill effects which hang on.

After the war is over

While looking around on a ship here in the harbor, I wrenched my right knee slightly though not seriously, and it has been something of a nuisance for the last few days, but I believe that it is much better now.

If you happen to run across a book of the title "Down From Corregidor,"[32] you might read it. It was written by Commander John Morrill who is now my commanding officer, that is, the Flotilla commander. The book, although I haven't yet had a chance to read it, appears to be quite worth reading and I plan to do so as soon as possible.

Dad's letter was a very pleasant surprise and I sure appreciate the enclosed clippings. As yet I haven't received the Fortune magazine that Dad mentioned though I did get a magazine from General Motors. The news about the conversion of the Saginaw plant[33] is most interesting — I wish you would find out, if possible, what they are going to make now— Dad suggested automobiles but that seems hardly plausible. Let me know what you hear about the plant.

G. M. PLANT HERE TO HALT WAR WORK IN 4 MONTHS

The Sarginaw Steering Gear Division of General Motors will cease war production here upon termination of its present contract "within the next four months," it was announced Thursday.

The Saginaw division has been utilizing approximately one-third of the huge Chevrolet assembly plant on McDonough Road in producing 37 mm. and 57 mm. armor-piercing shot. The latter is a high explosive.

L. W. Staples, war contract co-ordinator for Saginaw, said no definite date for the shutdown could be announced at present. He was not authorized, he said, to state the reason for the shutdown.

When the present contract is completed, "Saginaw will close out here and Chevrolet will take over the plant space we have utilized, presumably for other war work," Mr. Staples said.

The Saginaw division moved here in July, 1942, and entered upon the war contract production program. No figures are available to the public at present on production figures, or the number of employes involved.

Atlanta Journal, 1/20/1944.

---

32. Morrill's book is entitled *South From Corregidor*.
33. In July 1942, the Saginaw Steering Gear (SSG) Division of General Motors took over management of an unused Chevrolet plant in Atlanta for the production of 37mm and 57mm armor-piercing shot for anti-tank guns. Recently, Atlanta newspapers had reported that SSG would be turning the plant back over to Chevrolet sometime within the next four months. Before the end of the war, the General Motors Chevrolet-Atlanta plant, with approximately 750 employees working 48 hours per week, was producing ½-ton and ¾-ton, 4x2 standard military-style, olive drab pickup trucks at a rate of nine trucks an hour.

After the war is over

An advantage of living in this part of the country is that of seeing all the new movies almost as soon as they are released. The base here has a very nice theater so we are well taken care of. Some of the pictures I have seen lately are: "Mme Curie," "Desert Song,"[34] "Destination Tokyo,"[35] and others. Both the Curie picture and "Destination Tokyo" are good and factual to a degree.

It is no wonder that you couldn't find out about my voting when Congress can't even make up its mind—[36] maybe they will decide how and if we can vote in the next election.

I am enclosing a check which you can deposit or spend. I am sending it because it would be next to impossible to cash it.

Sometime before we leave I am going to send home a little money but I'll tell you about that later.

Your son

Bud

Autograph Letter Signed (ALS), no envelope.

---

34. *The Desert Song* was a 1943 American musical film shot in Technicolor in which the hero fought the Nazis. It was Warner Brothers' highest grossing film of the year.
35. *Destination Tokyo* was a 1943 black and white American submarine war film starring Cary Grant as the sub commander. The film was accurate enough to be used by the Navy as a training tool for submariners.
36. After months of bickering over such a bill, it finally passed and became law in April 1944, allowing members of the Armed Forces to vote by absentee state ballot. (See letter of November 7, 1944.)

After the war is over

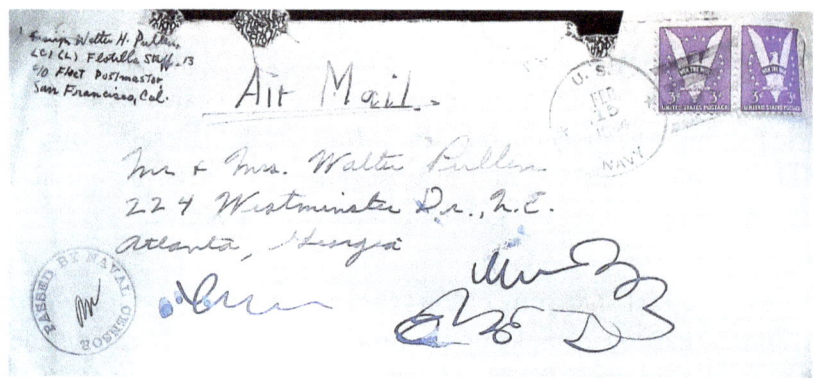

February 14, 1944

Dear Mom & Dad,

Sorry for the delay of a day or so in writing but maybe the phone call Sunday morning will atone for the neglect.

Our ships are back in now for good and consequently we are very busy — not so busy, however, as we will be tomorrow which is payday (the only day I work to hear some of the boys talk).

The day before the ships returned my partner and I took an all-day ride out in the countryside around here and were most agreeably surprised by the magnificent scenery. The Californians brag about the mountains up in the middle and northern part of the state, but seldom say very much about the range just east of San Diego. Starting out just riding we passed [through] the ever-present orange groves which abound in this section and soon began to climb on roads whose hairpin curves rival or even surpass those up around Lake Rabun & Vogel.[37] It is difficult to describe the terrain to you because we have nothing similar in Georgia or Florida. The mountains are very rocky and craggy but when one is some distance away they appear to be smooth and of a orange-brown hue studded with various forms of cacti and

---

37. Both in North Georgia, about 130 miles from Atlanta.

After the war is over

bushes. Great valleys with broad flat spaces are on either side of the ranges and one can see far distances seemingly impassable. We stopped after just entering the fringe of the Borrego desert which is a desolate, lonely place where nothing grows but the bushes. It doesn't look like the familiar conception of a desert with shifting sands and no vegetation, but nevertheless it would be a terrible place to get lost in. There is no farming and only an occasional dwelling; why anyone would want to live in such a place is difficult to understand. From one of the high peaks in the Laguna range, Point Inspiration, which is about 6000 feet [in] elevation it is possible to see the Imperial Valley and the Salton Sea, this huge lake is 241 ft below sea level; I haven't found out yet whether it is a salt sea,[38] but it is 60 miles across and shows plainly on the map if you care to look.

On the way back we came a different route and saw a lovely little lake, Cuyamaca, located high up in the mountains. It looked very blue and cold as our mountain lakes do. Notwithstanding the temperature which was many degrees above freezing, patches of snow were everywhere and to prove it I had my picture taken standing in a patch. Only a few minutes before we took pictures down in the desert. As soon as we get the pictures developed I'll send them home.

One of the boys went down to Tia Juana last night and bought a couple of pairs of stockings which I will send home soon.

It was wonderful talking to my folks the other morning—seemed as though I [was] there right in the hall with the dogs barking at the phone.

Your boy

Bud

Autograph Letter Signed (ALS), stamped envelope.

---

38. The water of the Salton Sea has a salinity greater than that of the Pacific Ocean.

After the war is over

Feb 18, 1944

Dear Mom & Dad

This letter is being written in bed so you will understand the scrawl.

Nothing noteworthy has happened lately except that I flew up to San Pedro yesterday and flew back today. San Pedro is one of the great shipbuilding yards on the West Coast and one could see row after row of merchant ships in varying degrees of completeness along the waterfront. It is impossible to tell when Los Angeles, Wilmington, and San Pedro begin and end but somewhere in the district I saw hundreds and hundreds of oil wells — most of them were being pumped so I presume that they are still yielding. The wells are only a hundred feet or so apart and are drilled everywhere except on the streets — small wonder that they haven't set up a derrick right in the middle of Wilshire boulevard or at the corner of Hollywood and Vine.

It takes over an hour on the Pacific Electric (a street car like our Stone Mountain line) to go from L.A. to San Pedro and in the past 24 hours I have ridden the following conveyances: Plane, buses of all assorted sizes, train, street car, ferrys, station wagon, small boat, bicycle, to get where I was going and return. The plane trip was very pleasant and provided an excellent opportunity to see what the terrain of Lower California looks like from the air. Such a trip also gives one an idea of the wealth of this state — no one need go hungry or ragged, particularly in these times. It looks as though half the people of California must own yachts since there are so many in the little coves along the seashore. Almost any place along the beach looks as though it would be good swimming — a far cry from the rugged New England coast which I saw last year.

After the war is over

Our mail service is still erratic — as yet I haven't received the candy you sent but certainly look forward to getting it because I like my Mom's fudge.

I don't remember whether I told you or not but Meddy[39] wrote me a letter and enclosed a card with a picture of Sue[40] which evidently was the family Christmas card. The little girl is very pretty and chubby. Also, I received a letter from Hugh dated Dec. 14 in which he said that he told Fay[41] (the present girlfriend) to go by and call on you-all. Has she ever come by?

I have some pictures we made on our little trip and will send them with two more pairs of stockings soon.

Your boy

Bud

Autograph Letter Signed (ALS), no envelope..

Sunday
February 27, 1944

Dear Mom & Dad,

I held payday today so it has been the usual hectic conglomeration of griping, shouting, and all the other associated evils that happen only twice a month— for which I am truly grateful. As usual, everyone seems to think he is overpaid or underpaid (mostly underpaid) and it is most difficult to retain one's temper. I hope that I don't keep this job too long because I am afraid

---
39. His mother's younger sister, Meldrin (Meddy) Hudson (1903-1961), who married Charles Gustavius (Gus) Caravalla (1903-1989) in 1937 and was living in the Tampa, Florida, area at the time.
40. Meddy's daughter, Sue Gene Caravalla, born in 1942.
41. Anna Fay Moffett (1924-2017), daughter of Herbert Rutherford Moffett of Atlanta, a former mayor of Dublin, Georgia. Hugh and Fay would marry on July 3, 1945, but divorce eight years later.

After the war is over

that my disposition will become warped and perpetually gruff; it isn't that any one instance of ignorance is particularly serious but when multiplied by about one thousand, one is apt to lose his temper and blow up over small incidents. Upon reflection, I always realize that compared to what some of our boys are undergoing, I have truly a picnic. I only have minor annoyances and not guns to contend with.

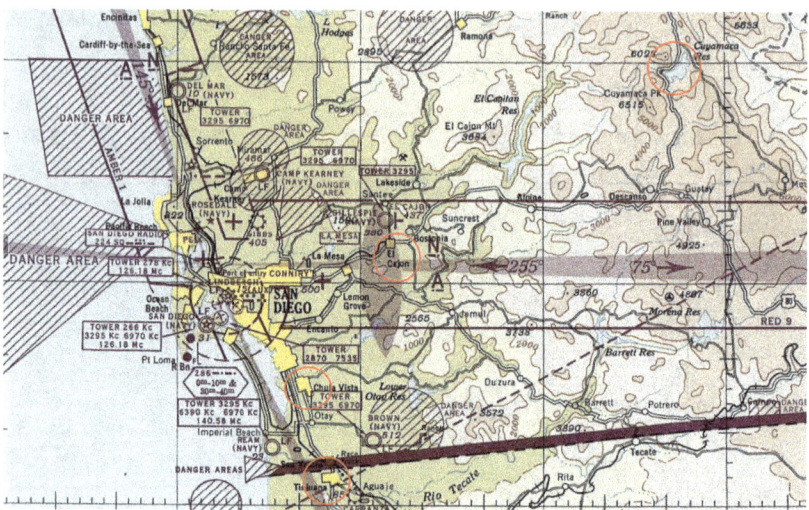

San Diego County Map (1944)

Last week I went out to have dinner with Ralph Willis and his wife — he is living at his mother-in-law's home because it is practically impossible to find one anywhere in San Diego — there are rewards offered in the newspapers for information leading to the securing of houses. But to get back to the dinner; it was very nice and homey and I enjoyed it greatly.

The following night Cliff and I had dinner at a friend's home out in El Cajon, a suburb of San Diego; the friend is Don Lindau,[42]

---

42. A native of Detroit, Michigan, Donald August Lindow (1916-2012) was in "Class H" with Cliff LeVee at the Navy Supply Corps School at Harvard. A 1938 graduate of Wayne State University, he worked for seven years as a payroll auditor for the Michigan Mutual Liability Company in Detroit prior to enlisting in the Navy. After the war, he returned to Michigan and rose through the ranks of Michigan Mutual (later named Amerisure) to become its chairman and CEO.

After the war is over

a fellow supply camp man who was at Harvard with us even though I didn't know him there. He has a tremendous disbursing office here and has all the problems I have, multiplied manyfold. However, he has the equipment and personnel to handle such a large volume and also an assistant ensign to help him.

Today I received a letter you all wrote to me on Christmas Day and mailed the following day, but most of your letters came through all right. Take good care of yourself, and don't forget to write to me leaving off the #474.

Your boy

Bud

Autograph Letter Signed (ALS), stamped envelope.

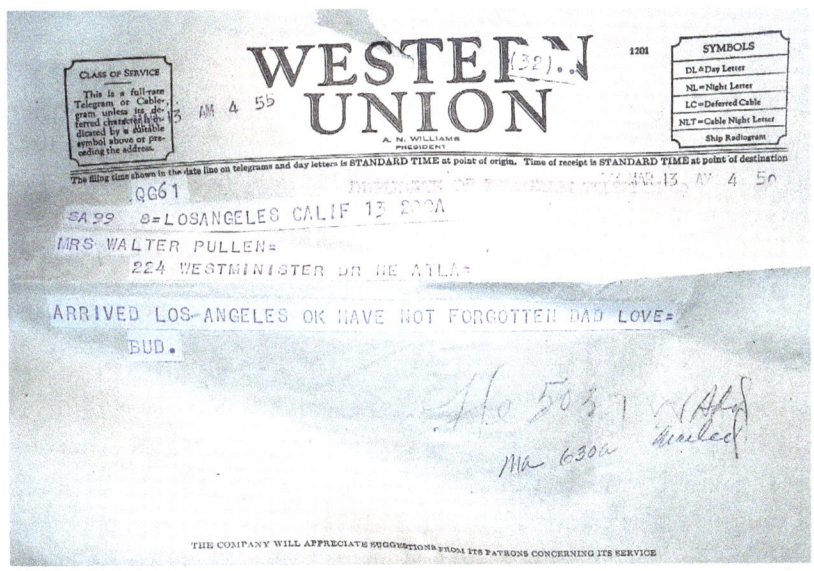

Telegram from Bud to Stella Pullen, March 13, 1944.

After the war is over

March 16, 1944[43]

Dear Mom & Dad,

I hope the telegram from my commander telling me to return didn't worry you — he thought that I was still at home and thought I should be here. Everything is all right now.

My trip back here was quite eventful and I'll tell you about it: I left Atlanta[44] about 10:00 that night and flew to Birmingham, Mobile, and New Orleans where the flight was canceled because of bad weather. After spending a night and part of the next day in New Orleans, I caught a ride to Brownsville, Texas which was a mistake — if you will look on a map, you will see that I was definitely off my route and practically out of the country. Brownsville is at the southernmost tip of Texas which is about the same latitude as Key West, Florida. The temperature there was very warm and a soldier told me that people were swimming.

The plane upon which I was riding was the private plane of a Major General who was flying to Panama. The general was very nice to me and gave me his father's address and phone number in Coronado, Calif. And insisted that I call up and talk to his father (also a general). I called the other night and his mother asked me to come out and see them — I don't think I will get a chance to go, however.

I caught a train from Brownsville up to Corpus Christi where I tried in vain for about 24 hours to catch a plane west but to no avail. From Corpus Christi I caught a train to San Antonio, Texas, where I was very lucky and after a layover of about 18 hours I caught a plane (army) straight through to Los Angeles. We stopped in Big Spring, Texas; El Paso, Texas; Phoenix, Arizona; and thence to L.A. where I spent the night sitting in the railroad

---
43. Bud had just returned to San Diego, after being promoted to Lieutenant (j.g.) on March 1, 1944, and given a 10-day leave to visit home.
44. On March 9, 1944. (See letter of March 19, 1944.)

After the war is over

station and finally arrived in San Diego on the 13th of March. Altogether I guess I must have covered 7 or 8 thousand miles on my trip home & back here.

I haven't forgotten Dad's birthday, but have been so very busy that I haven't had a chance to get him his tie & socks.

You son,

Bud

Autograph Letter Signed (ALS), stamped envelope.

Sunday
March 19, 1944

Dear Mom & Dad

I received your letter yesterday in which you were worried about whether I got back here on time and also you were worried about that telegram. Hope my letter has reached you by now and allayed your fears. It really wasn't a bad trip even though it did consume four days.

We are still very busy and with no let-up in sight. The best information now available which is never very reliable indicates that we will leave here somewhere between the 15th and 30th of April. It does look as though we must leave somewhere around that time, however.

Since this is Sunday afternoon our business is rather slack so I let the boys off for the afternoon and I am the only one in the office at the present time. Our radio is really a great blessing particularly

After the war is over

on Sunday afternoon when programs are so delightful. The other evening I looked up a girl that Louise Keel[45] asked me to call and took her out to dinner. I was sort of staggered when I saw the prices of a Turkey dinner ($3.50) which was the only dinner they had besides chicken ($3.00). It was too late to leave so I (we) had dinner but I could hardly enjoy it when I thought of the price.

Hope that Mom can find another operator for the shop but imagine that it will be a problem to find someone who would be satisfactory in all respects, maybe an ad in the paper will accomplish something.

Some more supply officers have arrived from Solomons to take care of ships which aren't ours to our great relief—we were taking care of all the LCI(L)s for a time.

Well, it is needless to say but I just want to remind you how wonderful [it was] to be home even if for so short a time. Tell the dogs that I miss them too. I am sending you the Commander's book which I told you about.

Your boy,

Bud

Autograph Letter Signed (ALS), stamped envelope.

---

45. Bud had taken Keel to a Sigma Chi fraternity dance in March 1942 when he was a student at Georgia Tech. Born in Macon, Georgia, August 20, 1920, Louise Keel was the daughter of Edward Burr Keel, Jr., a Milledgeville businessman. A graduate of Peabody High School and Georgia State College for Woman (now Georgia College), she was employed for several years in Atlanta, first in the accounting department of Southern Bell Telephone Company (1942-43) and later as a systems representative for IBM (1944). After she returned to Milledgeville in 1945, she married Army officer James Bertram ("Goat") Helton, Jr. She founded the Town and Garden Club and was active in it for many years. She was a member of First United Methodist Church, a charter member of the George O. King Sunday School Class, and an avid bridge player. Keel's sister, Myrtle, married on March 15, 1944, Joe Robert Tillman of Statesboro, Georgia, who attended Georgia Tech and was a member of the Sigma Chi fraternity.

After the war is over

Louise Keel in the
Atlanta Constitution,
4/12/1942, p. 41.

Saturday
March 25 [1944]

Dear Mom & Dad,

As is readily apparent, I am writing this letter at my office using our official stationery through the kind offices of the U.S. Navy.

The reason that those two letters were returned to you was because the number of the flotilla was omitted, in other words, your address read: "LCI(L) Flotilla" and not LCI(L) Flotilla 13. Probably just an oversight. We received information which indicates that some of our mail might have gone to Pearl Harbor which I believe must be true since I haven't received any mail

After the war is over

from home in several days. If that is the case, I should get the mail reasonably soon because we are very definitely going to leave in the next month and maybe earlier.

By the way, it is still possible to send your letters to me with a 6¢ air mail stamp — and vice versa; that is possible only when you write to a fleet post office.

I sent Dad a little present which should get there in a few days; if you don't receive it soon let me know; also I sent Belle a little "box" so she won't go up to Chattanooga to live.

My business is still very fast and the staff of another flotilla is forming here; we have drafted some of their storekeepers and thereby have been very lucky because we were literally swamped with work for a while.

As it is the end of another fiscal quarter, we are having to render returns again perhaps under more favorable conditions — from what we hear, the working conditions at Pearl Harbor aren't going to be too favorable.

The other day I recognized a familiar face from Tech; upon talking I discovered his companion was a fraternity brother from Tech and knew quite a few of the fellows that I know.

Well, hope all my mail isn't going to Pearl Harbor and I get some soon.

Your boy,

Bud

Autograph Letter Signed (ALS), stamped envelope.

After the war is over

Tuesday
March 28 [1944]

Dear Mom & Dad,

The mail is definitely confused somewhere because I have received no letters from home in quite a while — yet my official mail is coming through all right so maybe it is just unexplainably held up somewhere along the line.

I received a preliminary report on the set of returns which we rendered last December and am very well pleased with the report which, although not perfect, was incorrect only in one or two relatively unimportant instances. Of course the final audit by the General Accounting Office is the last word and I won't receive their report for 18 to 24 months.

Sunday, I went out and had dinner with the girl that Louise Keel asked me to look up—she lives out in Chula Vista which is sort of like Buckhead near Atlanta. The dinner was very nice and that evening we went to see the opera "Carmen" which was being put on by the San Carlo opera company who I had seen before in Boston. It was the first time I had ever seen "Carmen"; have you ever seen it? The woman[46] who had the leading role certainly was made to order for the portrayal and most of the singing was very good, that is, as far as I could tell.

The weather here is getting much warmer and out of the city the flowers, trees, birds, and other indications of Spring are plentiful. In fact, some birds built a nest in our office which we have had to regretfully remove.

I hope that Dad has gotten his little gift by now and also hope Belle has received her box.

---

46. Mezzo-soprano Coe Glade (1900-1985) sang the title role of "Carmen" when the San Carlo Opera Company toured the U.S. that year.

After the war is over

We got two new men several days ago—one is a former high school principal, the other was in pre-medical school when drafted so you see we have quite a bit of education.

I am sending a check home because it would be so much trouble to get it cashed, just deposit it at your leisure in the account.

Your son,

Bud

Autograph Letter Signed (ALS), stamped envelope.

Sunday
April 2, 1944

Dear Mom & Dad,

Please excuse my writing in pencil, but my pen is dry, and no ink is available. Also forgive the delay for a day or so in writing.

You ask me what I think about buying that little place over on Monroe Drive — it seems to me that $2550 is a little high for a place with no plumbing and not much else especially when there is only one acre of land in the whole tract. Of course, it is impossible for me to tell much about it from here such as: Is it on a paved road? Will the property increase or decrease in value? Could one live in the house if it became necessary? These are a few of the considerations to think about before purchasing the lot. Maybe I will try to call you tonight and get some more information on the whole deal.

It was certainly great getting Dad's letter and I do believe that he should write more often.

After the war is over

I hope that the birthday present has gotten home by now and you-all can find some time for it. Please let me know if it hasn't so I can check up here at the post office.

Well, it was a beautiful day here today and so a girl friend and I went out to the zoo in Balboa Park. The San Diego Zoo is renowned the country over as one of the most complete, and it certainly surpasses any I have ever seen. They have an aviary which is a tremendous wire enclosed place (really a small valley) where there are many different species of birds including eagles and buzzards. Peacocks and guineas roam all over the zoo at large and don't appear to be frightened at all by the spectators. On the whole it was a most enjoyable afternoon.

Let me remind you that you can still use a 6 [cent] air mail stamp if writing to a fleet post office address; however, I very often don't put a return address on my letters home so I won't have to bother with getting my mail censored. So, therefore, I must use an 8 [cent] stamp. By the way, don't mention to anyone that my mail isn't censored.

Will probably try to call tonight.

Your loving son,

Bud

Autograph Letter Signed (ALS), stamped envelope.

After the war is over

Friday
April 7 [1944]

Dear Mom & Dad,

I got you letter mailed April 3 today so I guess I must have most all of them; they seem to come in spurts of two or three.

It was wonderful talking to the family the other morning and it seemed as though I was right there at home. I received the picture of the dogs with Belle, the dogs with Mom, and the dogs with Dad— they sure are pretty and clean — I think the pictures of the family were exceptionally good, don't you? Everyone here in the office remarked how young Mom looks and say that it is almost impossible to believe that you are old enough to be my mother.

Oh yes, I meant to tell you that I got the letter from Kentucky all right.

Well, I have some news for you— it looks right now as though we are going to be here for another two months — of course, that is only an approximate date and nothing definite is available. We have reached the point where we would just as soon go, as stay around here never knowing from one day to the next when the plans will be changed. Since a good part of my ships have departed, our business has slacked off considerably and we are enjoying the unexpected respite, particularly when we think of the way and amount that our business will increase when we do catch up with the rest of the flotilla.

The weather here is getting warmer and warmer; however, most of the local people say that it doesn't get much warmer than it is now so it appears to be a pleasant climate all year round. It still isn't quite warm enough to go swimming at one of the

After the war is over

several good beaches, but I am looking forward eagerly to taking advantage of the excellent surf.

One of the captains of the ships just came in and invited us to dinner. Actually we would much prefer to eat at the officers' mess on the base, but I suppose we would hurt his feelings if we refused.

I sent Mom a little present for her birthday which is different if not so useful. Let me know when it arrives.

Your loving son,

Bud

Autograph Letter Signed (ALS), stamped envelope.

Tuesday
April 11, 1944

Dear Mom & Dad,

We have been very busy with our returns and are still pretty crowded for time, but I guess it will always be that way in this outfit. I haven't heard from you-all since I wrote the news home that we will be here maybe a couple of months more so I don't know what you think about it.

Easter Sunday I went out to Chula Vista and went to church with the Galligan[47] family (the whole family of the girl that I know out there) and then went out to her father's lemon grove which is about 25 miles out in the country in a valley.

---

47. Son of Michigan farmers, George Thomas Galligan (1871-1951) moved his family from the Hood River Valley in Oregon, where he was an apple and pear rancher, to Chula Vista in 1937, after he purchased a lemon grove. He had three daughters, including the youngest, Sylvia Jean, born 1925, who appears still to have been living at home at 466 E Street, Chula Vista.

After the war is over

You would certainly enjoy seeing the lemons, limes, oranges, and grapefruit hanging off the limbs in almost unbelievable quantities — I think of my folks every time I see such manifestations of nature because you both love the sight of things growing. It seems that as far as the lemon crop is concerned, there is no winter, and lemons are picked from the same trees eleven months out of the year. Of course, I would much rather have been at home with the family for Easter, but since I couldn't, it was most fortunate that I had some friends out in the country to spend the day with. You see, San Diego is so crowded that it is a struggle to do anything at all — there are about two or three times as many people out here as the city could reasonably take care of.

The news about Franklin and Imogene[48] going to Brazil is very exciting—please ask him to keep an eye out for a job for me after the war is over—I think I would like to go down there because the opportunities are so great. It is only a thought, however and probably I would change my mind if the occasion arose. Even so, I would like to know what Franklin thinks about the possibilities.

Hugh wrote me a letter giving me his new address but not much news except to say that he had been looking for me.

Wish I could have been home for Easter.

Your boy,

Bud

Autograph Letter Signed (ALS), stamped envelope.

---

48. Bud's Aunt Imogene and her husband Franklin Daniel Blackstock (1904-1977). Imogene and her three children, all boys, lived with the Pullens at 224 Westminster Drive, Atlanta, when her passport to Brazil was issued on October 24, 1944. Franklin worked for Goodyear Tire & Rubber Company in Akron, Ohio, and went to Brazil in the fall of 1944 as a *"técnico borracha"* [rubber technician].

After the war is over

Brazilian passport for Imogene Hudson Blackstock and children.

Friday, April 13 [14] [1944]

Dear Mom & Dad,

Well, at last I got a letter from home — it was mailed on April 8, and therefore didn't say whether Mom's birthday present had arrived yet or not, maybe it will get there in a few days.

Evidently, you haven't gotten the letter in which I said that I would be here until June or else you would more than likely have commented on the change in plans.

We are still extremely busy and can hardly keep our heads above water, but I think that we will be caught up in about two weeks.

The news about the flourishing business of the shop is most gratifying, however, I don't want my Mom to work too hard and would prefer that she didn't work at all. If you ever see a house which looks like a reasonably good buy, you could hardly go

After the war is over

wrong in paying the down payment because it looks as though it is going to be a long war and some degree of inflation is inevitable; the only protection against inflation is ownership of property and land.

The glasses that John sent me are just exactly what I wanted and it was certainly swell of him to go to so much trouble for me. I haven't thanked him yet, but intend to do so as soon as time permits.

The weather here isn't 10 degrees or hardly 5 degrees warmer than it was when we got here. The temperature apparently stays about the same the year round — I don't think anybody wants to go back to New England or the Midwest where the winters are so severe.

My easter eggs and fudge were most welcome and proved quite a success with all the boys in the office. I ate the whole bottle of olives in one sitting.

We went out to a friend's home out in El Cajon the other night and had dinner with him. He went to Supply school with us and runs a large disbursing office over in Coronado, and, therefore, is subject to many of the same grievances that I am. He has a nice little home out there and is very kind to us to have us out.

I am still waiting for a letter from Dad so I can see how the pen writes.

Your boy,

Bud

Autograph Letter Signed (ALS), stamped envelope.

After the war is over

Sunday
[April 16, 1944]

Dear Mom & Dad,

This has been a very quiet Sunday and I took a sunbath right out in the front yard of our B.O.Q. The sun is plenty hot, but the ever-present breeze kept it from getting too warm. The wind seems to blow almost continually — probably because we are right here on the coast.

We are still very busy and it looks as though we will continue to be that way for the next couple of weeks.

How is the shop coming along with all of the new business down there which you mentioned in your last letter? The figures you quoted in your letter certainly sound as though business is going right along at top speed. Maybe it won't prove too difficult to obtain operators at least some who can work on a part-time basis.

I have at last managed to accumulate $200. for which I am enclosing a money order. I want you to include this with our little kitty which is available for some kind of venture whether it be business or a house or farm. The thought of a little farm like we almost bought out there near Douglasville still sort of appeals to me. That is, provided the house on it is livable and could be used as a home if times ever really got tough. Of course, there is no hurry about doing anything yet it might be advantageous to keep an eye out for something that looks like a bargain.

The news that Imogene is coming to Atlanta to live for a while is nice to hear — especially so because you-all like a lot of family around and Imogene definitely has a lot of family. She will undoubtedly have to go out in[to] the suburbs of Atlanta in order to find a place to live.

After the war is over

Well, I guess that is about all the news from here so remember

All my love

Bud

Autograph Letter Signed (ALS), stamped envelope.

Thursday
April 20, 1944

Dear Mom & Dad,

We are still very busy and have been working almost every night up until 8:00 o'clock or 10:00 o'clock, but it looks as though we are about to get out from under the load and in the clear again.

Imogene sent me a picture of little Tuck[49] which is about the most entrancing I have ever seen of any baby— he actually looks like the advertisements in the magazines of babies after eating somebody's canned milk or baby food for a while.

I am very glad to hear that Dad is planting a garden out in the backyard— the very thought of those big tomatoes makes me homesick. I do wish you could see the citrus orchards out here; the railroad to Los Angeles passes through some of the largest orange orchards in the country and one experiences a desire to get off the train and eat about a dozen or so. I always thought the orange remained green or yellow until it ripened— these oranges are a rich orange color during the whole period of their growth and I don't see how one can tell when they become ripe. Evidently, the way they tell is to take a test of the amount of

---
49. Henry (Hank) Tucker Ansley Blackstock, who was born in Atlanta on April 23, 1943. Hank Blackstock founded in the early 1980s Blackstock & Co., an investment banking and brokerage firm in Jacksonville, Florida, with offices in Orlando, Atlanta, and New York City.

sugar content and when it reaches a certain point, the oranges should be picked.

It has been several days since I received a letter from home so I haven't heard what you have to say about the tornado which struck Georgia and North Carolina.[50] From what information is available, I don't think it was so severe as the two previous ones at Gainesville.[51]

Hope to get a letter tomorrow.

Your boy,

Bud

Autograph Letter Signed (ALS), stamped envelope.

Sunday
April 23 [1944]

Dear Mom & Dad,

Well, I didn't make it to church today — I probably could have if I had tried, but it didn't seem as though I could get away. As is usual it is cloudy today (Sunday) and therefore , my only chance to get out in the sun is postponed another week until next Sunday.

Our business has subsided at last and we are letting the boys take a leave of ten days and travel time for which they are truly

---

50. At least 40 persons were killed and more than 500 were injured by a night tornado that hit northeast Georgia and western South Carolina on April 16, 1944.
51. In what was one of the worst weather-related disasters in Georgia history, two separate funnel clouds converged on downtown Gainesville, Georgia, on April 6, 1936, killing more than 200 people, injuring 1,600, and damaging or destroying more than 1,000 homes. Another tornado killed more than 100 people in Gainesville in January 1903.

After the war is over

grateful — I'm certainly glad for them because they have been working long hours and on very tedious work — you can imagine how excited they all are about getting home.

Cliff and I are considering going out this afternoon and looking for a secluded golf course — it will have to be secluded though, because we are about the worst clubs that ever got loose on a golf course.

As happens every so often our mail is fouled up again. Someone sent the post office a notice to send all of our mail to San Francisco and, therefore, we haven't received any mail for several days. Maybe they will get it straightened out eventually, but it is most annoying to know that your mail is being misdirected.

This paragraph is being written eight hours later in bed and, boy, am I tired. We found our golf course out at the Chula Vista Country Club and I believe that it is the best course that I have played on; of course, I have played on only a very few, but this course is beautiful because it sits right in the middle of a group of mountains and the fairways and greens are in excellent condition. After playing eighteen holes, though, we were both pretty well worn out and very happy to come home and get in bed. The club there is one of the few places I have seen in San Diego which isn't so overcrowded.

Well, I have been thinking of my family all day and wondering what you are doing.

Your boy

Bud

Autograph Letter Signed (ALS), stamped envelope.

After the war is over

Thursday
[April 27, 1944]

Dear Mom & Dad,

Day before yesterday I received four letters from home including one from Dad so now I am pretty well informed on all the latest news from Atlanta.

I couldn't resist taking down our atlas just as soon as I found out Imogene and family were going to San [São] Paulo, Brazil, and seeing just exactly what part of the country it was located in — apparently, it is right on the coast in the most favorable zone as far as temperature is concerned and looks like a nice place to live. Maybe you can go down on the Clipper and visit them sometime after the war.

Last evening here we had a hard rain, and it is still a bit chilly — seems as though it will never warm up out here. The temperature hasn't changed more than 5° F since we have been here which is about three and one-half months now. Cuyamaca Lake which is 50 miles from San Diego had a storm with eight feet of snow.

Last night I went out to Ralph Willis' house for dinner and we played bridge afterward for several hours with some of his friends here at the base. It has been quite a while since I played bridge with any real players so I'm afraid I was a little rusty, but it doesn't take very long to remember the details.

We are sort of shorthanded here at the office this afternoon because three of our boys are on leave and will be gone for two weeks — it is too bad that I didn't get a few more days to stay at home. They are planning to make the whole trip by train for which I certainly don't envy them.

After the war is over

As I told you, I received the little pair of glasses from John, but as yet I haven't even written him a letter thanking him for his thoughtfulness. Maybe I will get an opportunity to use them at a local rendition of "The Student Prince"[52] which is playing here the next few days. Please tell him that I did receive the gift and really appreciated it.

As yet I have no word as to whether that $200 that I sent home has reached there yet. Let me know as soon as it does so I can throw away my money order receipts.

Well, there really isn't much news from here except that I would like to be home even if I had to dig up the backyard.

Your boy

Bud

Autograph Letter Signed (ALS), stamped envelope.

Sunday
April 30 [1944]

Dear Mom & Dad,

Well, here we are with another quiet Sunday — the Commander has gone for the weekend so I guess it [will] be possible for us to take the afternoon off and go golfing — as usual, however, the sun has gone into hiding for Sunday and won't be back until tomorrow. Hope that our game has improved since last week's venture. We lost seven balls last Sunday.

---

52. See letter of April 30, 1944.

After the war is over

Last night I went over to the auditorium to see "The Student Prince," an operetta, with Everett Marshall.[53] I believe that this was the first operetta I have ever seen and it was one of the most pleasant experiences I have ever known. Maybe it is because the whole thing is in English and the characterizations are so much more human. If you ever have an opportunity to see this performance don't miss it — I also believe that Dad would hugely enjoy seeing this operetta by Romberg.

The two little country places that you went out to see on the Howell's place[54] don't sound just exactly like what we want — if you can't get a piece of land that is reasonably fertile, there isn't much logic in buying it because you know that eventually you [will] want to plant something even if not on a commercial basis.

It isn't essential that the land be in Atlanta — perhaps you would rather wait until after the war and come out here to California and then you might never want to leave.

Love,

Bud

Autograph Letter Signed (ALS), no envelope.

---

53. Sigmund Romberg's operetta in four acts presented at the Municipal Auditorium of Long Beach, with American baritone and actor Everett Marshall (1901-1965) playing the role of Dr. Engel (the prince's tutor).
54. In anticipation of Stone Mountain becoming an attraction, Hugh Hawkins Howell, Sr. (1888-1979), prominent Atlanta attorney and three-time candidate for governor, amassed in the 1930s large parcels of land in the area.

After the war is over

Presidential candidate Franklin Delano Roosevelt in a motorcade, Atlanta, Georgia, October 23-24, 1932. At the time, Hugh Hawkins Howell, Sr. (pictured in center backseat) was chairman of the State Democratic Executive Committee.

Thursday
May 4 [1944]

Dear Mom & Dad,

I just came back from the dentist where I had a wisdom tooth extracted; the novocaine [*sic*] hasn't come out yet so I don't know whether it is going to hurt very bad or not — if the others I have had out are any guide, it will act up for a day or so pretty bad. I thought I had better have it done while we were still here in the U.S. before we get somewhere where they had to use primitive methods.

I got your long letter yesterday and was very happy to get so much news from home.

However, the news of your throat worries me. I am really hoping that this new doctor can find the root of the trouble — maybe, this is, at last, the doctor who can solve the problem and clear up all of your trouble.

Our business is very slow and we aren't kicking a bit because we were so rushed for a while— it is certain that once we catch up with our other ships, we will be terribly rushed for a while, and so now we are just enjoying the leisure time. It will be possible for me to get a few days' leave (not enough to come home) however, I am very undecided [about] what to do with it — I guess I'll just take a trip around here somewhere and see a little scenery; possibly I might go up to Yosemite National Park which is about one day's traveling time above Los Angeles.

The news from here is very meager, in fact, nonexistent, so you will have to excuse the scarcity.

I don't remember whether I told you or not, but I received a letter from Hugh the other day and among other things he said that part of my outfit was already at where he was located — he was looking for me any day. That gives me some idea as to where he is and maybe the same will occur to you.

Well, that's about all from here — try to keep the dogs out of trouble and tell Belle to send me some fried chicken.

Your boy

Bud

Autograph Letter Signed (ALS), stamped envelope.

After the war is over

Saturday
May 6 [1944]

Dear Mom & Dad,

Well, I had a nice long letter from home yesterday telling me all about the little farms out on the Howell's place. I'm not sure I can place the house that you are talking about — but I do have an idea which one it is. I'm not too sure I like the idea of buying a piece of the Howell farm even though it does sound pretty much like a good buy. There are several things I would like to know about the place such as: how much road frontage does the acreage have? What is the condition of the house? Can one live in it if the necessity [arises]? Is the soil suitable for gardening? Of course, if the house is anything at all, the price is extremely reasonable and I don't see how one could go wrong for $1700 dollars in any event. Let me know what Dad thinks about it.

About three hours after I had my wisdom tooth pulled, I went down to the officer's mess and ate a steak dinner; I wasn't bothered a bit by the extraction and was certainly surprised to get by with absolutely no pain or aftereffects. It was very different from the two I have had pulled recently.

We have had some warm weather recently (81°) which is the hottest May 5 since 1928 here in San Diego. I'm not complaining at all because it feels just like good ole Georgia weather.

When I sent that $200 home I didn't remember that I had registered an allotment for $125 which should start getting home about June 3rd or 4th. Consequently, I am a little low on funds and as I expect to take a few days leave sometime soon I will probably need a little money. If you don't mind, please send me $100. By money order in your next letter.

After the war is over

Will try to call home soon.

Your boy

Bud

Autograph Letter Signed (ALS), stamped envelope.

Wednesday
May 10, 1944

Dear Mom & Dad,

It was certainly swell talking to the family again on the phone the other morning — seems just as though I'm home with the dogs barking around my feet and good smells coming out of the kitchen.

I'm afraid that I padded the phone bill quite a bit though because we must have talked about fifteen minutes; it doesn't seem as though it could be more than two minutes.

I haven't gotten any mail in several days so I don't know whether my candy will arrive today or not — I hope that it does come because my mouth is watering at the thought of some good ole divinity. There is no hurry about my money order as it will [be] impossible for me to go on leave until next month.

The first place that the Howells showed you sounds a great deal like the old house Eddie Boles used to live in — it was sort of down in a hollow and was about a couple of blocks down toward Stone Mountain from the caretaker house; from what I remember, it was a pretty good house; however, the other lost sounds like a better bargain if the house could be put in shape for a reasonable cost. It might be that the land would increase in value due to the proximity of Stone Mountain; I am pretty sure that it would be a good buy especially if there is much wood frontage on the Stone Mountain highway. I don't recall whether you told me the amount of acreage involved but somewhere I got the idea that there [are] about 10 acres in the lot. Let me hear all the details about the place.

Our business is still very slack and it looks as though it will be that way until we leave which now appears to be somewhere around June 15.

Well, the mail just arrived and I received two letters from home dated two days apart; the news of the farms is a little out of date now that I have talked to you on the phone, but still, we haven't arrived at a definite decision so I guess I'll just wait until you have more information.

I hope that Mom is about to have her tonsils out real soon because, like the doctor, I think that they are probably the cause of much of the trouble, and very likely to cause much more trouble in the future. Please don't worry about the operation since it is only a very minor one and will be no worse than having a tooth pulled.

All my love,

Bud

Autograph Letter Signed (ALS), stamped envelope.

After the war is over

Sunday
[May 14, 1944]

Dear Mom & Dad,

Well, here it is Sunday again and we are taking it easy— I am here at the office, but only because there isn't anywhere else to go; I can just sit here and read the paper and listen to the radio— what more could one ask.

Under the persuasion of a couple of the other officers on the staff, I went to the Catholic services at the chapel here on the base. Although utterly ignorant of what the lengthy rites and ceremonies mean, I was very much impressed by the intensity and absorption of all the congregation— there is no doubt that the Catholics take their religion much more seriously than some of us protestants. Of course, it is all in the way one is reared, yet I believe that one can dispense with all the formal rites and still be as devout a Christian as the most rigid Catholic. However, whether or not I agree with the method of worship of their religion, I do appreciate the faithfulness with which they attend church and I believe that we Baptists could do well to emulate them in that respect.

Our weather here is perfect and I think that I may go out to the beach even though the water is still much too cold for comfort. The beaches here which I have seen do not compare with those farther up the coast at Los Angeles and up farther north.

Oh yes, as this is Sunday I have an idea that the family is out looking at a farm — a pleasant pastime [at] this time of the year even if one doesn't buy. The last word from home said that you were interested in a tract of land on a hill with a view of the mountain and an old house. I will be quite interested to hear what you have decided. Just out of habit, I look over the wantads

After the war is over

in the San Diego papers for farms and ranches; the prices that they ask are terrific and ballooned by the war workers who have expanded San Diego to just about twice its pre-war size.

The land here varies from one extreme to the other—an acre of lush, black soil may be surrounded by rocky waste-land good only for growing barley; water is the key to land out here—without water no land is productive and all the farms have some form of irrigation.

My bank money order arrived yesterday; thank you so much for your trouble. I am still looking for the candy which should arrive in the next day or so.

It would certainly be wonderful if I could be home with my Mom on this Mother's Day, yet you know that I am thinking of you and realize more every day how much you have done for me.

Yours

Bud

Autograph Letter Signed (ALS), stamped envelope.

Monday, May 22, 1944

Dear Mom and Dad,

Well, I'll give this typing a whirl for a change so you will just have to put up with the mistakes which are sure to occur as you can see. My typing doesn't seem to improve— maybe it is because I don't get enough but it seems as though my fingers get all tangled up in the keys.

Your candy arrived Sunday and the crackers came on Monday so the office is now well supplied with between meal subsistence.

After the war is over

The candy wasn't stale at all and you know how much I like divinity. Unfortunately everyone else likes it also.

The last letter that I have from home was written Sunday, a week ago, so I don't know the latest dope on the farm situation; for some reason or other, I don't particularly care to own a plot of ground too close to the Howell's especially if there [sic] house would be right up on the hill above ours. One of the prime purposes of owning property is the feeling of independence that goes with the ownership—therefore, I think that it would have to be a very good bargain to overcome the slight feeling that we are living on the estate of someone and the land was not completely all or own. On the whole, I don't think that the little farm is too much of a bargain and yet I know that the price of all land has gone up tremendously in the last year of [sic] so; consequently, it is difficult to determine what is a good buy and what is not. Your judgment is good enough for me so whatever you want to do will be perfectly all right with me.

Someone on business just commandeered my typewriter and gave another one to me which is in bad need of repair and what is worse, it cannot spell as well as the preceding one. Such [an] obvious remark was not necessary, however.

I am about convinced that the fountain pen that I gave to Dad recently does not work because I haven't seen a sample of it's [sic] work yet.

When I ordered the flowers for Mother's Day, the lady assured me that the flower I [specified] was in season on the east coast, but from what you tell me you received I can see that Colonial made a few changes and left out the particular flower which I specified which was Hyacinths (Pink and Blue).

I haven't been doing much of anything lately except working and going to the show at night. I believe that I told you we have all the shows here on the base even before they are released

After the war is over

in Los Angeles or Hollywood. I saw one last night which was utterly fantastic called "Between Two Worlds."[55] The only recommendation that I can give it is that [it] is very definitely different than the usual run of pictures that have been coming out lately. Also, I have been playing a good deal of bridge with some of the boys down at the BOQ. It has been a long time since I played and I am afraid that I have forgotten what little I ever knew.

Our date of sailing is still very indefinite but as I said before it will be somewhere around June 15. Cliff gets back from his leave in a couple of days and then I will be able to go away for a few days— as usual, I have no idea where to go or even if I will go anywhere at all. The last days that we are here are sure to be pretty hectic what with moving back on another ship and winding up all the loose ends.

Thanks again for the candy and crackers and remember— I sure miss everybody.

Your boy

Bud

Tell Belle to take good care of the dogs and to tell everybody up at the "Savoy" Hello for me.

Typed Letter Signed (TLS), no envelope.

---

55. Released on May 20, 1944, by Warner Brothers, this fantasy film concerns a London couple during World War II who decide to commit suicide instead of waiting to be killed in a Nazi air raid. After carrying out their decision, they awake to find themselves on a large, mysterious ship with several other passengers.

After the war is over

Friday
May 26 [1944]

Dear Mom and Dad,

Don't be alarmed by my using my personal stationery this time instead of the office stationery — there isn't anything wrong with me; I am just lying in bed and writing.

I caught a bad cold somewhere a couple of days ago and it is in full glory right now — you know how they affect me. Maybe it will leave as suddenly as it came in a few days.

Last Wednesday a fellow staff officer and I went out to a girl's home in La Jolla and went swimming. La Jolla is about the nicest residential section in San Diego and is, without doubt, one of the prettiest communities that I have ever seen. Although the beaches aren't the wide, white variety which we are used to, they are similar to the New England cliffs with a small stretch of sand at the foot. Flowers grow extravagantly everywhere and in so many varieties that it is impossible to remember the names of them. You-all simply must come to California after the war and see the scenery. I am looking forward to seeing Northern California which many of the natives insist is the most beautiful part of the state.

Cliff got back from his leave and took part of the work off my hands so I am again a man of leisure for a few days, at least. We are beginning to think about moving back on the ship in a week or so and setting up our office aboard. Please don't worry about my leaving the country as I have pretty definite information that I will be stationed at Pearl Harbor for quite a long time; it appears that I will have to be at Pearl Harbor in order to change over to the new pay system you remember I told you about.

I'm very glad to hear that the shop is doing so well and I sincerely hope that you can keep enough help to operate at top

After the war is over

efficiency. It seems to be the custom out here to jack up the price of everything so that not only the war workers but everybody makes more money; it is no exaggeration to say that any able-bodied person can make at least $200. Per month out here no matter what he does and almost everybody is making a good deal more than $200.

Well, hope I hear from home soon.

Your boy

Bud

Autograph Letter Signed (ALS), no envelope.

31 May 1944

Dear Mom and Dad,

I'll give this typing another go if your patience will stand up under the frequent mistakes. As I said before, my typing just doesn't seem to improve no matter how much practice.

Please forgive my delay in writing but it seems that every time I start to write, something comes up: I know that such an excuse is a very poor one and I will try to do better in the future.

The radio is favoring us with the most beautiful Hill-Billy music that I have heard in a long time—it sounds just like a bunch of good old Georgia mountaineers on WSB.[56]

---

56. The first radio station in the city of Atlanta, WSB was broadcasting 24-hours a day for two weeks awaiting the "D-Day" Allied invasion of German-occupied France. The popular radio program "WSB Barn Dance," carried by over 900 stations across the country, featured more than a dozen country music performers every Saturday night at the Erlanger Theater who played in the style of authentic "hillbilly" John William (Fiddlin' John) Carson (1868-1949) from the Blue Ridge Mountains of North Georgia.

After the war is over

The way things look now I think that I will be able to get away about the 2nd or 3rd of next month—I probably won't even know where I am going until I get there and since I can only be away 3 or 4 days, I can't go very far.

I was most agreeably surprised yesterday to get a letter from both my Mom and Dad. I know that when Da[d] writes it must be quite an occasion. You are undoubtedly right about the farm in that it is a bad time to buy any land and yet on the other hand it is conceivable that the value of a dollar might continue to fall instead of rising after the war. Under such conditions tangible property is the only way you can hedge against inflation. It wouldn't hurt a bit to keep an eye out for some little bit of acreage if for no other reason than the pleasure that you derive from going out on Sunday afternoons and looking at places.

```
On Your Radio
WSB Barn Dance
Tonight ... 9 P. M.
★  750 ON YOUR DIAL  ★
SONGS! LAUGHS! MUSIC! RHYTHM!
```

Atlanta Journal, 5/20/1944, p. 4.

My cold is about gone and I am ready to go swimming again as soon as we get some warm weather. It has been intermittently cloudy here for about two weeks; I am definitely convinced that the temperature never varies more than a few degrees.

Our date of sailing is still the same and a delay looks unlikely now—I will call you sometime soon and let you know more.

After the war is over

Cliff and I and one of the captains[57] of the ships went out to the San Diego Country Club Sunday afternoon and played a fast game of golf—we played so disgusted at our scores that we vowed never to play again and then proceeded to go out the following day and play again. Upon close examination, I believe that I can detect a slight, very slight, improvement though I still refuse to divulge my score to anyone. We are seriously tearing ourselves away from work this afternoon for a little while.

Well, I guess that is about all for now.

Your Boy

Bud

Typed Letter Signed (TLS), no envelope.

Wednesday
June 7, 1944

Dear Mom and Dad,

I know it has been an almost unforgivable time since I wrote home, but you see I just got back from my leave; and though, of course, I had plenty of time on my hands during the trip on the train, it is pretty hard to get around to writing.

The best way I know to tell you about my trip is to start right at the beginning and tell you in chronological order:

I left last Friday afternoon and caught the Navy plane to Los Angeles where I had to hang around until 1:00 in the morning

---
57. John William Peil. (See letter to Cliff LeVee, January 27, 1945.)

After the war is over

and they put me on a local train because I wasn't going all the way east. After a tough trip of about 20 hours, I arrived at Williams, Arizona, where I had to spend Saturday night before catching the bus the next morning up to the Grand Canyon, my goal, after so tedious a trip. The train that I rode from L.A. to Williams was a unique one — when the time for meals came around the train stopped and everybody in the two passenger cars got off the train and went in to eat at the nearest restaurant. We followed this procedure for the whole time until we got to Williams. I arrived at the Grand Canyon at about ten-thirty in the morning, which was too late to go on the trip about which I will tell you later so it was necessary for me to stay an additional day to take the mule trip down to the Colorado River. The first day, Sunday, I just wandered around and took a two-mile walk up to Yavapai Point where the park service has quite an educational exhibit set up with telescopes and binoculars focused rigidly on various points of interest so that all one has to do is to look thru the glasses and the object (about which the signs and explanatory matter is written) became immediately visible.

The next day (Monday) I took the one-day mule trip down to the bottom of the canyon where the mighty Colorado rages through gorge after gorge. The trip lasts from 9:00 o'clock in the morning until about 5. o'clock in the evening so you see that it is quite a journey; to be more exact the distance along the Bright Angel Trail is eight miles down and eight miles back making a total of sixteen miles.

After the war is over

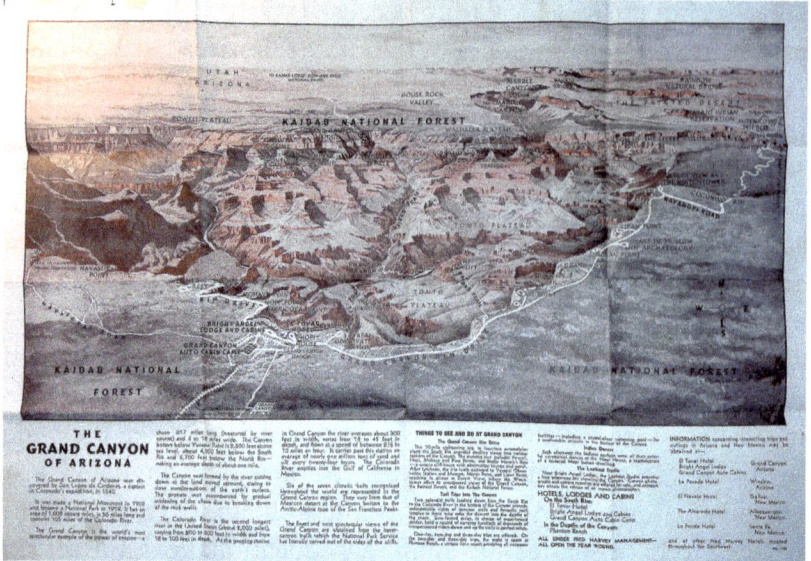

Enclosed in Bud's letter of June 7, 1944.

I won't be so ambitious as to try to describe the canyons where others of real ability remain mute. I can only say that one must see it to gain any idea of the grandeur and majesty of this work of nature. I am sending you a few postcards and a diagrammatic picture of the canyon[58] so as to give you a little idea of what I have had the privilege of observing; it is my most earnest wish that my Mom and Dad can get out to the West and see this magnificent spectacle of Nature's work after the war is over. Just for a souvenir I sent Mom a little Indian pocketbook — it doesn't look very practical and yet it might prove as useful as some of the modern hats you have.

To repeat, the whole family must consider such a trip as a necessary part of living and to miss seeing this sight would be to live an incomplete life.

---

58. Postcards not found, but "diagrammatic picture of the canyon" is enclosed.

After the war is over

Nothing much has happened outside of the news that you have there in Atlanta — the invasion[59]—I first heard it as I was sitting in the train station about 1:00 o'clock in the morning. It was welcome news and yet when we remember the inevitable casualties, we wonder if there was no other way.

Oh yes, I do have my Harvard yearbook[60] with me so don't worry.

No, Bobby and I aren't in the same outfit despite the same flotilla number.

If Hugh does get home tell him that I would dearly love to see him and may yet if he goes back to the Pacific.

We are still supposed to sail on the same date and there doesn't appear to be any reason for a change; I will call you sometime soon.

Your loving son,

Bud

Autograph Letter Signed (ALS), stamped envelope, enclosure.

---

59. D-Day, June 6, 1944, the Allied invasion of Normandy in Operation OVERLORD.
60. *The Rough Roll, the Accounts of the August 1943 Class of the Navy Supply Corps School,* Harvard University Business School, now in possession of Walter Hudson Pullen's heirs.

After the war is over

Saturday
June 10, 1944

Dear Mom and Dad,

It looks as though you will have to contend with my typing again for a while. The reason is that I can sit in the office and type and everyone thinks I am busy whereas it would be more difficult to explain writing a letter with pen and ink.

We are planning to move on the ship this afternoon; not our personal gear but all of our office equipment and furniture. You know how much I hate to move and now we will have to move both our office equipment and all our personal gear but maybe we will live through it.

We have been very busy the last few days registering allotments, for everybody waited [until] the last minute and there has been a continual stream of people pouring in here to accomplish various business: it will be a relief to get underway and clean up the mess and start on my fourth quarter returns, and after that to start changing over to the new system.

I regret to inform you that I am thinking of giving up the game of golf—it seems that every time I play, my game deteriorates. Also, the game is prone to ruin one's good disposition or at least tax one's patience severely. Of course, you know that I will be [out] playing at the last opportunity and no matter how much I cuss the game I will continue to play until the last few golf balls that are left have been lost over in the rough which seems to be the favorite destination of all my hits.

Perhaps you have received the travel folders by now from the Grand Canyon showing the scenes that I so inadequately described— you should receive the little pocketbook very soon

After the war is over

also. I am still thrilled by memories of the grandeur of the Canyon and can only hope that my family will be able to get out and see it very soon after the war.

A new officer reported [to] one of the ships yesterday and I discovered that he was from Decatur — unfortunately, however, he had the misfortune to go to the University of Georgia so you can see that he is no friend of mine. I don't remember whether I told you or not that there is a sailor on one of the ships named Pullen.[61] It certainly was a strange sensation one day to hear several sailors holler in a very disrespectful tone of voice "Hey Pullen." Of course, they were calling the seaman not me.

Well, there really is a paucity of news as you can see so I guess that is about all; I will call home sometime in the next few nights.

Your boy

Bud

Typed Letter Signed (TLS), stamped envelope.

14 May [June] 1944

Dear Mom and Dad,

I'm typing on a typewriter which is sitting on a couple of big books which is in turn sitting on a cot so you can get some idea of what we are doing — moving day is almost as hectic as

---

61. This was William James Pullen (1925-1986), a former student originally from Empress, Alberta, Canada, who enlisted in the Navy at Los Angeles on February 23, 1944, and joined the crew of the USS LCI(G)-729 as seaman second-class on April 11. He remained with the ship until February 1946, when he was transferred to Camp Elliott, San Diego, and was discharged as a quartermaster third-class on April 24.

After the war is over

anything I know. I never knew one could accumulate so much junk in so short a time. It is most difficult to decide just what to take — the only sure thing is that I can't possibly take everything that I have now. It seems that after we move it is impossible to find anything.

I sent Dad a little present yesterday; it isn't very original, but it isn't the traditional shirt and tie and I hope that you can find some use for it.[62]

Well, it becomes more convenient to dispense with the typewriter and fall back on my trusty pencil or else I shall not get very far with this letter.

As I was saying about Dad's Father's Day gift, I just happened to see something that I wanted and naturally assumed that Dad would like it also; hope my assumption wasn't erroneous.

To be part owner of a 43-acre country estate is certainly a novel experience for me and I am really excited about the whole deal— I truly wish that I could get home and see just how it looks although your description is quite complete and sounds like the place we have been looking for. I am particularly interested in the way you describe the long drive up to the house— tell me in your next letter if it is possible to see the house very well from the road. Also, I would like to know how long it will be before electricity becomes available. It is surprising that the former inhabitants didn't ever install electricity or plumbing. What are the possibilities of moving out there in the future? Another point I would like to hear is the amount of the taxes. We are leaving in a couple of days so I doubt if I [will] receive the pictures you made of the place before we shove off. I do hope that I get Dad's letter diagraming the farm today or tomorrow.

---

62. At this point Bud switches to pencil.

After the war is over

How much land is available for cultivation? And what kind of soil is the farm's cultivated plot? We might have to grow our own food someday so it would be a good idea to tentatively think about the possibility of setting up a few acres of vegetables.

It was wonderful talking to my family the other morning and I was glad to hear that you had found something that we believe to be just what we want.

I rather doubt if I will be able to write again before I leave but will try to.

Your boy

Bud

There will be a few days you don't hear from me —

Partial Typed Letter Signed (PTLS), with handwritten addenda, no envelope.

Chapter 6

"I try to do a good job."

Saturday night
June 24, 1944

Dear Mom & Dad,

I am going to mail this letter and a V-mail letter[63] at the same time so you will be able to tell me which is the more speedy method.

We have been to sea now for quite a few days[64] as you can see, and expect to arrive at our destination pretty soon — probably a couple of days. The trip has been very smooth and satisfactory up until yesterday when the sea began to get a little choppy; fortunately, most all of us have been in shape to work and a good deal of the time. I'm afraid that I don't do too much work, however, because most of the work is mere detail and it is just too easy to let the storekeepers do practically all of the stuff. Besides, my typing isn't of a good quality yet that it can be employed successfully.

Cliff and I spend a good part of our time up on the bridge of our ship absorbing sea lore and shooting the breeze. Our cabin is a little hot now that we are reaching warmer latitudes so we take our deck chairs on the deck, and prop our feet up on the rail and have little trouble persuading ourselves that we are on a pleasure cruise. Sometimes we are rudely interrupted by the buzzer sounding "General Quarters" or some other drill such

---
63. See V-Mail letter of the same date, below.
64. Bud was aboard USS LCI(G)-729, which, according to its War Diary, had left San Diego on June 16 enroute to Pearl Harbor, arriving June 26, 1944.

After the war is over

as "Fire," "Collision," or "Man Overboard." "General Quarters" means to man your battle stations and prepare to fight the enemy. Of course, the alarms are only for practice and there is little likelihood that we will undergo a real alarm anytime soon.

Oh yes, I must tell you about our office; it is about 6 feet by 20 feet and both sides lengthwise are lined with desks and file cabinets; maybe the diagram below will help you to picture it.

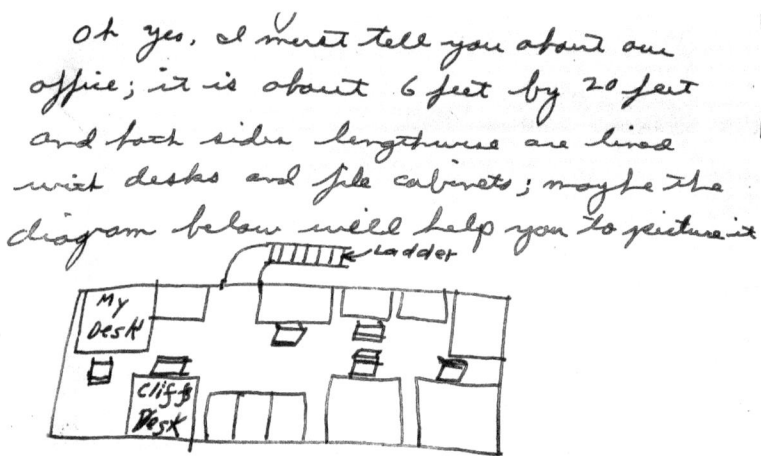

Excerpt of Bud's letter of June 24, 1944, showing the diagram he drew.

You can see that although we are a little crowded, there is plenty of room to work for everybody.

Today at noon Cliff handed me a letter from home that he had been carrying around since the day we sailed; he had forgotten about it. In your letter, you gave me the impression that there might be some hitch to your getting the "Hitching Post." I hope that everything goes all right because the place sounds very much like what we have been looking for. I am waiting impatiently for the pictures of the house to arrive so that I can tell more about it.

After the war is over

Needless to say, I would sure like to be at home and see the place, but I am sure that you know how much I would like to be at home for any reason.

Your boy,

Bud

Hope Dad [got] his Father's Day gift by now.

Autograph Letter Signed (ALS), no envelope.

[June 24, 1944]

Dear Mom and Dad,

I think that I will write you a V-Mail letter and a regular letter in order to see which gets home first. I will mail them at the same time so that we may decide which method is the most successful. I am using a noiseless typewriter for the first time and I find that it is a most peculiar sensation since one doesn't know when he is typing or not.

As you can imagine, there isn't very much to write about except that we are having wonderful weather for which I am truly thankful. We have been able to accomplish a good deal of work due to the favorable elements and have caught up with some of the back work. You no doubt recall that this is the end of the fiscal quarter and thus we have to render a set of returns to the Bureau of Supplies and Accounts. In the new pay system beginning July 1, 1944, the returns are rendered once a month instead [of] once a quarter, fortunately, they have been greatly simplified and won't mean nearly so much detailed work as before. The main difficulty involved will be acquainting all of the line officers with all of the new forms and procedures.

After the war is over

I will write you again tomorrow night and tell you more news. I can see that the paper is running out much too soon so just remember that your boy would really like to be home and hear about everything.

Love,

Bud

V-Mail Letter, signed, postmarked July 3, 1944.

Tuesday
June 27 [1944]

Dear Mom & Dad,

Only a few minutes after we tied up to the dock someone handed me a couple of letters from home; the next day (today) I received two more letters including that rare phenomenon — a letter from Dad. Of course, it is unnecessary to tell you how I felt at getting so many letters just when I wanted to hear from home.

Our family certainly has no equal in the matter of almost buying a country place. I was certain that this, at last, was a sure thing, but that was before I received a subsequent letter conveying the incredible news that we again had reconsidered at the very last minute. These latest affairs somewhat atone for our loss a couple of years ago of a $25.00 down payment so we can't possibly complain of the financial results. Frankly, I was hoping that you would go through with the transaction and buy the hitching post. But since you didn't, maybe it is just as well— as you point out, the place is definitely a retreat and not a farm or money-making proposition. Too, it would have been a good place to spend a lot of time and money; and the farmland was only one or two acres

After the war is over

so we could only use the rest of the acreage as a sort of hideout. Dad is undoubtedly right when he says that the farm prices are grossly inflated; the only indeterminate factor is whether we will continue to have the higher wages and prices after the war — if prices do continue to rise then our money actually buys less and a farm would be a good hedge. If prices drop then we would have done better to keep our money in the bank. So there we are in the dilemma. The only solution is to look for a good bargain and if you think it is not too expensive to buy it.

Another possibility which I hope you haven't discarded is the placing of our little nest egg in a place where it can multiply. Keep a sharp eye out for a little business and you may find another little bonanza like your shop.

Speaking of your shop — I hope that you have had success in obtaining an operator. It must be disheartening to have to refuse so many customers. If you can't obtain more employees, the obvious solution is to raise the prices. If your quantity drops off you are still making more money for less work. Don't be afraid to raise the prices because people think the price of an article or service is indicative of the quality, and in these times they have to spend their surplus funds somewhere. If you could see the way that some business owners are taking advantage of the times to raise their prices to fantastic heights, you could have no compunctions about a legitimate increase of a few cents.

Well, as I told you, I am going to move ashore here and set up an office — it is very indefinite for how long, but all indications point to a considerable stay.

I haven't had an opportunity to get off the base yet and see what the place is like— I did get up to the officers club last night to see a wonderful movie "Going My Way" with Bing Crosby.[65] I won't

---

65. A musical comedy drama by Paramount Pictures that became the highest-grossing picture of 1944, nominated for ten Academy Awards, winning seven, including Best Picture.

After the war is over

spoil your enjoyment of it by telling you about the substance of the plot. I <u>will</u> tell you that it is one of the best shows we have seen in several years and heartily recommend it for one of the "mileage" evenings.

I have seen several familiar faces here and expect to run into many more before long. Maybe even Hugh or Bobby will turn up.

This letter is becoming rather lengthy— I must save something for the next time so remember

I'm your Bud

P.S. It should not be very hard to find me on Dad's little gift.

Autograph Letter Signed (ALS), stamped envelope.

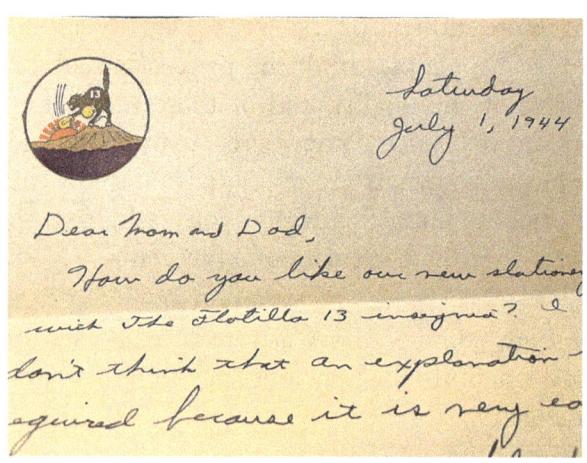

July 1, 1944, stationery and envelope (page 161) bearing the Black Cat USS LCI Flotilla 13 insignia.

After the war is over

Saturday
July 1, 1944

Dear Mom and Dad,

How do you like our new stationery with The Flotilla 13 insignia? I don't think that an explanation is required because it is very easy to determine what that black cat is doing.

We have been extremely busy since we arrived here and so busy that I haven't had time to get off the base. I plan to get away sometime soon, however. After a good deal of trial and error, I succeeded in getting Hugh on the phone yesterday; he said that he would be over to see me today sometime.

So far I have had very little success in finding a laundry. I was able to get my clothes washed on the ship where I am still living but it seems practically impossible to find any laundry service under three weeks.

The weather here is just fine — not excessively hot and, in fact, one even needs a blanket at night; it does become pretty warm in the daytime with intermittent showers which are to[o] short to get you wet. These little showers last only a few minutes and you

After the war is over

wonder where the moisture is forming because the sky is a clear blue with only an occasional white puff of a cloud.

As I said before, I have moved my office ashore, but am still living on the ship because it is so much more comfortable than the crowded BOQ where I would have to share a room with five other officers. Since this ship has reasonably good chow there just isn't any reason for living ashore until the ship moves and I have to get off.

I received no mail yesterday so maybe there will be some for me today— It seems as though my mail arrives here just as quickly as it did in my former residence. Obviously, it is being flown out here.

Would like to hear the latest dope on the farm or business situation. The more I think about it, the more I wish that we could find another little business which would make money and put our little bit of capital to work.

Goodbye for now,

Bud

Autograph Letter Signed (ALS), stamped envelope.

Monday
July 3, 1944

Dear Mom & Dad,

Although we have been here only one week, I am beginning to feel like an old soldier of fortune who has been away from his

After the war is over

country for many years. Not that the place is bad — it is just about as good as any place would be away from home and I expect that it is the next best thing to being home.

Hugh came over the other day and we spent part of the day together. I went over to his station that night and spent the night at his BOQ. He had quite a bit to tell of his experiences out in the islands and, of course, he is just living for the day when he can get back to Atlanta and see his "Fay." Evidently his family has told him that the farm has been sold because he said that he would have to buy himself a little farm somewhere and naturally he wasn't too happy over the sale. He doesn't know when he will get home but since he has quite a bit of time overseas to his credit, he has an idea that it shouldn't be too long before he either gets some leave or a tour of duty in the United States.

Still busy, we haven't had a chance to get off the base and see the rest of the land around here, but we plan to take off pretty soon and see what the town looks like — everyone says that one trip off the base is about enough and then you will be satisfied to remain on the base indefinitely.

I received your letter today saying that Jack Baldwin[66] called you— he is a nice kid and is going up to New London, Ct. for submarine training. I used to see him just about everyday at the officer's mess in San Diego.

As regards my golf — I told you that I had given up the game for good but it is possible that I might relent should the opportunity ever present itself and it might sometime.

Thanks for fixing me up with the church.

Your Bud

Autograph Letter Signed (ALS), stamped envelope.

66. A native Atlantan, Jack LeRoy Baldwin (1926-2003) graduated from the University of Georgia, where he was a member of Sigma Alpha Epsilon, and also graduated from the Georgia Military Academy. After the war, he sold real estate with Draper-Owens Company.

After the war is over

Thursday
July 6, 1944

Dear Mom and Dad,

Because of the omnipresent censor, I am unable to express myself about some matters; of course, I am not referring to information of any military value, but rather to personal feelings which just refuse to be written when a friend of yours is the censor.[67] There is an unfortunate lack of discretion in many young officers who suddenly have the job of censor thrust upon them. Please don't misunderstand me — I trust the staff censors implicitly, but personal observation has shown me that some officers have no qualms of conscience about divulging the contents of a personal letter to their fellows.

Well, enough about censorship—a task which only the most picayune mind could enjoy and a violation of rights which only a war could force us to accept.

As I told you, Hugh and I have seen each other several times and he seems to be in the best of health. I was truly surprised to learn that he will become an uncle in a few months. The next time we are together we will make a determined attempt to have a snapshot made and sent home so the Howells and Pullens can see their boys together.

The disbursing department is still going at top speed and will be for a couple more weeks when we should be able to pack up the returns and mail them with a minimum of regret that it will be the last time we render a set of returns in the present laborious manner; the new pay system requires a monthly rendition, but the detailed paperwork has been reduced by at least 50%. And the act of taking up and closing out pay accounts has been immeasurably simplified.

---

67. Envelope for this letter bears the stamp "PASSED BY NAVAL CENSOR" with initials "AJP."

After the war is over

You write that Bobby was in Hawaii for a time — he probably wishes that he were there now because it is said that Honolulu is the best place to be away from home; and when one hears the fellows who have spent a year or two on some little atoll recount their experiences, he looks forward to going most anywhere just as long as he keeps moving and doesn't stay in any one place too long.

Have you had any success in securing any new employees? If you keep running an ad in the paper you should get some results eventually. It seems a shame to lose so much business because there is no help available. Maybe the higher prices will adjust the number of customers so that you won't need a newer operator.

Well, tell ole "Belle" that I sure wish she was here to sew on a few buttons for me— I'm afraid that I will have to learn it before long. Goodbye for now.

Your son

Bud

Autograph Letter Signed (ALS), stamped envelope.

Saturday night
July 8, 1944

Dear Mom & Dad

We have only one chair in our room at the BOQ and it is occupied — some fellow is using it for a table of which we have none. Contrary to my usual luck, I lost the toss of a coin and deemed the upper bunk, my partner, Cliff winning the lower bunk. There are eight fellows in our room and the only time I have ever seen

After the war is over

most of them is when they are asleep. Remember I told you that we were working from six in the evening until midnight for four days because our office was taken in the daytime by a war bond drive. Two of our roommates have contrived by some devious means to secure a Navy "Jeep" which they ride around in at will. There is bound to be a reckoning someday, but until someone takes it away from them, they are living an enviable life.

To date it appears that you haven't received any of my letters— certainly, you should have one soon. Don't forget to tell me which arrives first — the V-mail or the regular airmail so I will know which method to employ.

Also, you might tell me whether the allotment check for June arrived. Because of a change in plans, I am stopping my allotment so don't look for any more after the June check.

So far, I have had very little opportunity to get off the Navy reservation and see the other part of the nearby countryside. Now that we are about to catch up with our work, I hope to get away sometime soon and take a tour though I will be unable to describe to you what I have seen.

One has his choice of four movies here almost every night; like at home the fare varies from good to exceedingly bad and they make the same mistake of thinking that two bads at one sitting can alleviate the suffering that only a double-feature can cause. I have yet to find anyone who professes to enjoy a double feature and yet still they come.

Hugh called me last night to say that he bumped into Bob Lang.[68] Unfortunately, he was leaving the next day and we were unable

---

68. Fellow 1942 Tech graduate, Robert McDonald Lang, Jr. (1921-1975), whose father played guard for the Yellow Jackets under coach John Heisman (1913-16) and was a World War I Navy veteran. Bob Lang was a Naval aviator serving as a carrier pilot on the USS *Bennington* (CV-20) in the Pacific.

to get together. It seems that if one is interested, he can find just about all of his friends sooner or later including boyhood chums.

Oh yes, I must tell you that we are able to buy the overseas edition of "Life" and "Time" here and the two magazines alone relieve a lot of the boredom that the otherwise spare time induces.

Writing on my knee is becoming a little tedious as I close: I trust that if "The Unholy Triumvirate" finds anything objectionable in these dispatches, they will enlighten me so the same mistakes do not occur again.

Your loving son,

Bud

Autograph Letter Signed (ALS), stamped envelope.

July 12, 1944

Dear Mom & Dad,

We are back in the normal state — our mail is being held up again somewhere along the line. I haven't received a letter for almost a week from home except one from Dad which arrived today.

Thanks very much for the clipping listing the victorious political candidates; I believe that I voted for the winner in every case except for the office of coroner. It appears that I was on the wrong end of an overwhelming majority for Mrs. Paul Donehoo.[69]

From your letter, I infer that the whole family is engrossed in a mad scramble to find a little farm — how the desires do fluctuate.

---

69. Margaret (Maggie) Dolvin (1906-1948) was first elected Fulton County coroner in 1941 over 47 male opponents, succeeding her late husband Paul Donahoo (1885-1940), whom she married in 1936.

After the war is over

I have about decided that it would be wiser to wait until after the war before buying a place because it is true that all prices of land are grossly inflated and all out of proportion to their intrinsic value.

I continue to bump into people that I know from home, from Tech, from Supply school, and familiar faces that are impossible to place.

For the last couple of days,[70] we have been eating ashore and the food is wonderful although we can't complain about the food on the ship, in fact, the ship's cook was rated as chief commissary steward (quite an honor for a small ship).

Our returns were mailed away this morning accompanied by no regrets — it is the last set to be rendered under the old system and eliminates the most irksome part of this job, though it is now necessary to render monthly returns which aren't nearly so detailed and lengthy.

Oh yes, the next time you see this lady who works in the capital, please ask her if there is anything further that is required for me to receive my ballot for the forthcoming elections.

It is certainly a loss not to be at home and argue with Dad about the various candidates; I would like particularly to hear the no doubt inflammable arguments for Roosevelt or the explosive vituperations against Dewey. It is really a toss-up between two evils and I have not decided how I will vote; of course it makes little difference in democratic Georgia, but then there is the

---

70. From July 11-14, USS LCI(G)-729 underwent repairs at a floating dry-dock at Pearl Harbor. The crossing from San Diego had cracked nearly a dozen welds in her flat-bottomed hull. Around midnight on July 15, after a "shake down" cruise, 729 was anchored in Mā'alaea Bay, Maui, when she was struck by her sister ship, the LCI(G)-404, tearing a big hole in her side above the water line. No one was injured, but LCI(G)-729 had to return to the Navy Yard at Pearl Harbor for additional repairs, July 20-29. The next day she was back anchored in Mā'alaea Bay.

personal satisfaction obtained from not approving of Roosevelt and "Eleanor."[71]

Goodbye for now

Bud

Autograph Letter Signed (ALS), stamped envelope.

Friday
July 14, 1944

Dear Mom & Dad,

Two letters arrived today from home after an interval of about a week during which I was convinced that I was a disowned waif. One, the V-mail, was mailed on July 5th; the regular air mail on July 10th, a difference of five days in time which proves that the regular air mail letter is the preferable method and there is no further good to be accomplished from experimenting with V-Mail.

From your letters I infer that the family is still afflicted with "farm fever" and I get the impression that you rush from one to another always looking for the greener grass just over the hill. As I said in a previous letter, Dad has about convinced me that now is not the most advantageous time to invest in land, whether improved or not, and one would do better to wait a while for the ballooning prices to drop.

Hugh and I and several other fellows from Atlanta who are friends of his got together yesterday afternoon and took a swim

---
71. Bud is referencing the forthcoming presidential election between Democrat Franklin D. Roosevelt and Republican Thomas E. Dewey. "Eleanor" is Mrs. Roosevelt, The First Lady. On November 7, 1944, FDR would carry Georgia, winning 81.74% of the popular vote.

After the war is over

in an outdoor pool near his BOQ, and, of course, the inevitable bull session later in the club followed. His quarters are something like the movie's version of officer quarters, but I guess he deserves a little luxury after spending many months in those desolate little islands that hardly ever show on the map.

Early this morning we played tennis, my first time in seven years. Need I say more?

Will write again in a day or so.

Your boy

Bud

Autograph Letter Signed (ALS), stamped envelope.

After the war is over

Monday, July 17 [1944]

Dear Mom & Dad,

Another letter from home arrived here today — it was written on July 2 so it must have been held up somewhere along the line.

You describe the farm out on Johnson Ferry Road so glowingly that I wish that you had purchased it immediately. From what you say, it is undoubtedly the best that we have seen, and make no mistake, we have looked at plenty. With electric lights and water and with 30 or more acres under cultivation it is difficult to see how we could go wrong for the reasonable price asked. Of course, you have probably changed your mind several times by now, but please give this one a lot of thought because I do believe that our needs are almost completely filled by the place you describe.

Just as we were cleaning up the debris after getting our returns mailed, a change in administration plans caused a tremendous increase in volume in the number of accounts we carry so we are truly grateful that the new system of pay I discussed previously has been put into effect. Were we still under the old procedure, the change would be near insurmountable — as it is now, we can handle the new accounts with our present complement, <u>I hope</u>.

I received a letter from ole McGinty and he intimates that he is in the very thick of an operation so he will be a battle-hardened veteran when and if I run into him.

Tell "Belle" not to raise too much devilment on her vacation.

Your loving son

Bud

Autograph Letter Signed (ALS), stamped envelope.

After the war is over

Thursday
July 20, 1944

Dear Mom & Dad,

If I were to take the letter from Dad which arrived yesterday at face value, I would consider myself part owner of a farm by now. However, knowing the vicissitudes of my family particularly as relates to farm buying, I am still skeptical and I will consider the deal closed only when we have the Deed in a firm grasp. The description and the accompanying map make the place appear to be a very attractive bargain, but I am curious as to the loss of enthusiasm for the place on Johnson Ferry Road; that place also sounded like about what we need and if I remember correctly, the location is ideal for a country place—Oh well—you have, no doubt, reconsidered several times by this writing and wax enthusiastic for yet another location.

I sent you a postcard[72] from here; however, there seems to be some doubt as to whether the censorship regulations will pass it so let me know if it arrives because I sent quite a few and am curious whether they will ever arrive at their destination.

Well, Today is our busy day, payday, with all the mailing and gnashing of teeth that accompanies it.[73] The only comment that we ever hear is negative; if the people are satisfied with the amount, they only grunt desultorily; if they aren't then they give forth with the most anguished groans. Of all the thousands of complaints that I have heard since taking this job, I can say

---

72. See series of Hawaii postcards postmarked July 26, with imprimatur by a censor with the initials HPJ, below.
73. The role of U.S. Navy Disbursing officers during WWII became a subject of postwar investigation. One study published by the American Sociological Association in the *American Sociological Review* of June 1947 revealed why they were frequently criticized: "First, disbursing officers handle matters of immediate personal importance to their clients. Navigation, gunnery, etc., may be more vital to the lives of the men, but their problems are vague to those not directly concerned. An error in a pay account or a delay in pay day is more quickly recognized and more loudly protested by the rank and file than deficiencies in most other departments aboard ship. Consequently, the disbursing officer and his staff are under constant bombardment for favors and incessant criticism for their mistakes—real or imagined—or failures to grant favors."

After the war is over

honestly that there hasn't [*sic*] been more than a dozen instances when we were actually in error—I say dozen because I don't remember more than two or three. I am just as guilty as everyone else, I guess, because here I am passing my grief on to you. It has been ever thus with the paymaster and I expect no improvement. The only outlook I can look forward to is the fact that no one can force me to be a paymaster after the Navy turns me loose. Then I, too, will be permitted to rant and rave at the <u>damn</u> paymaster and I probably will.

There is little news as you have discovered by now. Everyone is excited by the news of Tojo's demise[74] and the implications of the fallen cabinet in Japan. Let's all hope that we will be surprised by an early end to this war.

Hope to get a letter today,

Your loving son,

Bud

Autograph Letter Signed (ALS), stamped envelope.

74. Japanese prime minister Hideki Tojo (1884-1948) resigned on July 18, 1944, following the fall of Saipan.

After the war is over

Sunday
July 22, 1944

Dear Mom and Dad,

Only two letters (one of Mom's, one of Dad's) have arrived in the last week so I don't know just what the latest report on the real estate deal is. The last letter written on the 16th of July had you right on the verge of buying the 100-acre place out near Austell — I am waiting to hear whether the purchase was consummated or fell through as its predecessors.

Hugh, Cliff, and I are planning to take the afternoon off and go to town to look at the available scenery whatever it may be. Maybe it will be possible to tell you where we are now located when we move to another location. We will have to trust the vagaries of our estimable censors and, if they release their august approval, I can tell you more about the present location of our outfit.

I would like to recommend a movie for the next night off at home. "Wintertime" with Sonja Henie and others[75] is an above-average musical which is worth seeing, nothing spectacular, of course, yet somehow pleasing or should I say soothing to one who has to listen to the financial woes of 2000 people.

Well, I was interrupted and it is now Monday, July 23, one day later. As I said we got into the town for a few hours yesterday — today, I have been so extremely busy paying ships that this is the first opportunity I've had to continue my letter.

The two dolorous pictures which you have no doubt already received a fright and a laugh served us equally well by providing

---

75. A Twentieth Century-Fox musical film starring Norwegian figure skate Sonja Henie (1912-1969) and César Julio Romero, Jr., released on September 17, 1943.

amusement. The fellow with Hugh and I, rather I should say, the third ugly fellow with Hugh and I is, of course, Cliff LeVee, my partner and accomplice. Hugh has refused to send his (picture) home, therefore, I suggest you take them up and show them to his mother if she appears in such a state of health as can withstand the inevitable shock. I know that it would be useless to try to extract a promise not to exhibit the photos to my friends so I merely request that you confine the gallery to such of my friends who can overlook the unhappy result of our resolve to send a picture home.

It would be unfortunate if I failed to send you the customary travel folder, so you can expect one soon.

Your boy

Bud

Autograph Letter Signed (ALS), stamped envelope.

Wednesday
July 26, 1944

Dear Mom & Dad,

It has been nigh onto a week since I heard from home; obviously there is some hold-up somewhere. It is rather disconcerting not to receive mail which I know is due, and, it is definitely not conducive to a free spirit. Oh well, I have little of which to complain when so many go months without hearing from home.

Discussion on the farm would be rather dated so I'll just wait until I hear some news before pressing the delights of a country home.

After the war is over

During a hurried excursion into town the other day I bought a little gift for my Mom — the originality of the present must be becoming a little warm. I need go no further because you must have guessed by now what it will be if it ever arrives at home.

As I mentioned in previous communiques, our business is booming as never before, and we never know what the new day will bring forth— the only certain thing is that some change will take place. In this disbursing business planning ahead is vital, and thus we are often left hanging breathlessly at a recent change in plans. I become more convinced daily that I have the most repellent job in the Navy and then upon reflection, I decide that I should be deeply grateful for the considerable difference that a commission makes. However, I try to do a good job, for if I didn't, then it would be agony living with myself. Don't think me in the depths of despair. It is like many positions in that perfection is the expected and any deviation, however slight, is the cause for complaint.

We were treated to a unique movie last night; "Gaslight"[76] with the unsurpassed Ingrid Bergman and Charles Boyer is a psychological study which I won't spoil by divulging the plot. It is truly an absorbing story and well merits the next night off for the family.

I do hope that you have been fortunate in obtaining some help for the shop and don't have to work too hard yourself.

All my love,

Your boy Bud

Autograph Letter Signed (ALS), stamped envelope.

---

76. Released theatrically on May 4, 1944, by Metro-Goldwyn-Mayer, *Gaslight* garnered critical acclaim and box-office success, and received seven nominations for Academy Awards, including for Best Picture, winning two: Best Actress (for Bergman), and Best Production Design.

After the war is over

July 29, 1944

Dear Mom & Dad,

Well, at last you've done it— you have been teetering on the edge of buying a farm for a long time and now — the fatal step. How does it feel to look out over the fields and realize that it all belongs to you? I derive an intense feeling of satisfaction from knowing that there is someplace I can go — take off my shoes, prop my feet up on the railing of the porch, and watch everybody go by in a big hurry to do nothing while I just sit there and reflect on the futility of haste and quest after money. It is imperative that we have a porch rail and a screened-in porch for Georgia mosquitos are not proven for their ability to distinguish us country folk from those city dwellers, and a mosquito who has never tasted human blood is just as voracious as his city-bred cousin. Seriously, you ask me for suggestions as to fixing up the shack. I will oblige with the following helpful hints:

1. Screened porch
2. Old icebox
3. Fireplace
4. Good view
5. Not too close to the Nickajack Rd.
6. Quart of ice cream in [an] icebox.
7. Old radio
8. Comfortable chair.

Needless to say, I realize that most of these hints are unobtainable now and will be acquired gradually. Part of the fun of owning a country place is the satisfaction derived from the fixing it up to one's own individual taste and I expect that you-all have other suggestions though they are doubtless similar to mine.

I would be most grateful for some snapshots of the house, the barn, the fields, the branch, and other indispensable aspects of a

After the war is over

dacha. There is no substitute for the sense of sight; despite your more than adequate description; I would clearly like to see just what kind of a place I am joint-owner of.

A daily weather report of Atlanta is available here, and I have been amazed to see Atlanta in first or second place for the highest temperature almost every day. Surely our climate is being maligned by this propaganda — it just couldn't be so hot in the Gate city.[77] Possibly this can be explained by the fact that the temperature readings are taken at Candler Field where the heat really becomes unbearable. I will assume so anyway.

We have had a bit of excitement here just lately about which you will read later. Don't misinterpret me— nothing to do with the Japs. Merely political.

The last letter I received from home was mailed on July 24; as you see the mail service is either exceptionally good or poor. There is no doubt but that several of your letters have been mislaid because of the gap of a week during which I didn't hear from you at all. Hope you have gotten the snapshot of Hugh, Cliff, and me by now. It is undoubtedly a specimen for a collection. I need not elaborate.

Our business is relatively quiet since there was only one change of any magnitude today and we are only a few days behind.

I am exceedingly happy that we are the owners of a farm. Please tell me more.

Your son,

Bud

Autograph Letter Signed (ALS), stamped envelope.

---

77. Highest temperature reported in the *Atlanta Constitution* for July 29, 1944, was 95 degrees.

After the war is over

Aug 1, 1944

Dear Mom & Dad,

Payday again with the accompanying ills—fortunately, [fewer] people seemed to think that they were the victims of a hold-up, and on the whole things ran off rather smoothly. We aren't finished yet, however, and the next few days will bring forth another equally violent action. On the whole, people are reasonable, but the Navy method of figuring pay confounds anyone not initiated in the intricacies of disbursing — it is like beating one's head against Stone Mountain to attempt to explain "how" to the unfamiliar.

A letter from Dad with the enclosed postcard that I had sent you arrived today. It was mailed on the 27th of July so it is apparent that when the mail hits no snags, the service is no less than perfection. It has been close to a week since I heard from Mom— maybe tomorrow's mail will have a high yield. We can be certain of a good crop of official mail, regardless.

My fears were not groundless as your last letter so vividly relates: you-all will just have to take it easy when you go out to the farm. Save a little of the repairing and remodeling for me to do or else I will have nothing to do but sit on the front porch. You <u>must</u> not work so hard that you are stiff and sore the next day. I cannot offer any help as to whether [to] fix up the house or the shack unless I can see them — preferably a view from the road. As I hinted before some photographs of the various buildings on the place would be most welcome. If you don't send them I will have to conjure up a vision of my own and knowing as I do the typical, run-down, unpainted Georgia farmhouse, I am fearful of what my vision will reveal. Please do send a few pictures when the next opportunity arises. Another point that I would like information on is the amount of tax. I don't believe you explained what county it is in either.

After the war is over

Cliff and I stole away yesterday afternoon for a rather excruciating game of golf. Our scores still don't bear the light of the public gaze so we will just keep them darkened until still more improvement can be noticed. A golf ball is about the rarest commodity one can procure—we were forced to play with an assemblage of old "rocks" which certainly contributed nothing to our inflationary scores. Censorship precludes any description of the course, yet I can assure you that the possibilities of losing a ball are very high and one would require a diver to retrieve some of the casualties. If you do manage to escape the water, the fields of sugar cane await your sliced ball with great confidence that it will never be found in their mazes. However, I am happy to report that some improvement was noted and we still have a desire to continue our game so you can see there is still hope.

I would dearly love to be home for the watermelon season which is one way of saying that I would like to be with my folks right now.

Your loving son,

Bud

Autograph Letter Signed (ALS), stamped envelope.

Thursday
Aug 3, 1944

Dear Mom & Dad,

Mom's letter of July 29 arrived today somewhat restoring my faith in the mail service. You make no reference to the two little pictures which I sent home recently so I assume they have not yet arrived. Hugh, under my pressure, sent his home also — I can see where the Howells and Pullens will derive much enjoyment from these candid poses.

After the war is over

Of course, I am thrilled by the acquisition of the farm and I certainly don't expect a mansion for $2200.00. Half the fun of owning a place is the planning and arranging of your furniture (you have quite a bit of experience [with] that).

Cliff and I just got back from a very discouraging game of golf. So disconsolate are we that we threaten to give up the game. One contributing factor to the gloom was the loss of four golf balls each. As you know golf balls are now [more] scarce than electric irons or new automobiles. The only ones available are the old, battered, rocks bought from the little caddies who ask exorbitant prices. The golf course is or was evidently planned in the days when balls were plentiful because water hazards and other equally destructive hazards are most abundant with the inevitable loss to us dubbers. Oh, well, we will no doubt continue our fruitless quest of breaking 100.

I have reinstated my allotment of $125.00, and the first check should arrive about the 4th or 5th of September; if it doesn't, please let me know. I had to stop it for a month in order to catch up on my finances.

Hugh and I get together about every four days since he has a day off every fourth day. As is the usual case, our times of liberty don't coincide and we can do little but have dinner together at the officers club.

Tell Belle that I certainly am grieved to hear of her aunt's death and extend all my sympathy.

Don't be alarmed if at any time my letters stop arriving. The cause will be merely a change in location and certainly no course for worry. You do understand that such things are always possible.

Your loving son,

Bud

Autograph Letter Signed (ALS), no envelope.

After the war is over

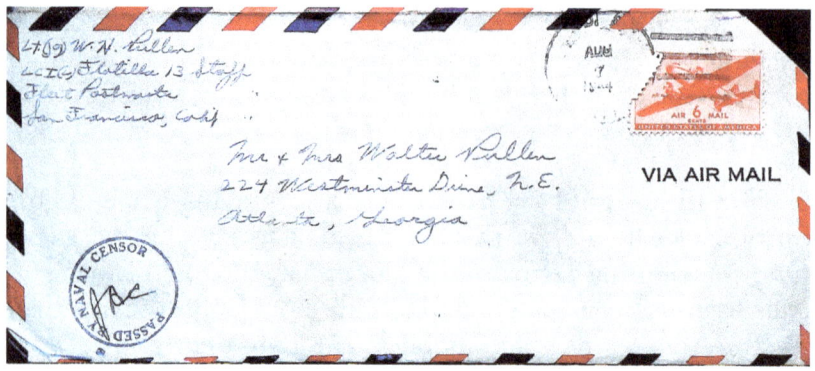

Sunday
Aug 6, 1943 [1944]

Dear Mom & Dad,

A letter arrived tonight from home dated Aug 3rd making an elapsed time of delivery of four days at the outside. Truly the mail service is better than when we were at other locations.

Cliff and I and the boys with all of our impediments have moved back aboard our ship adding one more time to now innumerable times which we have done this job. The very nature of our work requires that we have quite a few desks, tables, file cabinets, safes, and numberless records which are necessary to our work. One develops a decided distaste for moving when only his personal effects are involved; when we move, it is similar to moving from one house to another, and we know each time that we cannot go thru all the resultant confusion again without departing from our senses. However, after we are on the ship, it doesn't seem so bad.

I had a rather amusing experience with the piratical watch repair shop; the watch repairman to whom I took my watch merely held the timepiece to his ear and uttered "Eight dollars." After

After the war is over

leaving it with the shop for three days, I am still dubious as to whether the case was ever opened for my eight dollars. It seems a most appropriate occasion to use the cliché, "Time will tell."

There is no wonder in my mind that Mrs. Howell[78] reserved comment on Hugh's picture— I await with anxiety her comment on the ones that he sent home for they were certainly no improvement on the selection that you received.

From all reports the family appears to be getting full value out of the farm; I am a little fearful that Dad may work too hard in the spring. Oh yes, please inform me a little further on the availability of electricity, i.e., whether we must wait until after the war or maybe sooner.

The news that you obtained one synthetic tire appears to be sort of a mixed blessing; I'm afraid that we will be handicapped to some extent by the absence of tires on the other three wheels— Certainly, we are entitled to adequate tires to enable Dad to ride to work for his work is very definitely considered vital to the war effort.

Well, that is about all the news from here except to remind you that there will be times when we are at sea, and it will not be possible to mail any letters with the consequent period of delay there at home; I'm certain that you will not worry if there is any period of time when you receive no mail from me.

All my love to everyone,

Bud

Autograph Letter Signed (ALS), stamped envelope.

78. Ethleen Horne (1892-1988) of Jeffersonville, Georgia, married Hugh Hawkins Howell in December 1914.

Chapter 7

"I cannot tell you where I am."

Thursday
Aug. 24, 1944

Dear Mom,

We have been at sea for quite a while now and will no doubt continue to be so for a few days. For that reason, my letter will not be mailed today.

The deck gang is chipping paint exactly over my head on the deck above with the resultant pandemonium.[79] The sounds may be compared with a dozen low-speed riveting hammers, and I have not yet decided whether it is possible to write a letter under these conditions. You will have to be the judge.

As you can imagine, there is a great paucity of things to write about for the simple reason that every day is just like the one before except for progressing a few miles through the Pacific Ocean.

The days are marked only by inconsequential things that would not merit a thought under normal conditions. The ship ran out of milk the second day out; of bread the seventh day (this was a blessing since the cook is found to bake bread); of fruit the fifth day; of candy the eighth day; and so it goes. Our only hope is that we don't run out of water which shouldn't occur if everyone

---

79. Repairs had been completed too late for the LCI(G)-729 to be painted new Pacific dapple camouflage colors— brown, blue, gray, black, and white — a scheme that was designed to blend into the vegetated shoreline of islands in the background (from water level up). Old paint had to be chipped off before the new colors could be applied.

After the war is over

conserves his share. I have learned how to take a salt-water shower and find that [it] is not bad at all except that one feels a little sticky all the time.

USS LCI(G)-729 officers Max Fisher (left) and Frank Miller, ca. June 1944.

Cliff and I with our storekeepers have very little to do while under way; we have our battle stations, but otherwise our time is our own. This is a rather mixed blessing since it [is] much easier to be busy than it is to kill time and at times the boredom is is [*sic*] almost unbearable. However, we are reconciling ourselves to this mode of life for there is no alternative. Without exception, our fellow officers aboard this ship are the best of fellows. They include the Captain,[80] a young fellow with a comparatively long record of service in the Navy; he is highly competent and unlike some naval officers who are captains of these LCI craft, he knows how to work with the crew, a most important attribute on a small ship. The engineer,[81] an ensign, is

---

80. Lt. Byrne Fowler Martin (1918-2001), of Kansas City, Missouri, who enlisted in the Navy on August 1, 1941, after attending Yale University, where he played baseball and in the band. He retired as a commander in the Navy Reserve in 1959.
81. James Ardis Cornell (1911-1979), who was born in Havre, Montana, and enlisted in the Navy at Seattle on October 21, 1929. He formerly served aboard the minesweeper USS *Oriole* and the transport St. *Mihiel*, prior to being commissioned an ensign in September 1943.

After the war is over

a former enlisted man who has spent twelve years in the Navy as a machinist mate. He likewise is competent and liked by both officers and men. The other four officers[82] are all recent graduates

NAMES	RANK, TITLE, ETC.	DESTINATION
Byrne F. MARTIN	118849 Lt., USNR	
Max H. FISCHER	266942 Ens., USNR	
Edwin D. LAWLOR, Jr.	339753 Ens., USNR	
Clinton S. JONES, Jr.	358878 Ens., USNR	
Frank MILLER, Jr.	359025 Ens., USNR	
James A. CORNELL	304166 Ens., USN	

LIST OF NONENLISTED PASSENGERS OF U. S. S. LCI (G) 729 at date of sailing from Pearl Harbor, T. H. Date 8 August, 1944.

List of officers for LCI(G)-729, August 8, 1944.

of Navy Midshipman schools and are younger than I. One, a kid of only nineteen seems to have a reserve and dignity of bearing which belies his age. All of these younger fellows are quite affable and make up a very agreeable bunch to live with; we were truly fortunate to be placed on a ship where there is such good spirit for even the slightest fault or objectionable mannerism would become magnified in the cramped quarters which we occupy.

Needless to say, I am living for the day we next reach port and receive mail. If our mail has not arrived we will be a most dejected lot and somewhat tempted to grouse.

---

82. All four were ensigns at the time. Max Henry Fischer (1922-1991) was born in Trinidad, Colorado, and graduated from the University of Denver in 1943 with a degree in business. After graduation he enlisted in the Navy on April 5, 1943, and was released on February 10, 1946. Edwin ("Eddy") Daniel Lawlor, Jr. (1922-1981), originally from Chicago, attended College of the Holy Cross, in Worcester, Massachusetts, where he majored in business administration. Clinton Story Jones (1924-2006) graduated from Trinity College in Hartford, Connecticut. After the war he worked for General Electric Company, retiring in Indianapolis after 42 years of service. And Frank Miller, Jr., U.S. Navy Reserve, service number 359025, not otherwise identified.

After the war is over

Well, I'll write to Dad tomorrow and maybe by that time I will have recalled more newsworthy topics. How I miss everything at home!

Your loving son

Bud

Autograph Letter Signed (ALS), no envelope.

Friday
Aug 25, 1944[83]

Dear Dad,

As I told Mom in a letter last night, this letter probably is the first you have received from me in about three weeks; please don't worry about me because I can truthfully say that we are not in the dangerous part of the Navy and I couldn't be on a safer ship. Don't misunderstand me to say that I like it, however. In that attitude I expect about 90% of the personnel of the Army and Navy concur with me so don't think that I am mistreated. As a matter of fact, due to the nature of our work, there is very little for us to do when at sea and we spend our time learning the trade of the line officer and reading books. All of these ships and ours in particular are fairly stuffed with the pocket editions of books furnished by the Welfare branch of the Navy[84] and by private agencies such as the USO and the like. Surprisingly enough the books include both classics and best-sellers buried among the mystery stories and wild west sagas for the unsophisticated

---

83. On this date, though Bud does not say it, the convoy sighted the Solomon Islands. By the end of the next day, Flotilla 13 was beached and tied to palm trees on Tulagi Island across from Guadalcanal.
84. Navy's Morale, Welfare, and Recreation (MWR) program.

After the war is over

readers. To supplant my library I made a foray at the last place we stopped and procured ten or more really great books from a second-hand bookstore. Someone reminiscent of the days when you used to take me down to the bookstores on Walton St. and buy me an armful of Tom Swift novels[85] at prices from 25¢ up to $2.00.

You haven't written me since we bought the little farm so I assume that you are simply too tired from working on it. You must write and tell me what is growing or what has been grown there. Another point of interest is the availability of electricity. Still, another thing I would like to hear is the amount of plumbing that is in the big house. Is there a hill nearby where one could build a tank and utilize a gravity feed for the house? I am still curious as to whether you have yet walked all the way around the boundary or have you just assumed that it all looks the same all over as it does from the roadway. I really look forward to getting some snapshots of the place and would like it very much if you could arrange to include the whole family in one of the pictures. Please don't delay too long in making those pictures.

I guess you understand that I am not permitted to tell you much of what is going on so you don't worry [about] the lack of news.

Your boy,

Bud

Autograph Letter Signed (ALS), no envelope.

---

85. A popular series of juvenile science fiction and adventure novels. Included in Walter Pullen's books today is one such work entitled *Tom Swift among the Fire Fighters or Battling with Flames from the Air* (1921).

After the war is over

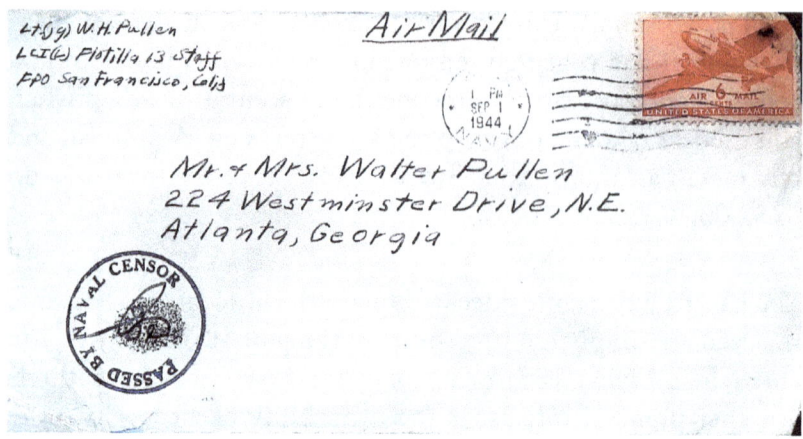

Aug 30, 1944[86]

Dear Mom & Dad,

I am writing this letter tonight with the hope that an opportunity will arise sometime tomorrow to mail it. You will be able to judge from the postmark whether or not I was successful.

Tonight is a rather pleasant interlude; we are anchored in some smooth water with a cool breeze flowing through our little wardroom, beautiful music pouring from our record player, and best of all I am noisily munching a raw carrot which I obtained from a stock we luckily received yesterday. You remember how I like raw carrots — just like old Susie. We also procured a supply of fresh apples so now I have nothing left to ask for except to be home. Some of the fellows are playing Acey Deucy,[87] a game that I have not yet mastered; unfortunately, we have only three bridge players aboard so it appears that I will have to learn "Acey Deucy."

---

86. The day before, Flotilla 13 moved out of Tulagi to the big island of Guadalcanal, where on August 30-31, 1944, they participated in a mock invasion with battleships, aircraft carriers, planes, and various amphibious ships. War Diary of LCI(G)-729 for August 26 – September 3, 1944, reads: "Logistics and dress rehearsal in the Tulagi - Guadalcanal Area."
87. A board and dice game that is like backgammon, a favorite in the U.S. Navy since the First World War.

After the war is over

We saw our first black natives a few days ago[88]— some of the fellows insist that they have red hair, a fact I cannot confirm. According to the best tradition some of them were climbing cocoanut palms after cocoanuts; but their incentive was not cocoanuts but shiny dimes of sailors so you can see that even out here money talks loudest.

As you see I haven't received any mail since the 6th of August — there is the possibility that we may get some on the 2nd of September or thereabouts, and you can imagine how eager I am to hear from home.

Just as an experiment, you might try writing a short letter to the ship on which I am riding at the present time; my address would be as follows:

Lt. (j.g.) W. H. Pullen
LCI (G) 729
FPO San Francisco, Calif

The ship is able to obtain mail frequently when the staff does not.

Several days ago I wrote a letter to Buie[89] at the Copenhill address— I hope he receives it even if it was rather devoid of news. It is so difficult to conjure up anything to say when one is prohibited from telling where, what, how much, or anything about his activities.

---

88. On Tulagi Island, on August 26.
89. Stella's brother-in-law, James Eston Buie (1897-1958), a pharmacist who married Etta Virginia Hudson (1901-1980), lived at 418 Copenhill Avenue, N.E., Atlanta. In February 1958, Buie would die of injuries he sustained when a car he was driving near Villa Rica, Georgia, skidded on an icy road and overturned. In the car with him were Etta V. Buie and her sister Stella Pullen, who were admitted to the hospital but later released.

After the war is over

Well, that is about all except to tell you that I am in perfect health (getting fat) and please don't worry about me and understand that the delay between letters is unavoidable.

Your boy

Bud

Autograph Letter Signed (ALS), stamped envelope.

Sept 1, 1944[90]

Dear Dad,

We finally got some mail yesterday for the first time since leaving our last port. There were four letters from Mom telling me that you had fallen off the Diesel and broken a collar bone and several ribs. The last letter written on Aug. 20 said that you had come home from the hospital— a fact which I was overjoyed to hear. It is most upsetting to receive such news and maybe it was good fortune that the four letters arrived at once alleviating my worries because Mom faithfully reported your progress and with good luck, you should soon be able to get back to work.

Please don't think of going back to work too soon because if I remember correctly, the Brotherhood[91] has made provisions for such accidents and you are certainly entitled to everything they offer.

One aspect of your accident concerns me very much; is your ability to write to me impaired? I hope that with some of your spare

---
90. On this date, LCI(G)-729 and other ships of Flotilla 13 were now anchored off Tulagi Island, where they took on more supplies of food, water, and ammo.
91. Grand International Brotherhood of Locomotive Engineers, Division No. 368, Atlanta.

time you can scratch off a few lines to me giving the lowdown on the Georgia Political situation. I received a card telling me that I would be mailed a ballot though Lord knows how long it will take to get here. I need your sagacious advice on the local candidates. Roosevelt is universally disliked in the Navy, but many people feel it would be a bad policy to switch presidents at the present time. What do you think? If the Republicans had a stronger man I think I would be tempted to vote for him even though it makes little difference how we vote in Georgia.

The pictures of the farm were tremendously welcome and give me a pretty good idea of what the buildings on the place look like. I would say that with a good coat of green paint, the house might not be bad at all. Did you say in your letter that it was occupied now?

I am going to write Mom a letter now so I'll tell her the news meager as it is. You'll share the letters anyway as usual.

Well, Dad, there isn't any sense to my telling you how sorry I am that you fell— you simply must be more careful in the future. I do wish that I could be there to look out for you.

Your boy,

Bud

Autograph Letter Signed (ALS), stamped envelope.

After the war is over

Sept. 1, 1944

Dear Mom,

I am writing letters to both you and Dad at the same time to ensure that at least one gets home.

The distressing news of Dad's accident has me deeply concerned and I am truly grateful for your frequent letters telling of his progress. You must impress upon him that he is not to try to go back to work too early because something more serious might happen. You can also allay some of my worries if you tell me a little of the financial end of the problem, i.e., does he receive full or partial salary from the Southern RR or the Brotherhood? You know without my saying that all of my little savings are to be used first if the necessity for a few hundred dollars arises. Which reminds me that my allotment should start arriving again bout the 3rd or 4th of September; please tell me in your next letter if it does not.

As I told Dad, we got our first mail yesterday in almost a month, and I hope that the service remains that good. We are a <u>long</u> way from home now and the farther one goes out into the Pacific, the worse the mail service becomes. A bit of information that you will be interested in and pass along to Mrs Mc[92]: Bobby wrote me a short V-mail and reported that he is or was in Guam; that was on August 8. The rapidity with which events move out here makes it appear doubtful that he is still there.

I am very happy to receive the photographs of our farm— of course, I will have to walk all over it to fully appreciate the area and that, as you can imagine, is my first desire upon getting home. Don't you think that it would be better to fix up the house

---

92. Mary Frances Gudger (1896-1995) of Calhoun, Georgia, who married Rowland Martin McGinty (1888-1967) in 1919.

After the war is over

rather than the shack? It looks as though the house could be put in livable shape without undue effort. Why don't you take Dad out to the farm to pass the time while he is mending those bones? And oh yes! You must examine the place closely to find a spot so secluded that it is completely out of sight of any road or other habitation. That is where I want to build a little shack to hide from the next war.

Well, we have had a few opportunities to step ashore, but most of the time we are out on the briny so it may be quite a time until I get more mail. You must understand that the same applies to my sending mail and don't worry about the lapses.

Take good care of my Dad and the rest of the family.

Tell Belle that I have seen some of her cousins out here and <u>not</u> at the Savoy.

Your loving son,

Bud

Autograph Letter Signed (ALS), stamped envelope.

After the war is over

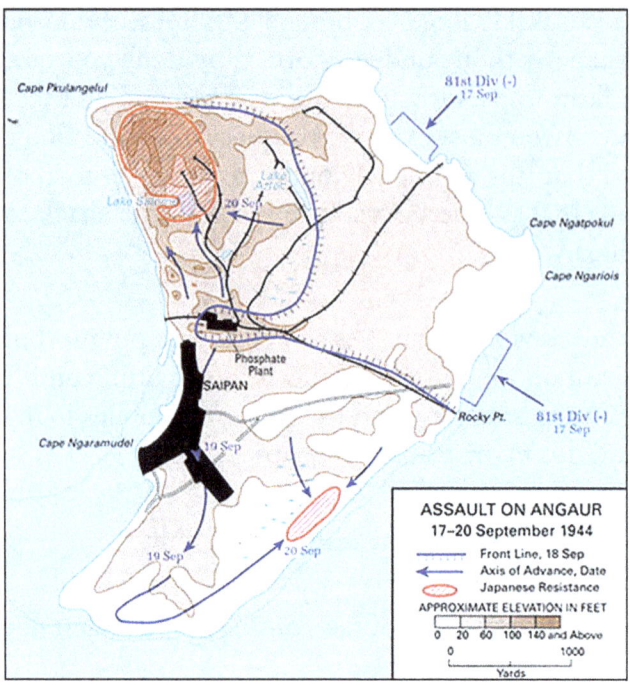

Sunday
Sept 3, 1944[93]

Dear Mom & Dad,

This is the last letter that you will receive for a while so don't be alarmed because you don't hear from me.

Your letter of August 23 arrived here yesterday with the reassuring news that Dad was able to ride out to the farm for an afternoon. I'll bet he is most exasperated that he cannot do a little planting now, but maybe in a couple of months, he will be able to set in a few plants. The pictures were a little blurred, yet I was certainly happy to get them. Please arrange for the apple and cherry trees

93. On this date LCI(G)-404 ran aground on a coral reef off Tulagi Island. A crew member on Bud's LCI threw a line to pull them off, but the line broke and fouled up one of 404's propellers. It had to go into a floating dry-dock to replace the propeller in time to join the 300-ship task force heading to the Palaus the next day.

After the war is over

to be loaded with fruit when I finally do get home. And don't forget the muscadines. You must know how much these pictures are appreciated since there is no substitute for the actual seeing of your folks. How about including a picture of Dad next time?

There is a minimum of news to relate—we held the payday for August with a little less than the usual amount of bickering; now we will settle back into the usual routine of doing the amount of accumulated work and then pass the time until the next place we stop.

The weather down here is of two kinds: either it is rainy and about the same general conditions as a rainy day at home this time of year or it is fair and hot and the heat is truly intense—something akin to a hot day in August in Columbus, Ga. is the best comparison I can offer.

One of the storekeepers is attempting to open a cocoanut right next to my desk; the only ones I have tasted have been green and much too bitter to eat. The natives will climb coconut trees for a slight fee; however, it seems that they always pull the green fruit. We obtained the almost unheard of delicacy of ice cream yesterday and will have some more for our Sunday dinner today in conjunction with the customary tough chicken which tastes like rubber. It is inconceivable what these Navy cooks can do to good food. It is just the same old story of slave labor I guess.

Tell Imogene and family when they arrive that I certainly regret not being able to see them; tell them that I would like to have a snapshot of all the boys because they have grown so fast that I would hardly recognize them. And don't forget to remind Imogene to look out for a job for me down there in Brazil. Maybe you will have the opportunity of taking a trip down to see her as soon as the war is over. By the way, it certainly appears that the Allied armies should cross the German border in a few

After the war is over

days. Then we will bring all of our power to bear on Japan — I'll be home before either of us expect it.

Well, Mom and Dad, you know how I miss you.

Your son,

Bud

Autograph Letter Signed (ALS), stamped envelope.

Sept. 20, 1944

Dear Mom & Dad,

I have just a very few minutes to write a line to tell you that I am all right and in good shape. There is a ship alongside of us which is going to take a few of our letters and promises to mail them tomorrow. You can understand that I don't have time to say anything except that I still have my proverbial luck and everything works out the best for me. I am farther away from home than Bobby is so you will have to put up with the consequent delay in receiving any word from me.

Please, please, don't send me any birthday or Christmas presents because the chances of my receiving them are infinitesimal. It will be miraculous if I get any letters for a while much less a package. Save it until I get home and I'll enjoy it just as much.

I do hope that Dad is about completely recovered by this time — it is most disconcerting to go so long without hearing from home, but I am extremely lucky in this war and have no complaints to make.

After the war is over

Remember how much I love everybody and tell the dogs and Belle hello.

Do forgive the atrocious penmanship, but the haste in which I write is the sole cause.

Your loving son

Bud

Autograph Letter Signed (ALS), stamped envelope.

Thursday
Sept. 21, 1944

Dear Mom & Dad,

Last evening an opportunity to scratch off a few lines presented itself so it is possible that you may get that letter <u>sometime</u>. I have my doubts about this one reaching home anytime soon,[94] but I am writing it just in case another chance to send mail arises.

One lazy afternoon about two weeks ago we were rolling along through the middle of the Pacific Ocean, and one of our sister ships pulled up alongside and tossed over a bag of mail including a letter from Hugh and your letter of August 28 (the last I have received). Literally a bolt from the blue, this unheard of luck will probably not occur again soon. As I said before, we haven't touched land since the 1st of the month and future prospects for sending and receiving mail are very dim. You must understand this and not worry— I can assure you that there are thousands— millions, of us in the same predicament.

We are getting along just fine troubled only by the lack of anything to do; it is so difficult to pass the time under such <u>conditions. Mu</u>ch to my delight the ship is stuffed with books

94. The envelope for this letter is postmarked September 27, 1944.

After the war is over

many of which are classics and books that I have long wanted to read but lacked the time. Also before leaving one of our ports I was able to procure a small library of my own. My only worry is that this existence doesn't reward ambition and inculcate lazy habits which may be hard to discard when I get home. You all will really have reason to call me "Lazy" then.

Our food supplies were a little bare until yesterday when we replenished our stores from a big transport — now it is difficult to walk about the ship without stumbling over a box of fruit juice or a sack of potatoes. We are so well supplied that we could easily remain at sea for two months and never suffer any scarcity— except, of course, that rare delicacy, ice cream.

By this time Dad should be pretty spry and able to go back to the run. I suggest that he take an easier job if obtainable, at least for a while until his arm and collarbone are completely knit. As I have said earlier, it is trying not to hear anything at all from home.

I told you in my last letter not to send me a birthday or Christmas present because to be perfectly truthful I don't think I would ever get it. Take a look at the distance out here in the Pacific and you'll understand why. Just keep it until I get home and I'll have something else to look forward to after the war.

When you received this letter my allotment checks for August and September should have arrived — use them if necessary, otherwise, put them in the "Pullen trust fund."

Well, Mom & Dad, I hope that I am able to mail this letter soon— I don't even hope to get one for a while yet. Don't forget— I am in one of the safest spots in the Navy so don't worry.

Your loving son

Bud

Autograph Letter Signed (ALS), stamped envelope.

After the war is over

Thursday
Sept. 21, 1944

Dear Mom & Dad,

This is the second letter that I have written today. The first I gave to an officer on a transport which we were alongside for a while. I don't know when I will mail this one, but rumor has it that we may go to a mailboat tomorrow, and I don't plan to miss any opportunity to let you all hear from me. If and when you receive the three letters that I have written in the last two days you will have to overlook the repetition of news, the sameness of expression, and the relating of the same stories which are the extent of my experiences.

About two weeks ago a sister ship pulled up by us and passed over a few letters including one from you dated Aug. 28. It was indeed a happy surprise and completely unexpected making it the more welcome. That letter is the last one that I have gotten from home; I fear that it will be some time before any more letters arrive because we are a long way from home — farther even than Bobby.

It is a quirk of circumstances that although we are out here where the news is made, we have to find out how the war is going from the San Francisco news broadcasts and really know less of the progress of our efforts than the people in the United States. It would gratify my hunger for local news if Dad would write one of his rare gems with the usual enclosed clippings relating to the contortions of the Georgia politicians. In my small section of the Navy I estimate that the Dewey supporters outnumber Roosevelt's by about 2 to 1. The Republicans would certainly win the election on this ship.

After the war is over

Just for an experiment you might address an occasional letter as follows:

Lt. (j g) W H Pullen
U.SS. LCI (G) 729
FPO, San Francisco, Calif.

The reason that I don't ask that you address all my letters as illustrated is because I may sometime have to move to another ship. Incidentally, the "G" after the LCI is an abbreviation of "gunboat." You may have seen references to this type of ship in the newspapers.

We are in excellent shape as regards food and other comforts; I have even learned to take a salt-water shower with equanimity. A specially prepared salt-water soap makes the lathering possible.

One advantage of being on a small ship is that one always knows everything that is going on, and we frequently give the captain advice — a condition not tolerated on a larger ship where the captain is of higher rank. I must have informed you that we are not riding on the same ship as our boss, the Flotilla commander.

The surest indication that Dad is back in good shape will be for him to write me a letter so otherwise I will just have to hope that everything is all right at home — and wish that I were there!

Your grateful son,

Bud

P.S. <u>Don't</u> send any presents or packages! I'll never get them here.

Autograph Letter Signed (ALS), stamped envelope.

After the war is over

Friday
Sept. 22, 1944

Dear Mom & Dad,

The letter I wrote yesterday hasn't been mailed yet, but we have just been informed that we may write a good bit more news [about] our activities since we left Pearl Harbor. I might mention that the Port is the last real outpost of civilization in the Pacific and when one leaves it he is more apt to appreciate the comforts that were available there. After leaving Pearl Harbor, we proceeded to the Solomons Islands where the great battles of Guadalcanal, Tulagi, Lava island, and others were fought back in the first days of our offensive in the Pacific. In sailing to the Solomons you can see by examination of your globe that we crossed the equator where I ran afoul of the shellbacks[95] aboard the ship. All pollywogs, luckless victims who have not crossed the equator, are initiated into the rites of Neptune who is "the ruler of the raging main." The initiation consists of cutting one's hair and other indignities such as dumping a tub of salt water over one's head and surprisingly enough there were more than twenty-five shellbacks out of the crew of about eighty. Now we are all shellbacks and privileged to perpetuate similar punishments on subsequent victims when and if we ever cross the equator again.

---

95. On August 23, 1944, while enroute to the Solomons Islands, Commander Morrill, the Black Cat Flotilla commander, in keeping with Navy tradition, had the flotilla observe the Navy's line-crossing hazing ceremony. Sailors who had already crossed the Equator were nicknamed "Shellbacks," "Trusty Shellbacks," "Honorable Shellbacks," or "Sons of Neptune." Those who had not crossed were nicknamed "Pollywogs," or "Slimy Pollywogs," or sometimes simply "Slimy Wogs." As he indicates, among the initiated, Bud and some two dozen others were given haircuts shaved to the scalp and sent through a swat line with a fire hose spraying on them, becoming shellbacks. Officers got the worst of it. It was hot, over 100 degrees, and both he and Cliff had to stand for some time on deck at their assigned battle stations in their full-dress blue uniforms and line officer hats, instead of their usual LCI basic duty uniform that consisted of khaki short sleeve shirts, lightweight shorts or cut-off dungarees, and a baseball GI cap. Several months later Bud would receive his shellback diploma from the Navy Department, signed by the skipper of LCI(G)-729 and dated with exact longitude and latitude coordinates of his crossing, certifying that he had been duly initiated into the "Solemn Mysteries of the Ancient Order of the Deep."

After the war is over

From Florida island we proceeded to the invasion described in the enclosed news. Obviously, I cannot tell you where I am so you will have to be content with the description of the action.

The danger in the invasion was all for other units of the Navy and principally for the landing troops. It is no exaggeration to say that our LCI (G)s were in the safest position of anyone mainly because the Japs were not interested in retaliating [against] us.

Well, I merely wanted to tell you the latest news, and I expect to mail these letters tomorrow or maybe even today. I will write more details next time.

Your lonesome boy,

Bud

LCI Flotilla 3 line-crossing ceremony ca. 1944.

After the war is over

> **NEWS**
>
> Army forces swung a one-two punch at the _____ Group, following up the _____ assault by slashing into _____, southernmost island of the _____ Group. Landings were carried out smoothly after ferocious preliminary bombardment by Battleships, Cruisers, Aircraft, landing craft, especially the fire-spitting LCI's which raked the beach mercilessly with rockets. Veterans of 4 or 5 Pacific landings said barrage outweighed anything they had seen before. In the 3 previous days, warships had poured 14,000 rounds of projectiles, 5 inch or bigger into _____. On assault day in early morning, 12,000 more were fired, building up into continuous rolling drumfire as the first waves rolled into the beach. Unbearable fire had swept Japs back from shore and first organized resistance was met 150 yards in, but one pillbox at extreme left of Red Beach came to life as bombardment slacked and opened up with machine guns. Pillbox was one of Jap's best, built around natural limestone caves hollowed out and reinforced with mine timbers, entrance covered over interlaced coconut logs and rocks bound together with filler of reinforced concrete and covered with earth and vegetation.

"Enclosed news" in Bud's letter of September 22, 1944.

Autograph Letter Signed (ALS), stamped envelope, enclosure.

Monday
Sept 25, 1944

Dear Mom & Dad,

We finally had the chance to send a bag of mail [the] day before yesterday so at least a few letters are on their way home; it now appears that another opportunity may present itself so I am writing again just in the event we are near the post office soon.

After the war is over

It seems even longer than it actually has been since I heard from home—you too know how paralyzing it is to go so long without and answers and then to keep on writing and hoping. We really don't have much hope of getting any mail for quite some time yet though there is always the chance of being agreeably surprised as I was once before which I related previously.

Because it no longer matters I can tell you that we spent quite some time at Pearl Harbor and I was able to get into Honolulu several times. Cliff and I and a friend of ours made two trips out to the Waialae Golf Course[96] (defective spelling no doubt) where we immediately discovered that our game? had definitely not improved since leaving San Diego. That is, of course, a gross understatement. The course sprawls over a large area near the famous Diamond Head point which is the first bit of land the approaching traveler sees of the island of Oahu. The scenery is magnificent — many of the fairways are bordered by the emerald sea on one side and small purple mountains on the other side; one is apt to overlook the attractiveness of the bordering sea, however, when his golf ball invariably slices off and lands with a splash in the surf separated from the fairway by generous rolls of barbed wire (a reminder of the days when Pearl Harbor was actually in danger of attack). The city of Honolulu is something like a dingy edition of any American city of 200,000 population and is truly a melting pot of the races. In a stroll down any block you can easily pick out Chinese, Japanese, Hawaiian, Filipino, Whites, negros, and the various mixture of these races. At the present great hordes of sailors, soldiers, and marines jam the city streets and bring all the troubles that are common to our overcrowded cities in wartime. There is also a tremendous influx of war workers from the United States who are handsomely paid for their leaving home and coming out here to work.

---

96. Wai'alae Country Club in East Honolulu, Hawaii, was founded in 1927.

After the war is over

Well, folks, just a little picture that you might find interesting. I am sending another copy of a news flash[97] to [ensure] that you get one.

Your son,

Bud

Use my new address until I tell you otherwise.

Autograph Letter Signed (ALS), stamped envelope, enclosure.

Sept. 28, 1944[98]

Dear Mom & Dad,

We haven't mailed my last letter yet, but I am just writing you to bring the news, however sparse, up to date. It has been exactly one month now since I heard from home, i.e., the date of your last letter was Aug. 27. You probably know that we are one day ahead of you out here having crossed the international date line quite a while back so actually it has been only one month to the day despite the date being August 28 out here.

Our first delivery of mail in about a month arrived today, but unfortunately, I received only one letter which was from Bobby. Most of the other fellows received two or three letters arousing my envy no end. Maybe our next delivery will be more successful.

Our engineering officer opened a letter from his brother[99] which was an expression of sympathy over the death of his wife. (The

---

97. Same enclosure as in his letter of September 22, but without underlining.
98. War Diary of LCI(G)-729 for September 28, 1944: "Joined other LCIs on eastern (lee) side of Angaur."
99. Possibly his next to youngest brother, Francis Dell Cornell (1913-1968), also born in Havre, Montana, who lived on Camano Island, Washington and attended Stanwood schools, graduating in 1932. In 1940 he worked for New York Gas and Electric in Elmira, and before that as an auto mechanic. His youngest brother, Alvin Kenneth Cornell (1918-1999) was serving in the Navy.

After the war is over

wife of Cornell[100] our engineering officer.) Since this was the first notice that had come Cornell is almost crazy with grief and anxiety because the brother mentioned no details assuming that previous letters had reached here explaining the circumstances of her death. We are so far away from the United States that it is impossible to fly home or even to communicate with his relatives. The only thing he can do is just stay here on this ship and hope that another delivery of mail will give more details. Of course, we do all we can to console him, yet there is absolutely nothing that can be done really except to wait for another letter.

The seas have been an exemplification of the gentle Pacific until last night when one of the tropical storms blew up[101]— it is now about as rough as the ole Atlantic was during that voyage to San Diego— I have to hold the table with one hand and write with the other. My activities today have consisted of sleeping and playing checkers of which game I am the undisputed champ aboard.

Let me reiterate once more not to attempt to send any packages out here; needless to say, we are in the very front rank of the Pacific [*illegible*] and the chances of our ever receiving any packages are infinitesimal.

My only complaint is that of inaction and a slight inclination to becoming fat. You would at last admit that I am heavy enough could you see me now. I will most certainly be among the best read people you know when I get back because that is both work and recreation. Luckily we are well supplied with all types of books.

---

100. Ensign Cornell's wife, 35-year-old Josephine Ann Varin Cornell, drowned after her boat capsized in Lake Oswego, Oregon, on August 27, 1944. Her body was found by two fishermen two days later. The Cornells had been married for only about 15 months.

101. War Diary of LCI(G)-729 for September 28, 1944: "… a rough night at the buoy." September 29: "Rough weather continued," pushing the ship some ten miles off Angaur Island out to sea.

After the war is over

Use my new address as shown on the envelope.

Your loving son,

Bud

Hope Dad is about recovered by this time.

Autograph Letter Signed (ALS), no envelope.

Sept. 30, 1944[102]

Dear Mom & Dad,

We are alongside an LST which is going to take some mail so I will just <u>literally</u> scratch off a <u>few</u> lines to tell you that I am fine though I still haven't received word from home.

Landing ship tanks (LSTs), on the beach at Leyte Island in the Philippines, October 1944.

102. War Diary of LCI(G)-729 for September 30, 1944: "Lay to as before...south of Angaur." Envelope postmarked on October 1, 1944, and stamped "PASSED BY NAVAL CENSOR."

After the war is over

We are doing nothing in particular which is the same story that I have related many times before. As I said my sole occupation is reading and shooting the breeze. Fortunately we get the news daily so I am well posted on international affairs if not local news.

We frequently listen to the Jap radio programs because they play much popular music — something that our own stations fail to do.

On board this ship we have a former barber, tailor, presser, cook, et al, so you see that a big ship has no advantage over us.

Well, folks, pardon the haste but I couldn't resist the chance to tell you how I am getting along.

Hope to hear from you soon.

Your boy,

Bud

Use my new address

Autograph Letter Signed (ALS), stamped envelope.

After the war is over

Oct 2, 1944[103]

Dear Mom & Dad,

At long last — a letter from home — with tremendous relief and joy I got Dad's letter written on September 18 which was the first that had reached here since your letter of August 27. You can doubtless understand my concern, for the last letter left me in some doubt as to Dad's condition; now I rest more easily because, at least, I know that he must be in good shape to write such a long letter.

Our two deliveries of mail since the invasion have obviously been flown out and are only one days mail leaving the void from Aug. 27 to Sept. 18 completely blank; also the period from Aug. 3 to Aug. 15.

Dad's clippings were most welcome particularly the column by Gladstone Williams berating Dewey.[104] I have used it effectively to refute the anti-Roosevelt men aboard.

In the same mail I received a letter from my friend Woody Smart[105](my buddy at Boston Navy Yard and Supply Corps school) who aroused the envy of everyone; he says that he is now located in England although he was temporarily stationed in Cherbourg, France; he also said that he has been able to travel

---

103. War Diary for LCI(G)-729 for this date: "Left for Kossol Passage after sunset and arrived daybreak. Anchored near USS PROMETHEUS for repairs."
104. Possibly the column that appeared in the *Atlanta Constitution* of September 16: "Dewey Misunderstands His Title of 'Buster.'" A native of Swainsboro, Georgia, Williams (1899-1968), who graduated from Mercer University and Harvard Law School, was the *Constitution's* Washington newspaper correspondent since 1930. In 1944, he wrote several columns critical of Thomas E. Dewey, New York governor, who was the Republican Party's nominee for the presidency that year.
105. Atwood ("Woody") Ora Smart (1917-2007), who was in Bud's "Class J." A graduate of the University of Maine at Orono (1940), he worked as a credit manager for Sears, Roebuck & Co. in Lewiston, Maine, prior to receiving his commission in the Navy at Cornell University and attending Navy Supply Corps School at Harvard. After the war he returned to Sears, retiring in 1977 as a zone manager.

After the war is over

around France extensively and harbored a thought of visiting Paris. All that while we just sit out here on the endless Pacific.

My only diversions are the frequent times when we tie up to the large transports and oilers for provisions and fuel. We scamper off the ship hardly before the lines are taut and look up the supply officer of the larger vessel who always makes us at home and swaps grievances with Cliff and I. Even an opportunity to look over another ship becomes a pleasure due to the monotony and confinement on such a small vessel as ours. We have frequently encountered LCI (L)s which used to be in our outfit, but left the United States long before we did; it is quite interesting to hear of their experiences— many of them have participated in several invasions not all of which came off so smoothly as did ours.

MARRIED IN HOULTON—Miss June Lawrence and Ensign Atwood O. Smart, USNR, both of Houlton, were married Sunday afternoon at the First Baptist church in Houlton.

Woody Smart's wedding announcement, Bangor Daily News, 9/9/1943, p. 11.

After the war is over

Although we are not in the slightest danger, it is brought to our attention occasionally that the Japs have not forgotten that we are getting close to their homeland.

Although the address:

USS LCI (G) 729
FPO San Fran, Calif

Appears on the outside of my envelope you should change back or continue to address my letters to the same old place, i.e.

LCI (L) Flotilla 13 Staff
FPO San Fran, Calif.

Because there is always the chance that we may move ashore on some island or move to another ship and then my mail would be confused, if possible.

It is reassuring to hear that everyone is well at home — hope that my letters are getting through all right.

Your loving son,

Bud

Autograph Letter Signed (ALS), stamped envelope.

After the war is over

Tuesday
Oct. 10, 1944

Dear Mom & Dad,

As usual, it is a doubtful matter when this letter will be mailed, but there is the chance that we might go alongside another ship so I am going to be ready in the event an opportunity does arise.

Still, the only letter that I have received from home since leaving Tulagi[106] was Dad's letter of September 16 which leaves me quite in the dark as to what is going on at home. We are most fortunate in that we are able to hear the news broadcast daily, and we were shocked last night to hear of the death of Wendell Wilkie[107] — the radio failed to explain the cause of his death so I assume it was from natural causes and not an accident. Several of the fellows home received their ballots; since mine has not yet arrived I guess it is held up in my mail somewhere between here and home.

Do you remember my telling you about the tragic situation of our engineering officer who got a letter consoling him on the death of his wife but giving no hint of the cause or circumstances surrounding the death? He received a subsequent letter saying only that his wife had drowned and still maddeningly omitting the circumstances. It requires no imagination to picture his concern and anxiety over his personal property and the disposal of his furniture. After quite a bit of wrangling, he secured orders to go home (Portland, Ore), but the only method of arranging it was to pass him off as a mental case which, of course, he certainly is not. I sincerely hope that the ruse doesn't cause him to be placed in a Naval hospital before he gets home for observation.

---
106. September 4, 1944.
107. Lewis Wendell Wilkie (1892-1944), the 1940 Republican nominee for President, died on October 8 after suffering over a dozen heart attacks.

After the war is over

I cannot, of course, tell you what we are doing, yet I can assure you that it is completely devoid of any interest so that my only diversion is still reading and sleeping. There were a few hints that we might move ashore on one of these islands — a mixed blessing of most uncertainty because of the necessity of fighting all the innumerable varieties of tropical insects and the ever-present threat of diseases. On the whole — I believe that life aboard this ship is preferable to that of a jungle island.

Please mention in your next few letters whether or not my allotment is reaching home. We left Pearl Harbor too soon for me to definitely ascertain that it had gone through satisfactorily.

I do hope that we get another delivery of mail soon. Likewise, I sincerely hope that I hear from you.

Your loving son,

Bud

Autograph Letter Signed (ALS), no envelope.

Thursday
Oct 12, 1944

Dear Mom & Dad,

You have probably often heard of the ship's "log," a written record of events kept in chronological order. After each officer-of-the-deck comes off watch, he writes a summarization of noteworthy occurrences on his watch. Of late, the only entries to be found in the log are: "Anchored as before." It requires no alteration to tell you of my news. My only real news is just "anchored as before."

After the war is over

Occasionally one of the ships of the flotilla comes alongside so that we might pay the crew. Of course, there is no opportunity for spending the money except for the few cents necessary for cigarettes and candy. The remainder of the money is used for gambling and money orders home.

No longer able to stand the mustiness and rust, Cliff and I held Spring house-cleaning in our cabin yesterday. We first painted the deck yellow, but later rather reluctantly switched over to green when the yellow paint ran out. Our other two room-mates, or better, cabin-mates occupy the upper bunks so they were not so interested in the house-cleaning as we were. I believe that I would be lonesome if I didn't have at least three roommates in our capacious cabin which stretches about 5' by 8' and has approximately 5 square feet of available floor space to lounge around in.

With the use of several large canvas curtains, I have rigged up a small reading place in our office and spend a great part of my time here. My study is quite a popular place and it is sometimes necessary to eject several persons before I can find a place to sit.

Still, no letters from home since Sept. 16 which makes almost a month that has transpired— I hope that you are receiving these letters I write. We send them over to a larger ship anchored nearby for mailing, but dark suspicions have been voiced that our letters still repose in the big ship's post office.

I have no way of knowing whether you bought Franklin's automobile—if the purchase is still possible, I heartily recommend that we take advantage of such a bargain. As you know, it will be a year or more after the war before one will be able to buy a new car, and then only at a greatly inflated price.

After the war is over

Well, Dad should be back in the harness by now if everything is going all right. I would like to hear the circumstances of the financial settlement that is made with the Southern R.R. It is, of course, unnecessary to reiterate that all of the money in the bank is at your disposal for any purpose.

I am in supreme health and have absolutely no worries except how long this thing will last. Hope everything is all right at home.

Your loving son,

Bud

Give my love to Belle and the pups.

Autograph Letter Signed (ALS), stamped envelope.

LCI(G)-729

After the war is over

Sunday
Oct. 15, 1944

Dear Mom & Dad,

I don't know whether you have gotten my last letter or not, but if you have, you will understand what I mean when I repeat "anchored as before."

Yesterday and the day before, however, were red-letter days: after a most refreshing swim in the ocean, we upped anchor and pulled alongside a tanker for water and provisions. Some of the crew of our ship (including me) as always made a thorough search of the big ship to determine if they sold ice cream. Oh, joy! I think that I must have downed at least a gallon of pineapple and chocolate ice cream before the supply was exhausted. It appears that the love of ice cream is hereditary because certain parties of my immediate family are a little partial to that delicacy also, aren't they?

This ship [LCI (G) 729] received a batch of mail yesterday; of course, there was none for me because my mail first goes to the flagship and is later handed to me at infrequent times. Several of the fellows received letters which acknowledged the receipt of the first letter that we mailed from this area so I assume that you have certainly heard from me many times by this writing.

It must be rather tiresome to read that I suggest that you again address my mail to the ship I am riding on as I previously suggested and then later retracted.

Lt. (j.g.) W. H. Pullen
USS LCI (G) 729
c/o FPO San Francisco, Calif

After the war is over

I will let you know when to change back to the original address, i.e., Flotilla 13.

Today is Sunday with the inevitable chicken and as an added attraction— ice cream. You can see that any sympathy would be utterly wasted on us as far as cuisine is concerned since we have everything that one could ask for — except maybe a piece of lettuce with Thousand Island dressing.

Our nightly news broadcasts fail to report any of the national news particularly about the progress of the presidential election. For one who was alway[s] so interested in political affairs this is a serious loss— if you could send a few clippings occasionally they would be most welcome assuming, of course, that I ultimately receive a delivery of mail.

Please let me say just once more that the chances of any package reaching here [are] very small. You see, the mail is flown out here; and, naturally, only the letters are considered. A package would just rest on some island somewhere until someone burgled it.

It still is so difficult to continue writing you-all when I haven't heard from you in quite a while. You will just have to overlook the paucity of news and repetition of my advice.

Your loving son,

Bud

Autograph Letter Signed (ALS), stamped envelope.

After the war is over

Chapter 8

"I am in the Pacific."

Wednesday
Oct. 18, 1944[108]

Dear Mom & Dad,

The days continue to march by with no change — I still haven't received any mail from home which makes about three weeks since I heard from you-all.

All the fellows on this ship are getting letters regularly now except our staff whose mail goes to another ship which is a good way off from our present location. Don't forget to address my letters to the LCI (G) 729 from now on.

One of the officers received a "Time" magazine of October 2, 1944, which had a great deal of interesting news: I heartily recommend that you be sure to buy one of that date and read it thoroughly particularly the Pacific theater of war.[109]

We had a big fishing party the last few days and caught enough fish to serve at two meals. I must reluctantly admit that I didn't catch any, but maybe it is because I don't have the patience that is required. At least, I had a nibble since my bait was stolen off the hook. The fish "we" caught were tentatively identified as mackerel, bluefish, and one barracuda which weighed 14 pounds. Fishing from the deck is about the only recreation available except the

---
108. This was the 45th day in a row that LCI(G)-729 had not touched land.
109. The magazine's section, entitled "World Battlefronts: BATTLE OF THE PACIFIC: The Beach Approach," dealt with the U.S. amphibious landing at Angaur.

After the war is over

ever-present electric phonograph, and radio news in the evening. The crew has a perpetual poker game in progress and for the last few nights, I have seen a raucous game of "Monopoly" drawing quite a few spectators.

I made an attempt last night to teach Bridge to my storekeepers and they catch on exceedingly quickly— either due to my pedagogical prowess or their mental alertness, more likely the latter.

Oh yes, I forgot to tell you that the fish dinner mentioned earlier was very tasty and would have been well-nigh perfect if we had had a little lemon juice and some of your wonderful tartar sauce. I think that I will give the fish just one more chance to bite my hook this evening and if not successful, I shall give up the sport.

Hans Butzon, Boys' High School Army R.O.T.C. cadet colonel, 1936.

A strange LCI (G) came alongside of us the other day to be paid; the captain was a native of Atlanta and went to Boys' High

After the war is over

at the same time I did. His name is Hans Butzon.[110] Another captain of yet another LCI (L) is also from Atlanta though he was so unfortunate as to go to the U. of Ga. His last name is Hansard[111] and he lived out in West End I think.

Well, there is a chance that I may get a little mail soon so I am still hopeful—

Your boy

Bud

Autograph Letter Signed (ALS), stamped envelope.

Vic Hansard, Milton High School, 1954.

110. Hans Hermann Butzon (1918-1992), whose parents moved from Dusseldorf, Germany to Atlanta, Georgia, via Medicine Hat, Alberta, Canada in 1916. Commissioned an ensign in Chicago in August 1942, by October 1944 Butzon was a lieutenant and in command of LCI(G)-460. A veteran of three invasions—Saipan, Tinian, and Peleliu—he returned home in December 1944. He retired as a commander in the U.S. Navy Reserve in December 1968. At the time of his death in Decatur, Georgia, he was a lector and eucharistic minister of St. Thomas More Catholic Church.

111. Lt. Victor Bond Hansard (1912-2003) played football, basketball, and baseball for Georgia Military College in Barnesville before transferring to the University of Georgia, where he graduated in 1938. After the war he coached football and baseball at West Fulton High School, winning the state baseball championship in 1947, and then served as principal at Milton High in Alpharetta (1949-63) followed by North Springs. He was principal or coach at high schools in Mableton, Sylvania, and Canton, Georgia, before retiring in 1978.

After the war is over

Saturday
Oct. 21, 1944

Dear Dad,

At last, I received your letter of Oct. 2, 1944, which greatly relieved my mind of the anxiety caused by such a long time without a word.

We are getting along well here — my only problem is finding something to occupy my time. You see we haven't been ashore since we left Tulagi (Solomons Is.) making over a month and a half that we have been confined to the narrow limits of this ship. This morning I went rowing in our dinghy just to obtain a little exercise, but I am always afraid to go very far from our ship because there is always the chance that she will have to move somewhere immediately.

You have undoubtedly answered this question in previous letters that I have not gotten, but I still don't know whether someone is living in our house at the farm. My question is prompted by your frequent references to repairs to the shack and very little mention of the larger house indicating that someone may be using the house now.

Your clippings were accorded a moot enthusiastic ovation, particularly the one containing all the football scores; if it wouldn't be too much trouble, I think that all of us would deeply appreciate your sending of the scores each week. As you know, everyone has some team which he follows and pulls for even though he may not have attended college. At this writing I have not gotten the clippings which explain how to make a farm pay — I am waiting for them with anticipation. What do you think of the possibilities of raising hogs or cattle?

After the war is over

Your letter reported that you were going back to work in the next day or so; I hope that the work won't be too hard for your still weak arm and newly healed ribs. You must be extremely careful at first in order not to strain the unused muscles and ligaments.

It is unfortunate that you had to lose some money, but I guess the offer of half pay is not so bad for the time lost due to your accident. It could have been much worse. I assume that the Brotherhood stood the cost of all your medical expenses.

Well, I guess [the] swimming call will sound soon and I will take advantage of it. We dive off the side of the ship and climb back up a rope ladder which is quite a feat itself.

Hope to get the missing letters and packages soon. Wish I were there to help you plant those grape vines at the farm.

Your boy,

Bud

Address my mail to the:

USS LCI (G) 729
FPO San Fran, Calif.

Autograph Letter Signed (ALS), stamped envelope.

After the war is over

Saturday
Oct. 21, 1944

Dear Mom,

As I just told Dad your letters were most welcome affording a break in the depressing monotony of our life on the ship. Your letters of Sept. 19, 24, and 29 arrived at the same time with Dad's letter of Oct. 2. Obviously, several letters have gone astray. I do sincerely hope that the packages aren't pilfered before they arrive. You really shouldn't have gone to so much trouble because there is a good chance that I will not receive them. Nevertheless, you were wonderful to send me not only a Birthday present but also even a Christmas box. If and when the packages arrive, I will be the most popular man on board for a short while.

How is your bad cold? I do hope that you don't have any after-effects from it as you sometimes do. I am definitely convinced that colds are caused by contagion rather than exposure because no one has had a cold since we left the United States four or so months ago. That is one of the very few advantage[s] of which we can boast.

I regret to say that the pictures of Little Tuck and Johnny[112] out at the farm have not yet arrived, but I am waiting for them with pleasure. Who was the little blond tow-head in one of the earlier pictures?

Of course, you must have mentioned it in several letters, but I still don't know whether my allotment which I reinstated has been arriving at home. You should have gotten the check for August, September, and maybe even October by the time this letter reaches you.

---
112. Imogene's sons, cousins Hank Tucker and John Franklin Blackstock (1940-1995).

After the war is over

Please let me hear in several consecutive letters whether the checks are reaching you satisfactorily or not.

Your report on the progress of our payment of the notes on the shop and the farm [is] certainly inspiring. It is gratifying to hear that the shop is doing so well. Can you tell me in your next letter how much money we have in the bank? I trust your judgment completely and would like to suggest that we keep the notes on the shop and farm at their present value rather than increase them so as to pay for our purchases sooner. I believe that it [would] be wise to have some money in the bank as a cushion to fall back on after the war. Let me know what you think.

A letter from Bobby arrived simultaneously with yours and indicates that he is faring well except for eating K rations and fighting monotony as all of us do. He has an excellent idea where I am located — maybe he told his mother.

Well, Mom, everything is fine here and I would like to remind you that your boy loves you more than ever.

Your loving son,

Bud

Autograph Letter Signed (ALS), no envelope.

After the war is over

Sunday
Oct. 29, 1944[113]

Dear Mom & Dad,

Today has all the indications of being another one of those indistinguishable Sundays which seem to occur more often than at home; it is a paradox since time should pass more slowly because of our confinement and monotonous life, yet the days do go by rapidly and one is hard put to remember how he spent yesterday.

The last letter that I have from you-all was dated Oct. 2, 1944, so you see it has been close to a month that I have not heard from you.

It was a rather uneventful birthday for me yesterday despite all the felicitations of my fellow officers. However, your package will be just as welcome when it does arrive. I prefer to be optimistic and expect that it will get here soon.

A few priceless copies of the "Pony" edition of "Time" magazine[114] continue to reach the ship spasmodically and as I always devoured them at home, it is no innovation for me to read them almost in their entirety. A shipment of books arrived yesterday for the ship and, strangely enough, one of them dealt in great detail with the area in which we are operating.

Unfortunately, I cannot inform you as to the title and I doubt whether it would be available anyway.

---

113. War Diary of USS LCI(G)-729, for October 28-31, 1944: "On picket station between Kossol Passage anchorage and Konrei Point, Babelthaup."
114. This edition was specially printed for members of the U.S. Armed Forces overseas, beginning in November 1942.

After the war is over

How is Dad getting along now that he is back at work? I hope that he draws the Diesel engine because he always said that it was much easier to operate, and too great a strain will not be suddenly thrown on the newly healed ribs and collarbone.

From a news sheet obtained from a larger ship I see that Tech defeated Navy[115] in the football game a couple of weeks ago— I hope that they can go through the whole season in such good form.[116]

Well, the news is non-existent and a boat is alongside to take on mail so I'll just tell you that—

I am your boy,

Bud

Autograph Letter Signed (ALS), stamped envelope.

Friday
Nov. 3, 1944[117]

Dear Mom and Dad,

It has been a few days since I wrote last, yet I'm afraid that the news here doesn't merit a letter. I have spent the last two days building myself a desk chair from an unusual army cot. The labor involved is no small matter but the reward is more than ample. The chair inclines somewhat between the horizontal angle and

---
115. In the game played at Grant Field on October 21, 1944, # 8 Georgia Tech scraped by #9 Navy 17-15, to go 4-0 for the season.
116. The Yellow Jackets would finish 8-3, ranked #13 by the AP and winners of the Southeastern Conference.
117. War Diary of USS LCI(G)-729 for November 2-5, 1944: "Anchored in Barnum Bay, Palau Islands."

the angle of an ordinary lawn chair. It gives one the dignity of being considered awake and it affords all the advantages of a bed. I am highly pleased with my efforts.

As I told you in a previous letter, the last I heard from you-all was about Oct. 12, and much to my chagrin the packages haven't arrived yet.

We (the LCI (G) 729) move around a good deal, but we never go very far and are anchored most of the time. It is an easy life. To get used to working again for a livelihood will probably be a difficult change though there isn't one of us who wouldn't swap at an instant notice. The climate here is tropical yet the heat isn't so unbearable as it is in other localities. The temperature here corresponds roughly to that of a typical July day at home except that it doesn't get so cool in the evening as it usually does in Atlanta.

Our provisions are holding out well through our constant replenishment at the expense of larger ships. Of course, no one in the area has any fresh vegetables and only a few fresh apples are still available. We have plenty of frozen meats and canned vegetables, but there is no denying that the diet often becomes rather heavy and monotonous. The cooking is about all that anyone on a small ship can expect due to the inexperience and lack of enthusiasm of the Navy cooks. I am quite buoyed up right now because we had the rare delicacy of pineapple ice cream for dinner today.

Have you ever determined in your frequent guesses where my present location is? None of your guesses so far have been very good — maybe you don't read your "Time" magazine very well.

It's too bad that Imogene didn't get to go to New York to embark for Brazil; I had so hoped that you would be able to go with her. Many summers have gone by since the Pullens, and dogs and all, have taken a real vacation. Maybe the farm will prove a substitute if it doesn't cause everyone too much work. Well, Mom & Dad, thank you for my birthday package—wish I were home to thank you in person.

Your boy,

Bud

Tell Belle I'm glad I don't have to eat her ice cream.

Autograph Letter Signed (ALS), stamped envelope.

Monday
Nov 6, 1944

Dear Mom and Dad,

There is a chance that we may go alongside the flagship of the flotilla today and I am eagerly looking forward to doing so because there is the probability of mail and maybe even packages for me.

After a little more than two months we have, at last, been able to get ashore and at what a place! It (the beach) is nothing but a few square miles of tumbled lava of a long-extinct volcano. As you know, these Pacific islands are nearly all volcanic in origin and take the usual form of a chain of small atolls surrounding a lagoon. Of course, time has worked endless variations in the appearance of the islands leaving only the irregular mounds of lava which are usually surrounded by a coral reef formed by the skeletons of countless millions of tiny sea animals. These reefs make navigation very dangerous because we frequently have no charts to consult. I don't really mean dangerous, but rather hazardous and necessitating careful attention to surroundings and currents. The reefs are easily seen being usually only a few feet under the water and often above water at low tide.

To get back to "our" island. The only indication of habitation is the small clearing which our construction gangs have managed to wrest from the jungle. Despite the forbidding aspect of the island, everyone rushed ashore to a little beach which was quite pretty—that is at low tide—and plunged into the water. Later, many of us walked up and down the shoreline looking for rare shells. Yesterday, I commandeered the dory and rowed around the shoreline finding many attractive spots for a picnic if only we had the ingredients. Later in the evening, there was a unanimous attendance at an impromptu beer party at which all hands were issued [their] ration of three bottles. You can easily realize that no one required a second invitation. We are back at anchor now so we will have to look forward to going ashore again soon. The islands are a welcome diversion for a day or two, but their attraction would diminish very soon if one were forced to live on them and work in the jungle. The food is miserable, the bugs interminable, and the monotony unbearable—so I would much rather stay on the ship; at least, until we find a more improved island. Well, goodbye for now.

Your grateful son,

Bud

Autograph Letter Signed (ALS), no envelope.

After the war is over

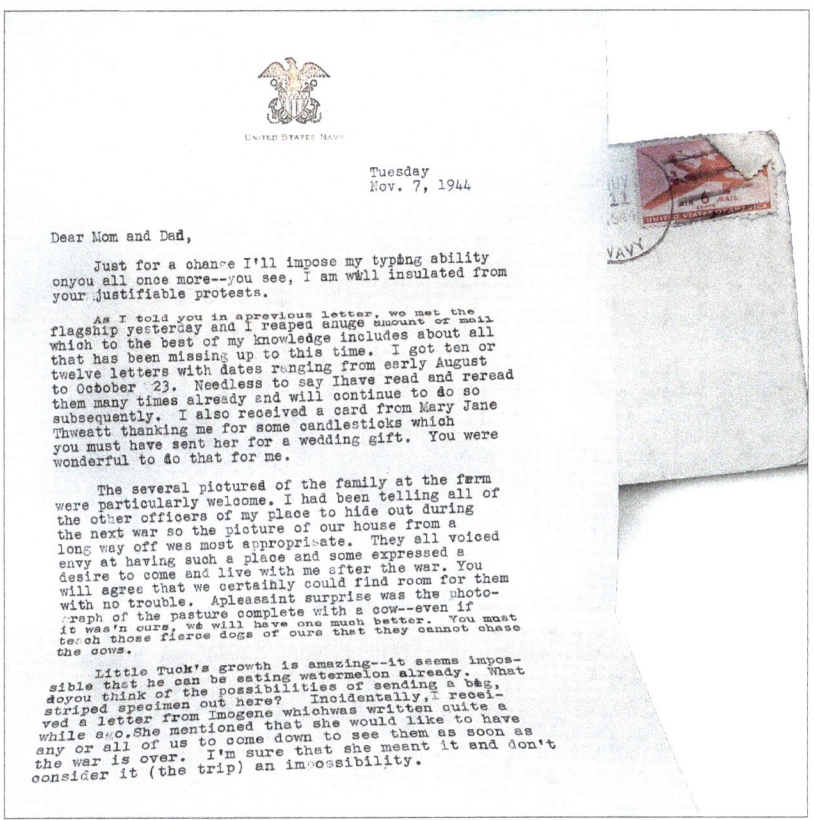

Tuesday
Nov. 7, 1944[118]

Dear Mom and Dad,

Just for a change I'll impose my typing ability on you all once more— you see, I am well insulated from your justifiable protests.

As I told you in a previous letter, we met the flagship[119] yesterday and I reaped a huge amount of mail which to the best of my knowledge includes about all that has been missing up to this

---
118. Diary of USS LCI(G)-729 for November 7-8, 1944: "Anchored in Schonian Harbor, riding out storm."
119. USS LCI(L)-732, which also served as the Fleet Post Office.

After the war is over

time. I got ten or twelve letters with dates ranging from early August to October 23. Needless to say I have read and reread them many times already and will continue to do so subsequently. I also received a card from Mary Jane Thweatt[120] thanking me for some candlesticks which you must have sent her for a wedding gift. You were wonderful to do that for me.

Miss Thweatt Is Engaged To Lt. D. F. Bachler, U.S.N.R.

Society's interest is centered today in the announcement made by Mr. and Mrs. H. M. Thweatt of the engagement of their only daughter, Miss Mary Jane Thweatt, to Lieutenant Dudley Francis Bachler. Jr., USNR, son of Mr. and Mrs. Dudley F. Bachler. The marriage of this popular young couple will be solemnized on March 15 in New York city.

Miss Thweatt's mother is the former Miss Abbie Murphy, daughter of the late Mr. and Mrs. E. J. Murphy, of Birmingham, Ala. Her paternal grandparents are the late Mr. and Mrs. J. M. Thweatt, of Talladega, Ala.

The lovely bride elect is a graduate of Washington Seminary, where she was a popular member of the Sigma Delta sorority, Tallulah Falls Circle and a member of the May Court in her senior year. She completed her education at the University of Georgia at Athens, and at Emory University.

Lieutenant Bachler is the son of Mr. and Mrs. Dudley F. Bachler. His mother is the former Miss Edith McLaughlin, daughter of the late Mr. and Mrs. H. M. McLaughlin, of Pennsylvania. His paternal grandparents are the late Mr. and Mrs. Leonard Bachler.

The groom-elect graduated from Tech High school and from the Georgia School of Technology in architecture. While at Tech he was a member of the Sigma Chi fraternity. Before joining the armed forces Lieutenant Bachler was connected with the Gulf Oil Company. He is now stationed at the Brooklyn Navy Yard, New York.

Constitution Staff Photo—Kay Cain.
MISS MARY JANE THWEATT.

McDaniel-Depew Wedding Plans

Atlanta Constitution, 3/5/1944, p.28.

---

120. On May 25, 1936, Mary Jane Thweatt was Bud's date to the K.D.K. fraternity trans-Atlantic dinner and ball at the Druid Hills Golf Club. Thweatt (1919-1988) attended the University of Georgia and Emory University before marrying on March 15, 1944, Lt. Dudley Frances Bachler, Jr., an architecture graduate of Georgia Tech and Sigma Chi fraternity member, at the chapel of the Naval base at Brooklyn, New York, where Bachler was stationed.

After the war is over

The several pictures of the family at the farm were particularly welcome. I had been telling all of the other officers of my place to hide out during the next war so the picture of our house from a long way off was most appropriate. They all voiced envy at having such a place and some expressed a desire to come and live with me after the war. You will agree that we certainly could find room for them with no trouble. A pleasant surprise was the photograph of the pasture complete with a cow — even if it wasn't ours, we will have one much better. You must teach those fierce dogs of ours that they cannot chase the cows.

Little Tuck's growth is amazing — it seems impossible that he can be eating watermelon already. What do you think of the possibilities of sending a big striped specimen out here? Incidentally, I received a letter from Imogene which was written quite a while ago. She mentioned that she would like to have any or all of us to come down to see them as soon as the war is over. I'm sure that she meant it and don't consider it (the trip) an impossibility.

At the same time all your letters arrived, I received a letter each from Bobby, Hugh, and Arnie Haynam[121] (my close friend at Saginaw, Mich.). Hugh was incorrect in his assumption that he had seen the ship I am riding on although we were operating in the same general area. He was permitted to tell me which carrier he is now attached to[122] so his mother no doubt has the same knowledge as I. Bobby is still at the same location and urged me to come by to see him if the chance ever presented itself. He was at his usual top form in grousing about the living conditions at his station, but I'm sure that he likes his duty better than he would lead one to believe. My good friend, Arnie, is now an ensign in the Navy and is stationed on an LST, the big brother of the LCI (G). He too expressed the hope that we might run into each other soon.

---
121. Arnold Wayne Haynam (1917-2008), a graduate of Case Western Reserve University.
122. USS *Enterprise* (CV-6).

After the war is over

Because of the failure of my Georgia ballot to arrive on time, I was forced to vote by means of an official war ballot. Not quite a satisfactory substitute since only the national elections are listed and no provisions are made for voting for the local offices. However, I should not have known enough about the candidates to vote intelligibly at any rate.

The "Official Federal War Ballot" required servicemen to write the names of the candidates they wished to vote for.

After the war is over

Please let me again thank you for the pictures of everyone at the farm — I believe that the picture [of] you all and Franklin and the boys standing under a big tree is the best picture that I have ever seen of Dad. You must send me some more as soon as practicable.

I'm definitely convinced that we will have a more satisfactory correspondence if you address all my mail as follows:

Lt. (j.g.) Walter H. Pullen
USS LCI (G) 729
FPO San Francisco, Calif.

Don't work too hard at the farm.

Your loving son,

Bud

Typed Letter Signed (TLS), stamped envelope.

Tuesday
Nov. 14, 1944[123]

Dear Mom & Dad,

It has been only eight days since I received that large batch of letters from home, yet for some reason it seems longer; maybe I am just getting a little bored with this existence.

---

123. War Diary of USS LCI(G)-729 for November 9-14, 1944: "Anchored on picket station, Kossol Passage."

After the war is over

USS LCI(G)-472 of the Black Cat Flotilla receiving supplies while alongside a larger ship.

My activities during the last few days have been a mite interesting — I have been jumping around from ship to ship (I mean larger ships, not LCIs) trying to secure some money so that I wouldn't become the most useless of all personnel — a paymaster without money. My success was only partial since I was able to obtain only fifty-thousand dollars which won't last too long. It is next to impossible to predict how much money one will require due to the ever-changing number of our organization.

Yesterday we (our ship) had the good fortune to go alongside a stores ship to replenish our supply of swabs, brooms, mess gear, line, etc. We took on enough for several ships and find ourselves loaded to the gunwales with the above-listed items.

The clipping that you-all sent to me concerning the commercial farming of grape arbors and scuppernongs sounds most interesting. I'm afraid that I would be tempted to devour the whole fruit of a season, however. It is possible without too much

After the war is over

labor, I hope that you-all will be able to set out a few experimental bushes in order to determine whether our soil is conducive to the growth of grapes. I can assure you that my appetite for any variety has not abated. Also, have you considered planting a plum tree?

I am delighted to hear that the shop is doing so well. If you can only keep a full staff of operators, I don't see why you can't make a start toward a reasonable bank balance, and always keep your eye out for any promising businesses — beauty shops or otherwise. Remember, it is always easier to let someone else work for you. That applies everywhere including the Navy.

With some trepidation, I reluctantly e[n]sconced myself in a dentist's chair several days ago and was informed much to my amazement that I had no cavities. I explained that one of my molars was sensitive, and the dentist decided to remove the present filling and look at it. You don't have to overwork your imagination to determine how fast I escaped from that chair just in time.

Heres hoping that we get some mail soon and that I am among the lucky ones.

Your son,

Bud

Autograph Letter Signed (ALS), no envelope.

After the war is over

Saturday
Nov. 18, 1944

Dear Mom & Dad,

Still no letter since the large batch I received almost two weeks ago. Our mail service is intermittently good and bad — mostly bad, however. The only exciting thing that has happened recently[124] was the discovery of an old abandoned Japanese barge which we salvaged. The barge is approximately 70 feet in length and is not much more than a heavy wooden box pointed at either end. Nevertheless, we are extremely proud of our prize and enthusiastically spent a whole day in salvage operations such as pumping out water and plugging up the bullet holes caused by our firing at it before we found it to be empty. Someone may find a use for it — I hope so — so that we may feel that we accomplished something useful. I am most grateful for anything which interrupts our undeniably monotonous role in this war.

It is axiomatic that everyone in the Navy feels that his job is not a good one and that he would willingly trade places with almost anyone in another place. Of course, it is merely an instance of seeing greener pasture on the other side of the hill; I realize when I stop to think that I have one of the softest jobs in the armed forces and I do believe that I don't complain unduly as do some of my fellows.

Several days ago we were privileged to witness a tropical storm which approached typhoon proportions. Fortunately, we were anchored in a small sheltered anchorage[125] or we should have been buffeted unmercifully by the storm. For sheer irresistible power and intensity, I have never seen its equal. The wind fluctuated

---
124. War Diary of USS LCI(G)-729 for November 15-17, 1944: "Picketing Toagel Mlungui [Passage]. Went alongside empty 75-foot Jap coal barge, and took it in tow after shelling it." For November 18-19: "Towed barge to Barnum Bay and anchored there."
125. War Diary of USS LCI(G)-729 for November 9-14, 1944: "Anchored on picket station, Kossol Passage."

After the war is over

from a mild prevailing trade to a howling gale of at least forty miles an hour. The rain surpassed anything that the temperate zones could muster coming down in great sheets which stung the skin unbearably when the wind was high. The storm or hurricane continued for about two days before gradually abating to a mild rain.

There is a chance that we may get ashore this afternoon and I am buoyed up by the hope.

Goodbye for a little while,

Your loving son,

Bud

Tell Belle and the dogs that I don't want them to forget me.

Autograph Letter Signed (ALS), stamped envelope.

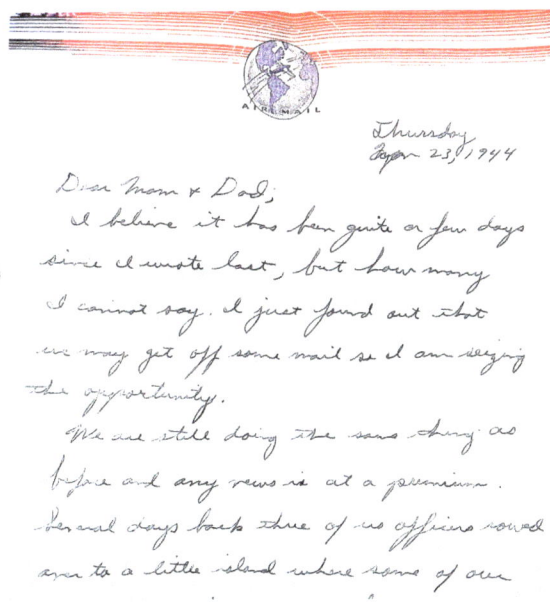

After the war is over

Thursday
Nov 23, 1944

Dear Mom & Dad,

I believe it has been quite a few days since I wrote last, but how many I cannot say. I just found out that we may get off some mail so I am seizing the opportunity.

We are still doing the same thing as before and any news is at a premium. Several days back three of us officers rowed over to a little island where some of our soldiers are garrisoned; they had many interesting stories to tell and they also had some rather picked-over Jap souvenirs which they were eager to sell or trade. The only thing that I could procure was some Jap money which I cannot send through the mail yet. I will send it as soon as I can so that you-all can see the gaudy little piece of currency which were taken off dead Japs.

After seeing the soldiers' camp, I am more than ever convinced that I have a good job and that the most uncomfortable ship (or landing craft) in the fleet is vastly superior to the best shore base in these desolate islands.

As you know I am extremely anxious to hear how Dad's arm is healing up and also how everything else is going at home. It is difficult to imagine that it could be cold there because [the] temperature here is consistently warm with only an occasional shower. I would [also] like to hear also what you have been doing out at the farm recently. I assume that as the tenant moves out of the house, you will move all the equipment and furniture from the shack.

I take the collection of pictures out of my desk drawer almost every day and remind myself of the delights of spending my time walking through the fields that belong to me.

After the war is over

I see that the mail sack is just about closed so I will have to hurry to get this note in before it is too late.

Your loving son,

Bud

Use my new address.

Autograph Letter Signed (ALS), no envelope.

Monday
Nov 27, 1944

Dear Mom & Dad,

The only mail I have received in three weeks was a letter from Bobby that arrived today. Evidently one of the too-frequent mix-ups has happened again and I will get a large batch all at one time. He seems to be suffering from the same malady as I (no mail).

Since I last wrote you, I have had several opportunities to go on the shore [for] business purposes. It is amazing how quickly our forces can build up a living place out of the jungle. Of course, their living condition would seem most rigorous to you, but it is surprising how much one appreciates a few creature comforts after their absence for a while.

We are engaged in a little activity[126] different from our usual monotonous duty, and everyone welcomes the diversion. It is impossible to tell you the nature of our activity now but maybe I

---

126. On joint operation with 81st Infantry Division forces in the reconnaissance of Kayangel Atoll, November 27-December 4, 1944.

After the war is over

will be allowed to later. Suffice it to say that there are more faces to look at and fresh topics of conversation. What more could one ask?

Quite inadvertently I ran into a supply school classmate of mine a couple of days back and strangely enough he sat next to me for a good part of the course. His name is Prewitt[127] so you can understand the proximity of our seating.

I have just heard the sad news of the Tech-Notre Dame game.[128] It seems that it is almost impossible for us to ever win that game. I believe that I can await with little doubt for a smashing defeat of Georgia which will salve the wound of the Notre Dame loss somewhat.[129]

Please remember to send me the newspaper clippings which show how each state went in the election. We have been unable to obtain the detailed results out here.

Well, Mom & Dad, it is so hard to write when I haven't had news from home in such a while. You see there isn't much to write about unless I hear from you.

We aren't celebrating Thanksgiving until next Thursday so I can't even tell you of our dinner. I will do so in my next letter.

Your loving son,

Bud

Autograph Letter Signed (ALS), no envelope.

127. Joseph (Joe) Sidney Prewitt (1921-1972) was in Bud's "Class J." Born in Martinsville, Indiana, he graduated from DePauw University (1942) at Greencastle. After the war he worked as a sales representative for Tappan Co. of Mansfield, Ohio.
128. The Irishmen won 21-0 on November 25, 1944. It was Georgia Tech's 13th loss out of 15 meetings with Notre Dame since 1922.
129. Tech beat the Bulldogs 44-0 on December 2, 1944.

After the war is over

Dec. 7, 1944

Dear Mom & Dad,

Santa Claus arrived yesterday a trifle early but just as welcome as on Christmas Eve. All of your packages came at once and literally flooded the market with candy and fruit cake. It is unnecessary to tell you that you shouldn't have gone to so much trouble because I have already told you that several times. Please believe me when I say that I am magnificently happy to get these gifts and I must ask you to thank John & Elisabeth and also the Andersons[130] for me for their thoughtfulness.

Mrs. John W. Hudson, the former Miss Elizabeth Anderson, daughter of Mr. and Mrs. W. K. Anderson, whose marriage took place in Conyers, Ga., in early summer.

Atlanta Constitution, July 18, 1937, p. 30.

---

130. John W. Hudson, his wife Elizabeth, and Elizabeth's parents, William Knoll Anderson (1886-1947) and Edna Christine Nies (1888-1973). W. K. Anderson, Sr. was associated with Davison-Paxson Co. department store in downtown Atlanta, while Edna retired from the National Weather Service.

After the war is over

Oddly enough, only two letters arrived with the packages and they were both from Dad. You see, this delivery of mail was sent to the old address (Flotilla 13 Staff) and I suspect that all the other letters are contained in 13 bags of mail which this ship has ready but has not been able to pick up. Oh yes, the picture postcard from Miami came inspiring some envious thoughts I'm afraid.

I was very pleased to hear that you were able to go to Miami with Imogene. I remember how much you enjoyed your last trip there. Of course, my inevitable question is: How much money did you win from the Slot machine? Do you recall that I was in Key West about this time last year?

Another bit of information I was glad to hear is that Dad is going to get a vacation with pay sometime around Christmas; he said that he plans to set out trees at the farm, but don't you think that it will be a little cold to plant young trees?

All of the Georgia fellows in the flotilla are anxious to hear the results of the Tech-Georgia game so please enclose your usual clippings about that game.

Dad related that he didn't think he would be able to see the Notre Dame game; I do hope that he can see at least one game this season.

The news from here is still meager excluding the excursion to a native village which I narrated in my last letter. You-all haven't made any guesses as to where I am in the Pacific[131]— I would like to hear from you where you would place me on the map. You have received several clues.

---

131. War Diary of USS LCI(G)-729 for December 5-8, 1944: "Anchored on picket station one half mile south of Urukthapel [Island, in the center of Palau] and west of Yoo passage."

After the war is over

Thanks again, Mom & Dad, for all the welcome gifts, and remember how much I love you-all.

Your boy,

Bud

Don't try to spend the money I'm enclosing or you may be jailed for [being] a fifth columnist.[132]

Attached to this letter by cellophane tape is a Japanese 10 yen occupation note and a coin, supposedly "taken off dead Japs."

Autograph Letter Signed (ALS), stamped envelope.

---

132. Someone who secretly supports and helps the enemy.

After the war is over

Dec. 8, 1944

Dear Mom & Dad,

I am just digging myself out from under another deluge of letters. Four letters from Dad with dates ranging from Oct. 9 to Nov. 18 arrived today with six letters including a V-mail from Mom covering the period Oct. 6 to November 16.

There seems to be very little that we can do to change the method of delivery of your mail so I guess we will continue to receive letters in batches of two or more weeks accumulation. From your reference to receiving four of my letters at once, it appears that the service is erratic going both ways. Dad, I certainly do appreciate all the clippings— please continue to send them whenever practicable.

Let me thank you for clearing up the allotment data. I wasn't quite sure that everything was going right but now I am satisfied that everything is in order. It looks as though we will be able to save quite a bit of money at the present rate.

It is unfortunate that you are troubled by a cigarette shortage;[133] that is one commodity which is always available out here and that is doubtless the reason for the scarcity at home. However, if the shortage causes you to cut down on your smoking, it may well be that the lack is beneficial.

Although you required a little prompting from the newspapers and magazines, I think you made a very good guess at our present location. Was Dad the one who made the guess?

---

133. Cigarette smokers faced critical shortages in late 1944. Part of the reason for this was American tobacco companies shipped 30% of their output to the armed services as part of GIs' C-rations. Others blamed hoarding and black marketing. Lines formed outside stores on the one or two days per week that cigarettes were available for purchase. By December 1944, signs lamenting "no cigarettes" turned up in store windows everywhere. (See letter of January 26, 1945.)

After the war is over

Halbert A. Hudson, University of Cincinnati, 1949.

I am delighted to find out that Hal Jr.[134] is in the Officers' Training Unit at Fort Benning. Maybe he is so late getting into the war that he will not be sent overseas. It is a rough life at best for the Army. It is inconceivable that he could be old enough to be an officer in the Army.

What does Dad think of the political beliefs of Big Halbert since he has lived up North for so long?[135] We have a new engineering officer aboard our ship now who comes from Birmingham, Ala. and who is a much-needed democrat aboard this Republican infested bucket. I am inclined to agree with Big Halbert except that I do not like to change presidents at this time.

Well, Maw & Paw, you know the extent of my happiness upon receiving so many letters so it is unnecessary to thank you. The

---
134. Bud's first cousin, Halbert (Hal) Austin Hudson, Jr. (1923-1994), was commissioned a second lieutenant on November 29, 1944, and was wounded in action in Germany on February 11, 1945. Discharged from the Army on April 9, 1946, he later worked for Proctor & Gamble as a mechanical engineer for thirty years until his retirement in 1983.
135. Halbert Austin Hudson (1898-1977), Stella's younger brother, was working for Southern Railway and living in Cincinnati, Ohio at the time. Prior to then he was in Alexandria, Virginia for five years.

After the war is over

letter-writing set is an ideal birthday gift and is due for a great deal of use.

Your loving son,

Bud

Autograph Letter Signed (ALS), stamped envelope.

Wednesday
Dec 13, 1944

Dear Mom & Dad,

Three more letters from home arrived dated Nov. 27th and Nov. 29th. They were written from Miami and home.

I am so glad that you enjoyed your trip down South; I know you are a little partial to warm weather and pretty clothes. Are there still as many Army Air Corps trainees there now as there were earlier in the war? Didn't you have any difficulty getting train accommodations?

I remember that you once mentioned buying Imogene's automobile because they were forced to sell it before leaving this country. What was the final result of the proposition? If it isn't too late, I suggest that we buy it, but I suppose it has already been disposed of by now.

Yesterday we discovered an old Jap wreck piled up on a reef several miles off a supposedly Jap held island. After anchoring our ship we put over our small boat and a rubber life raft which we use as

After the war is over

a small boat to investigate the wreck. As far as I know, we were the first Americans to inspect the sunken hulk. The wreck, from what we could tell, was a Japanese craft about one hundred feet long and had been stripped of all the guns and everything else that one could carry away. Of course, we couldn't explore the holds as they were underwater, but I doubt if anything of value was still aboard.

The incident related above has been the only deviation from the usual life out here — we are ready for something else to develop to break the monotony.

One of the storekeepers receives his copy of the pony edition of "Time" regularly (our most recent Nov. 27) so there isn't any reason for you to send it to me. In addition, I have su[b]scribed, but have yet to receive the first copy.

We finally had our belated Thanksgiving dinner last Sunday and gorged ourselves with chicken a la king and ice cream. Our ship, [like] all the others, has been provided with plenty of turkey for Christmas. Our only lament is the loss of our good cook. Maybe Santa Claus will bring us one who can bake.

The stamps Bud enclosed in this letter.

Someone on the staff sent over the Japanese stamps which are enclosed; the story is that the stamps were taken from a captured Jap Post Office. Maybe you know a stamp collector who would like to see them. What does Belle think of the Nipponese money which I sent you?

After the war is over

Be good there at home and don't forget to tell the Hudsons, Andersons, et al thanks for their gifts.

Your loving son,

Bud

Autograph Letter Signed (ALS), stamped envelope.

Dec 17, 1944

Dear Mom & Dad,

Dad's letter of Dec 5 arrived today indicating that several previous letters are missing. They will turn up soon though as usual I suppose.

Let me thank you-all just once more for that delightful fruit cake. I somewhat reluctantly invited all the other officers to have a piece and only one out of the seven declined. I'm afraid that I greedily ate his slice before he changed his mind.

Dad's letter says that both of you are bothered by rheumatism; do you suppose it is the cold weather or just a periodic attack which seems to afflict almost everybody at one time or another?

To hear that the tenant is not cooperating makes me rather angry and I wish I were there to "dicker" with him. My advice is to get him off the place even if it does mean the loss of a few dollars each month. One can't call the house his own when someone else is living in it especially such an ambitionless character as you describe. There must be some way to eject him without creating a scene.

After the war is over

Is it not possible that Dad can get his Christmas vacation in spite of the rush of work? I hope that he can at least get off Christmas day.

The soul-satisfying score of the Tech-Georgia game has elated me tremendously. As you know this is the first time that Tech has ever downed Georgia at the Athens stadium. The victory atones in some measure for all the lickings they have given us in the past years.

Today has indeed been a day among days: It began with a delicious Turkey dinner including candied yams and all the usual accouterments and terminating in an incomparable apple pie. I could barely pull myself up the ladder to sit in my semi-horizontal deck chair. Hardly had the pleasant effects of the dinner begun to disappear when a small boat brought us mail including several letters and Christmas cards for me. Sometime later I answered the evening chow call with my usual alacrity and was rewarded for my promptness with a gargantuan dish of ice cream which as you know is the best thing that could happen to me.

Well, it has been six months since we left home and although I, as much as everyone else, would like to get home, I cannot complain if the rest of my tour of duty out here is no worse than the first six months. Our only lament is of confinement and boredom which is encountered at home as well as here. We have lately been enjoying a newly-rigged Public address system over which one can play records. As Dad can no doubt imagine such an arrangement may prove to be a mixed blessing, however.

If this letter reaches home by Christmas, I wish everyone all the happiness and joy possible.

Your loving son,

Bud

Autograph Letter Signed (ALS), stamped envelope.

After the war is over

Saturday
Dec. 23, 1944

Dear Mom & Dad,

I'm so sorry to hear that Mom has another bad cold — I do hope that it doesn't linger on as some of the others have done.

It is surprising to hear that you didn't get a letter in the week ending Dec 11; I try to write about every three or four days, but our mail service is still sporadic and undependable.

Your guess that I might be close to Dudley[136] is not very good— Dad's conjecture several weeks ago was much closer. Don't you all consult before you make a guess?

What do you think the possibilities are [for] buying that house next to our farm? The idea is exciting if the house is a good sturdy one, but you say that the people don't want to sell. Maybe after some thought they will reconsider. Like you-all, I think we ought to have a livable house because I am planning on living there some day. After Dad surveys the land on Christmas day, I wish you would send me a diagram of the plot showing where the present buildings are and where you propose to erect a new house when the materials become available.

I am losing patience with that tenant — if he is such a lazy and worthless character as you describe, I can't see that any advantage is to be desired from retaining him there. You tell him that when I get home I'll move him out <u>fast</u> and I would certainly like to do it now if I were there. It is preposterous not to be able to use one's own house however shabby it may be.

---

136. Probably Lt. Dudley Frances Bachler, Jr., who had married Mary Jane Thweatt on March 15, 1944.

After the war is over

After consulting with the farmers on this ship of whom there are several from Arkansas and Texas, I have obtained the information that an acre of pasture will support at least one — maybe two cows from the spring to the late fall and that one should just about double his money on the deal. I don't know how much acreage we have in our pasture; I would like to hear your estimate of how many heifers our pasture will support.

Well, Mom, it is quite a struggle to keep operators at the shop. Perhaps you will get one who will stay permanently. By the way, how many operators do you have at the present time?

I am getting along fine except that there is absolutely nothing to do most of the day. Nothing diverting has occurred lately to write you.

Your loving son,

Bud

Autograph Letter Signed (ALS), stamped envelope.

Monday
Dec. 25, 1944

Dear Mom & Dad,

Don't feel sorry for me this Christmas— I just had dinner almost as good as I would have had if I were home. Magnificent slabs of turkey were almost crowded off my plate by the wonderful candied yams that reminded me strongly of your Sunday dinner. After stuffing myself with the olives and chicken broth, I hardly had room left for a huge dish of vanilla ice cream accompanied by fruit cake the equal of any I have ever tasted (except yours).

After the war is over

Our dinner was to be topped off by a couple of cans of beer—but somehow no one could find the necessary space. I guess I'll save mine until tonight.

Everyone aboard is imbued with the Christmas spirit of wellbeing and a few gifts where possible have been made.

You didn't tell me whether you were going to have the usual family tree on Christmas Eve as we always do— Is there enough family left there to make it practical?

As you-all know, I lean over backward to avoid any sentimental expressions but I cannot miss this opportunity of telling my Mom & Dad that everything that is good in this life I owe to you— I am humble in my debt to you for your constant love and inspiration.

Your grateful son,

Bud

Autograph Letter Signed (ALS), stamped envelope.

Thursday
Dec. 28, 1944

Dear Mom, & Dad

For a change the mail is arriving regularly now at this end probably due to the fact that we have been able to get on the beach and pick up our mail at the post-office. While on the beach several of the fellows were able to procure fifteen cases of cocacolas. Our real purpose ashore was to obtain fresh provisions; we were so fortunate in finding fresh meat that we exceeded the

After the war is over

capacity of our ice-box and were forced to give away quite a few cases to another ship.

I am very happy to hear that little damage was caused by our fire and wish to extend my congratulations [on] your fire-fighting ability. What a versatile mother I have!

Hugh wrote me a long letter relating to that he is stationed on another carrier and that he participated in the same operation that we did three months back. He also said that their ship had received the Presidential Unit Citation[137] which as you may know is an award made to ships or units of the Army or Marines who have performed exceptional work in the prosecution of the war. His ship must have taken part in some hazardous operation to merit this coveted award.

Don't expect to receive any pictures soon because we may be a long time running into some place where the negatives may be developed. I was caught in a rainstorm on the trip back to the ship from the small island and I am afraid [that] the prints were spoiled.

Over a month ago, a fellow named Buck[138] showed up as Cliff LeVee's relief,[139] but I didn't tell you then because he wasn't sure

---

137. On May 7, 1943, the *Enterprise* had been presented with the Presidential Unit Citation for "consistently outstanding performance and distinguished achievement during repeated action against enemy Japanese forces in the Pacific war area, December 7, 1941, to November 15, 1942."
138. George Crawford Buck (1918-1992) graduated from Meriden High School, in Meriden, Connecticut, in 1936 and from Amherst College, Massachusetts, in 1942. While at Amherst he ran track and played on the golf team, in addition to excelling in the classroom, graduating *magna cum laude*, and being inducted into Phi Beta Kappa. He completed training with Pullen at the Navy Supply Corps School at Harvard University in August 1943. Three months later, he married while stationed in California; a union that ultimately produced three children, his first son born in August 1944 while he was on duty in the South Pacific. After his discharge from the Navy in 1946, Buck earned his M.A. and Ph.D. degrees from Yale University. A specialist in Germanic languages and literature, he taught at Columbia University and after 1950 at the University of Washington in Seattle. While at UW he pioneered distance learning in the late 1950s using television as a teaching medium with his nationally-broadcasted program "Spoken German." Before his retirement, he also served as associate dean of the College of Arts & Sciences and as president of the local chapter of the AAUP. (See letter of February 25, 1945.)
139. On November 10, 1944, Lieutenant (j.g.) Clifford LeVee was aboard the seaplane tender USS *Pocomoke* (AV-9) in transit from Kossol Passage, Palau Islands, to San Francisco, California. (See letter of January 26, 1945.)

After the war is over

he would get back to the States. Received a letter from him today telling me that he arrived in San Francisco on Dec. 16. He knows no more of the circumstances which occasioned his transfer than anyone else. About all he does know is that he is awaiting assignment to a new duty station. He might be so lucky as to be assigned a billet within the continental limits. I asked him to call you-all on long-distance and tell you where we are and what is going on—I do hope he has the opportunity to do so. It is possible that he may have already called by the time you get this letter. Please don't ask me why he was transferred and I am still with Flotilla 13 because I have not the slightest idea.

Well, folks, the news is scarce. Send me a little of that snow.

Your boy

Bud

Autograph Letter Signed (ALS), no envelope.

After the war is over

Chapter 9

"Here I am — half way around the globe."

30 December 1944[140]

Dear Mrs. Pullen,

Am enclosing several snapshots of Walt. After looking them over, I would suggest you send them on to him. Note the titles on the back which titles may cause him some amusement.

The larger pictures were spoiled by the heat according to the printer and developer.

Note the high shoes and green shirt in the three smaller pictures. Note also the shoes are several inches above the head usually. The chair is located in one of the more open areas of the ship but in the background are a cylinder of acetylene gas, signal gun locker, swab, 20 mm gun shield and ammunition box, several boxes of dry cereal under a cover, a stay holding up the mast, and a box containing a spare 20 mm gun barrel. In the background of the three-man picture is Schonian Harbor, 2 LCI's, and Eil Malk Island which was then, and may still be, held by the Japs.

Kossol Passage is an anchorage area in which repairs are made. Breaks in the dotted line indicate entrances in the reef. Ulithi is 300 miles northeast. Angaur was our objective and we landed at Blue beach.

If you have any questions just let me try to answer them.

Cliff LeVee

---
140. Letter from Cliff LeVee, postmarked Chicago, January 2, 1945, 6 p.m. Also, written on envelope, postage due 2 cents.

After the war is over

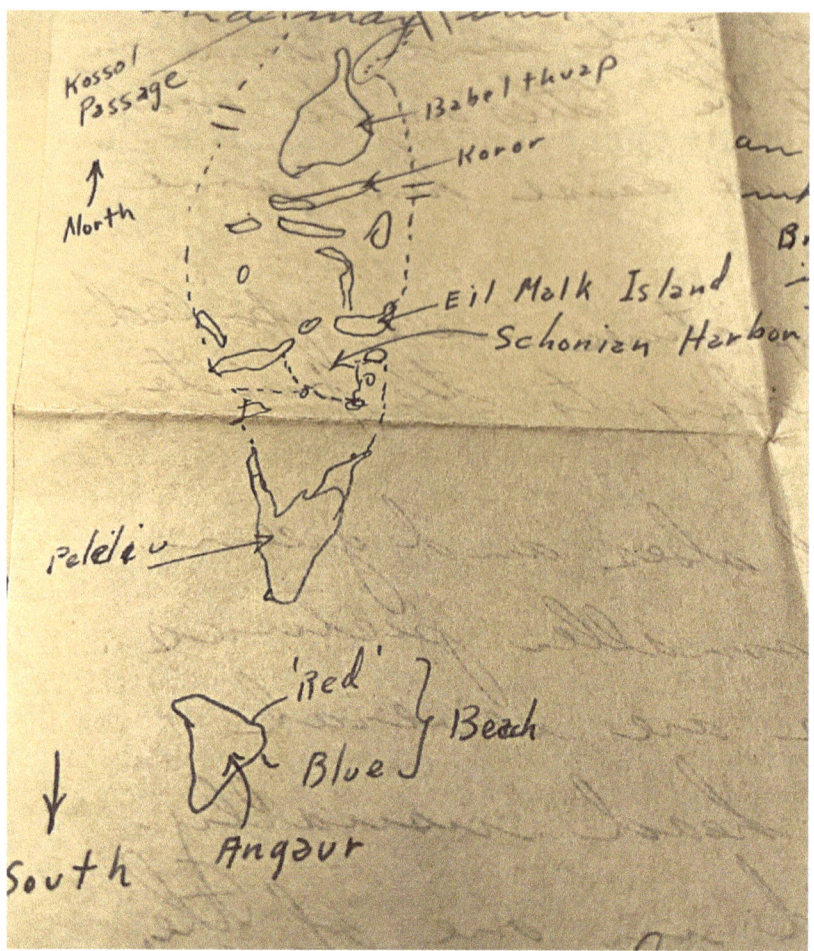

Map drawn by Cliff LeVee on the back of his letter of December 30, 1944, to Stella Pullen.

Autograph Letter Signed (ALS), stamped envelope.

After the war is over

Jan. 1, 1944 [1945]

Dear Mom and Dad,

You are familiar with my typing ability by now so you can overlook the profuse strike overs and various other errors. After all, how can I ever learn if I don't practice?

As I told you in my last letter, my partner, Cliff LeVee got a change of duty which required him to come back to the United States for re-assignment. He promised me that he would call you on the long-distance phone as soon as he found time. It is possible that he might have already called you by this time. If he has, you have a better idea of where we are located in this vast Pacific.[141] I tried to explain that I had no clue as to the reason [for] his relief and he had no better information than I. The disbursing officers of the LCI (L) Flotillas that preceded this one have not been relieved so I have no expectations in the near future and that this is all right with me because this duty while often boring has certain compensations which are not to be found on larger ships of the fleet; of course, this is not to say that I would not enjoy a tour of duty in the States. However, it makes no difference what I want so one just has to be philosophic about the whole thing.

Our mail addressed to the LCI (L) 729 has been coming through very well but the mail sent to the Flotilla Staff address has gone awry again proving that my request that you send my mail to this particular ship has merit. I'm not sure that all the packages you have sent me have arrived. One fruit cake arrived but it was not packed in marshmellows [sic] as you described one you had sent so I'm still looking for another perhaps in vain.

You never have told me whether you were able to buy Imogene's automobile before they left for Brazil. I suppose that you would have informed me if you had bought it so I assume that some hitch prevented you from purchasing it. How are the tires holding out on our buggy? Have you been able to buy any more since [the] last one you picked up several months ago?

---
141. See letter from Cliff LeVee to Stella Pullen, December 30, 1944.

After the war is over

The storekeepers have been very busy the last few days on the end of the year business; we had to close out all the old pay records and open up new ones and this involves a prodigious amount of typing and calculation. The work is just about completed by this writing— tomorrow we expect to be very busy paying some of the ships of the flotilla.

As you can imagine, I am very anxious to hear if you have had any success in talking the owner of the house next door to our farm into selling his small acreage and house to us. From your description, the house sounds about like what we are looking for— something livable yet not too expensive. What do you think of the possibilities of buying the place? I hope that by this time you have succeeded in expelling the tenant from our house. I am also looking forward to receiving the plan [for] the land that Dad was to secure on Christmas Day. Don't forget to send me a drawing of the place as the survey shows it.

We had a delightful turkey dinner today with an unexpected luxury, Waldorf salad. The repast wound up with some delicious mincemeat pie that tasted "just like Mother made." Our salmon salad tonight was something of a letdown but it was rescued by three fresh apples. It is perfectly obvious that we have received a transfusion of fresh food so I won't elaborate on the contents however important they may seem to us.

Well, folks, we are anchored as before[142] and the news is even less than usual if possible so I'll just send you all my love and say goodbye until the next time.

My love to Belle and the dogs.

Bud

Lt. (jg) W. H. Pullen

Typed Letter Signed (TLS), stamped envelope.

---

142. War Diary of LCI(G)-729 for December 31, 1944: "Anchored on picket station north of Eomogan [Ioulomekang] Island."

After the war is over

Ja n. 4, 1945

Dear Mom and Dad,

In the past two days I have received three letters from you all up to the dates of December 23 bringing me up to date pretty well on all the home news. I'm glad that you got the Jap money and stamps--don't let Belle try to spend them down at the corner grocery store or they might lock her up as a spy.

Maybe it is just as well that we didn't get to buy Imogene's automobile if it was rusting away underneath. We might have had the trouble with the muffler that we had with some of the others. The pictures of our car look as though it were still in excellent condition probably because I haven't been around to drivee it lately. When I do get home, it will fall to pieces all at once just like the old One Hoss Shay.

I believe that I told you that I am one of the most popular men on board since I began receiving my copy of " Time" magazine regularly. It requires only about a week or ten days to reach here. As you know the "Pony" edition is mailed from Pearl Harbor so the magazine gets here in shorter time than my other mail. We are able to swap books quite frequently withe the other LCI's around this area so our selection is constantly being replenished by this method. My main difficulty is deciding what to read before it is traded off by some of the m impatient crew members.

In a letter which I received two days ago from Bobby, he indicated that conditions at his present location have improved somewhat, but you know he was never one to see the better side of any situation and he is still dissatisfied and yearning for a change, but aren't we all.

The new map which you bought sounds justlike a commodity which was badly needed there at home. Both of your guesses have been good lately and I recommend no further hazarding of guesses because you couldn't do much better.

My typewriter was drafted for business reasons so I'll continue with the old familiar scrawl that

After the war is over

Jan. 4, 1945[143]

Dear Mom and Dad,

In the past two days I have received three letters from you all up to the dates of December 23 bringing me up to date pretty well on all the home news. I'm glad that you got the Jap money and stamps— don't let Belle try to spend them at the corner grocery store or they might lock her up as a spy.

Maybe it is just as well that we didn't get to buy Imogene's automobile if it was rusting away underneath. We might have had trouble with the muffler that we had with some of the others. The pictures of our car look as though it were still in excellent condition probably because I haven't been around to drive it lately. When I do get home, it will fall to pieces all at once just like the old One Hoss Slay.

I believe that I told you that I am one of the most popular men on board since I began receiving my copy of "Time" magazine regularly. It requires only about a week or ten days to reach here. As you know the "Pony" edition is mailed from Pearl Harbor so the magazine gets here in shorter time than my other mail. We are able to swap books quite frequently with the other LCI's around this area so our selection is constantly being replenished by this method. My main difficulty is deciding what to read before it is traded off by some of the impatient crew members.

In a letter which I received two days ago from Bobby, he indicated that conditions at his present location have improved somewhat, but you know he was never one to see the better side of any situation and he is still dissatisfied and yearning for a change, but aren't we all.

---

143. War Diary of LCI(G)-729 for January 4-5, 1945: "Picking up spare engines at Orange Beach, Peleliu."

After the war is over

The new map which you bought sounds just like a commodity which was badly needed there at home. Both of your guesses have been good lately and I recommend no further [typing ends here] hazarding of guesses because you couldn't do much better.

My typewriter was drafted for business reasons so I'll continue with the old fashion scrawl that you are used to deciphering.

I'll have to hurry if I want to get this letter in today's mail so you must pardon the brevity.

I hope Cliff has been able to call you by now.

Your loving son,

Bud

Typed Letter Signed (TLS), with handwritten addenda, stamped envelope.

Jan. 7, 1945

Dear Mom and Dad,

Your two nice letters written on Christmas Day arrived yesterday letting me know that you received my small gifts. It was very little, but at least you know that I was thinking and maybe I'll be able to do a better job next Christmas. I'm happy to hear that you were so fortunate as to locate a turkey; I understand that they were very hard to buy there at home this year and many people were not so fortunate. As I told you, we feasted after the manner of the old traditional Pilgrims and lacked nothing but possibly the church services which even the Pilgrims didn't enjoy. All in

After the war is over

all, it was a very happy day and one not soon forgotten. It just occurs to me that the Pilgrims mentioned above should be called Puritans—I forget which is correct.

As yet we haven't received the scores of the New Year's Day games, but I am hoping that Tech beat Tulsa as bad as they [Tech] beat Georgia.[144] I guess that Dad is sending me clippings of the scores so there is no use reminding you not to forget. There are several Atlanta boys in the Flotilla and we are all anxiously awaiting the results.

The news we are getting from home is certainly sobering; the war in Europe is beginning to look more and more like the last war. Of course, we all realize that the longer the Germans hold out the longer the war out here will continue and everyone who knows the news is greatly disheartened by the stagnation on the German front. How is the morale of the people there at home? The magazines we receive nearly always exaagerate [sic] the successes of our forces and the news broadcasts are even more flagrant in there [sic] artificial optimism. I would really like to hear what the folks there at home think of the present state of the prosecution of the war.

After experimenting with several men on the ship who had had cooking experience, we have at last hit on a successful combination and we are now eating as well as we ever were which is very good compared to the usual run of food on these small ships. For dinner, we had some delicious baked chicken, but I prefer the other methods of cooking chicken because I am to[o] lazy to cut it up.

The letter you all wrote on Christmas Day didn't say anything about the survey that you were going to make in company with the next-door neighbor out at the farm. Was it postponed or

144. Georgia Tech lost to the Tulsa Golden Hurricane 26-12 in the Orange Bowl in Miami on January 1, 1945.

After the war is over

did you get out there after all? What is the latest information on our tenant? Has he moved out or is he still defying us by not answering the door whenever we call on him for the rent?

There is a possibility that I may make a trip to another group of islands out here in the Pacific on business reasons. It is just an idea so far and I don't have any definite information as yet. The trip would only be of a few days duration and would be made by plane. I rather hope that I do get to go if for no other reason than merely to break the monotony. There is the possibility that I might get around to see[ing] Bobby at this place.

Hope everyone had a very happy New Year's Day and Dad enjoyed his vacation.

Your loving son,

Bud

Typed Letter Signed (TLS), no envelope.

```
19 January.  Anchored on picket station "Easy".
20 January.  On picket station "How". Left for Kossol at 1800.
21 - 24 January. Replenished fuel, water, and provisions at Kossol.
25 January.  Went to Barnum Bay to transfer personnel.
26 January.  Took station "Peter-Mike".
27 January.  Anchored on station "Queen".
28 January.  On station "Dog".
29 January.  On station "George".
30 January.  Anchored on picket station "O".
31 January.  Moved to station "Queen".
```

BYRNE P. MARTIN, Lieutenant, USNR
Commanding

War Diary of LCI(G)-729, January 19-31, 1945.

After the war is over

Sunday
Jan. 21, 1945[145]

Dear Mom and Dad,

This is the first time I have been able to write in about eight days as I have been away on a trip up to another island.[146] Of course, I have seen a lot of interesting things and could write quite a letter— if I were permitted to. I met Bobby [on] the second day that I was there and stayed with him [for] about three days. No doubt he has already informed his mother that we were together for a while and I no longer sympathize with him whenever he complains about his hard life there on his island. Compared with some of the shore bases that I have seen, he is living in the lap of luxury; any of his complaints are purely imaginary and I so informed him. Naturally he doesn't see eye to eye with me and bemoans his fate continually. He is living in a Quonset hut with several very likable fellows and has only a short walk to his office where he reposes on a leather sofa which is scandalously soft. In the evening he has only a short stroll over to the movie theater; however, I must admit that the caliber of the movies that were shown the two nights that I attended was truly deplorable. It is impossible that they could be that bad consistently though.

My trip which was made by air was uneventful and differed little from a trip on a commercial airliner back there home. As you know, the Army and Navy fly transport planes all over the Pacific with schedules as punctual as the American Air Lines.

One of the officers here on this ship tells me that Cliff has sent his family some pictures which he took out here. Have you received any from him yet?[147] We would like very much to see

---

145. War Diary of LCI(G)-729, January 21-24, 1945: "Replenished fuel, water, and provisions at Kossol."
146. Bud had traveled to Guam. (See his letter to Cliff LeVee, January 27, 1945.)
147. See Cliff LeVee's letter of December 30, 1944, to Stella Pullen.

After the war is over

them if you have gotten any; he made quite a few including some of the storekeepers in various lazy poses not to mention those he took of me in complimentary postures.

Only one letter arrived from you-all while I was away; Dad's letter of Jan. 7th or 8th telling me of the efforts we have been making to eject our reluctant tenant. How I wish that I were there to add my weight to moving him out. You can tell him for me that if he is there when I get home (your guess is [as] good as mine) there are certainly going to be some fireworks because we didn't buy the place to provide a free lodging for a lazy bum who won't even pay a pittance for rent. You indicate that more than one person is living there — I thought that only one man was occupying the house. I am somewhat fearful of the attitude that the OPA[148] may take toward the ejection of this fellow so you must be sure of the legal ground before you act. I repeat, however, that you can promise him that I'll get him out when I get back.

Dad's drawing of the place gives me a better idea of the layout of the farm. I would like to know more about the spring. Does it give enough water to supply a plumbing system for the house? If not, it will be necessary to have a pump installed at the well for our water. I have invited Bobby to live out there after the war though I doubt whether I could get much work out of him. I am planning to live there when I get home for quite a time before I try to get a job; in fact, I may not try to get a job. Ha Ha.

Your package containing the olives, Yardleys,[149] candy, nuts, comb, etc. arrived yesterday. It was certainly a strange coincidence that the Yardleys shaving bowl arrived at such a propitious time. In my next letter, I was going to ask you to send me a shaving bowl because the one I am using at present is just about exhausted.

---
148. The Office of Price Administration, which was empowered by executive order to deny landlords trying to evict tenants.
149. Yardley & Co. brand toiletry items, such as shaving soap, after shave, and cologne.

After the war is over

Thanks very much for anticipating my desires and needs. I haven't yet eaten the fried chicken or the pecan roll. Is the fried chicken a commercial product or did someone can it at home? It is the first time that I have seen canned fried chicken.

Well, folks, the news is still scarce— we are still doing the same thing at the same old place in the same old way. Hope you get this letter soon.

Your loving son,

Bud

Typed Letter Signed (TLS), no envelope.

Jan. 26, 1945

Dear Mom and Dad,

I'm so glad that Cliff sent you the pictures he took at Pearl Harbor, that is, Honolulu, and at our present location showing me at that favorite spot of mine— sitting i[n] the comfortable chairs out on the deck. Don't bother to send all of them out, but I would like to see at least one of the ones taken on this ship. Oh yes, don't show them to any of my friends or they shall receive the wrong impression of my arduous duties out here in the Pacific. I must admit that I do spend a good part o[f] my waking hours in the chair you see in the picture. I received a letter yesterday from Cliff enclosing a few pictures and telling me of his latest activities. When he arrived at Chicago the temperature was 17 degrees below 0. He is probably having a little trouble getting used to the cold after the hot climate out here. His new address is as follows:

After the war is over

Lt. (jg) C. G. LeVee
Naval Supply Depot
Spokane, Washington

The news about the cigarette shortage is alarming; maybe I can return some of your gifts by sending you a few cartons of Luckies[150] from our ship's service here on the ship. If your ration allowance is not enough, let me know so I [can] send you some.

I am awaiting expectantly the picture of Dad of which you wrote [about]; I still don't understand just how you ever managed to get him in the studio however. As you say, I would like to have some of the proofs, which are not used.

Doubtless Mrs. Mac has called you by this time to tell you that I was up to see Bobby at his station. It seems that no matter how f[a]r we get from home we are still able to get together: first [in] Boston then at Solomons Md. And now finally at his present location. I wonder where I will see him next.

After considerable agitation, we finally succeeded in expanding our office space here on the ship. My partner, Buck, who relieved Cliff, moved off onto another ship yesterday and I took the same opportunity to request more space. The result is highly successful—I have a space curtained off about eight feet by twenty feet which is completely my own, that is, for my own personal use; the storekeepers have a similar allotment of space directly adjoining my office.

Dad's latest letter reported that our or should I say "his" tenant is still defying us and has the audacity to get a supply of coal for future consumption. What is the most recent report on

---

150. Lucky Strikes, the dominant project of the American Tobacco Company, whose slogan in 1944 printed on the bottom of a pack was L.S.M.F.T. ("Lucky Strike Means Fine Tobacco"), which after FDR's death sometimes turned into the political statement: "Lord, Save Me from Truman."

After the war is over

this tenacious fellow? What do the legal powers that you have consulted have to say on his ejectment? I should think that it would be a very simple matter to have the justice of the peace issue a warrant or whatever the legal document required is to get rid of this leech.

Mom's letter described a spot for a house so glowingly that I can hardly wait to see the waterfall and tall shade trees that make this such an ideal location for us to build a house or country place. Have you ever heard any more on the subject of when they plan to bring electricity out to our road? As you know, that is a most important consideration because it would be folly to build a house before one had definite assurance that power was available. Both of your diagrammatic sketches were most welcome as my idea of the general layout of the farm is still a little hazy; I believe that I now have a pretty good conception of how it would look from the air. Please let me know if the next-door neighbor decides to sell his place to us.

Our life here rolls on; we have had several exciting events to happen lately, but the security regulations prevent me from telling you all any of the particulars. Of course, the main topic of conversation is the same on every ship, viz when are we going home? Or when are we going to a new location? No one had any real news, but the inevitable rumors float around exciting everyone unnecessarily.

My "Time" is coming through regularly now so I am quite well-posted on what the current news has to offer. The news for the past few days has been heartening; the Russian advance to within 134 miles of Berlin is truly exciting because the sooner the war in Europe is completed, the sooner we can throw all of our weight into the Pacific war. I have been very lucky so far in my Naval career with all that duty there in the United States; perhaps that is why I cannot get used to this dull, monotonous life out here.

After the war is over

Well, as Dad usually says "that is all for this time["]— will write more later—

Your loving son,

Bud

Typed Letter Signed (TLS), stamped envelope.

Envelope that contained Bud's letter to Cliff LeVee, January 27, 1945, which Cliff forwarded to Stella Pullen, with the following handwritten note in blue ink.

Dear Mrs. Pullen,

Believe you are interested in this fellow; here is what he says to me!

Yes, it was a very interesting letter to read and almost wish I could go back to see the boys! I've reread the letter 3 or 4 times each time imagining the place and ship as it was. My hope is that the next time I go to sea, I'll be lucky enough to travel with such great friends and congenial fellows as were those on the 729!

After the war is over

Capt. Piel[151] of the 396 was the third member of our golfing group [in] San Diego last spring.

Kirnak is the one member of the flotilla for whom neither Walt nor myself ever lost respect.

Our duty here is most interesting although unusual. I'm assigned to the packing department and have to watch 200 or so people (civilians) from 15 to 65; most of them are former housewives, farmers, lumberjacks, trappers, school kids, shoe clerks, restaurant waitresses, etc. They provide me with entertainment in plenty. For instance one of my jobs is interviewing returned absentees. Such fantastic reasons are unbelievable!

Am working one week on the early day shift (6:40 A.M. to 3:10 P.M.) and the following week (from 3:10 P.M. to 11:10 P.M.) on the swing shift. Neither one is good for night life because rising time is 5:00 A.M. on the early shift. Oh, well, I should kick!

Sincerely,

Cliff LeVee

Typed Letter Signed (TLS), with notations, stamped envelope.

---

151. John William Peil (1917-2001), the commander of LCI(G)-396, which struck a mine on January 18, 1945. A graduate of Westminster College, Peil was associated after the war with Glidden for 35 years until his retirement in 1984. He was an avid tennis and handball player, duck hunter, and trap shooter in St. Louis, as well as a husband for 50 years, father of three boys, and grandfather several times over.

After the war is over

Handwritten annotations in margins:

Top left: "Dear Mrs. Pullen, Believe you are interested in this fellow; he is what he says to me!"

Top right: "— addressing envelope"

Left margin: "Piel - Capt. of fcl 496 Kirnak - flotilla gunner"

Right margin (near "weaker sex?"): "what could he mean?" and "(?)"

Right margin lower: "no lurid details! so envelope would be big"

Left margin bottom: "Guam? advance base Pacific?"

Jan. 27, 1945

Dear Cliff,

Wait a minute—none of your cracks about my flawless typing. The two mistakes that I have made so far must have been unusual because I don't often make two in one line. — *Doubtful statement; usually makes more than 2!*

I received your nice letter yesterday containing all of the complaints about the tough duty you have been assigned there at Spokane Supply Depot. Piel and Kirnak tell me that they also have heard from you lately. This comparatively new interest you manifest in women has me baffled—does the recent estrangement at Boston have anything to do with this sudden upsurge of feeling for the (weaker sex?) By the way I am sorry to hear of your parting with the little girl in Boston; she certainly looked like a lucky choice in all the pictures you had of her. Perhaps this is only a temporary separation. *Is Permanent!*

Needless to say I am deeply grateful for your phone call and letter to my folks; you could tell, of course, how much it meant to them to hear from someone who had seen me recently. I can imagine how wonderfully surprised your mother must have been when you walked in just in time for Christmas dinner. That is the most propitious moment for the return of the prodigal son; I'm so glad that you could make it on that day.

Did the clipping your letter contained about Capt. Skillman mean that he was going to be the supply officer at Spokane? Well if so, you are in for some tough times are you not? It appears that you were given just the kind of duty that you requested. I cannot understand why you didn't ask for East Coast duty however. Everyone here merely groans piteously when I inform them of your new assignment. Incidentally almost the entire flotilla has asked me for news concerning your activities. You must send me some lurid details of your night life so that I may satisfy at least vicariously the many interrogators.

A couple of weeks ago I made a trip up to another island to get my pay records reproduced by V-Mail equipment, there being no such equipment available at the present location. The trip actually was necessary in addition to providing me with a little vacation. First they make a picture of the pay record with a regular V-Mail camera and then reproduce the record. The result is the same size as a regular V-Mail letter. As a supply officer you should recognize the value of having the retain copy of all the pay records right at your own office.

Bud's letter to Cliff LeVee, forwarded to Stella with Cliff's annotations and remarks in blue pen. In his letter, "Walt" mentions Capt. John Henry Skillman (1893-1956), who commanded the Naval Supply Depot at San Diego when LeVee and Pullen were stationed there. He left that assignment and transferred in December 1944 to the large Naval Supply Depot in Clearfield, Utah.

After the war is over

page 2

The second day that I was there Bobby McGinty came over and picked me up in his jeep. After finishing my work, I spent better than two days with him just rubber-necking, drinking beer, seeing movies, drinking beer, eating ice cream, and drinking beer. You can understand me when I say that I enjoyed my vacation immensely. Sober as it was. Of course, I am prevented from telling anything of the island, but I was truly amazed by the things I saw there.

Buck, strange to say, is getting along great with the old man after several events which would have had you or I on the carpet. He has even bearded Neff and has embarassed him in front of the Commodore. He is as loquacious as ever — my belief in his veracity has had many severe jolts and I 'm afraid that he does embroider the truth a little when he discusses his sea experience; however we get along wonderfully since I straightened him out on a few details. The Commodore ordered him to move off this ship and to take up residence on the mail ship so he would be able to get around better. He tried to talk me into moving with him, but I am staying here until I get definite orders. With the room left after he moved off and the addition of the little space on front of my desk, we now have a very capacious office. Many improvements have been made to the ship since you left including a seltzer bottle, a P. A. system with an outlet in the wardroom, and other creature comforts. The captain has become more liberal letting the crew have an occasional party in which the officers have to join to preserve order. Am I too subtle?

We have had quite a bit of excitement lately, but I'm afraid that I cannot tell you any of them, events which happened because of the security involved.

Please let me thank you for the pictures that you sent to my home and to me here. Capt. Martin says to convey his thanks also. As you can imagine I made some appropriate comments when I presented his to him. Frank begs me to thank you for as writing his folks and says that he will write to you soon. Lawlor also send his best wishes and appreciates your seeing his father.

Have you any clue as to why we were not relieved at the same time? It is still a mystery to me. Tom Sharp is still in his same billet and is still sending us his usual fouled up pay accounts. Rumor has it that he is heading this way; I sincerely hope not. He causes enough trouble where he is.

Well, Cliff, we all certainly do miss you and would enjoy hearing from you as often as possible. Let me hear all the hot dope.

Your ole buddy.

In the next to last paragraph, "Walt" mentions Philadelphia native Thomas Monterville Sharp (1919-1990), who graduated from the University of Virginia, identified by LeVee as "Disbursing [officer] for Flotilla 3."

After the war is over

Feb. 4, 1945

Dear Mom and Dad,

Today I received letters from Mom, Dad, and Belle, and last but not least, the dogs. Belle's letter was quite a surprise and afforded me much pleasure [in] describing the little scene which occurred when the car went into the ditch on a trip out to the farm. I see that my family has not changed appreciably since I was home.

How long do you estimate that it will take for the grape vines which you planted to bear fruit? I can hardly wait until I can sample the first grapes which make their appearance so you can understand my concern. Though you didn't say, I assume the grapes to be of the large purple variety— the name escapes me at the moment, but you know the type of which I am speaking. It might not be a bad idea at all to set out several different varieties so that we may discover which is the most favorable to our particular soil and climate.

So we have at last evicted Dad's tenant. That is something of a victory in itself, is it not? I am sure that we concur in our jubilance at his departing and will be most wary of ever renting the place to anybody else. It is my personal opinion that we shouldn't rent the farm or house to anyone. Of course, I am not speaking of the pasture or of the barn for obviously it does no harm to let the people next door use our pasture, especially when they continue to furnish us with fresh butter and other staples. To get back to the farm— I cannot see that the little rent that we could get for the house would justify our being deprived of the right to fix up the house just as we want it and to use it whenever we choose for a picnic or maybe even overnight. If I remember correctly, the amount of rent we were receiving <u>when</u> we received it was something like nine dollars. That is a pittance which we can well afford. Even if we only went to the place once a month,

After the war is over

the presence of a tenant would not be agreeable and I must confess— arouse something akin to anger in me. There may be other considerations with which I am not familiar and defeat my arguments, but first I must hear you expound them. The only one that occurs to me at the present is that someone there to look over the place would be worthwhile. I cannot think of anything there on the place which is so valuable that we must have a per[s] on there to watch it. Even if we did have someone there he could not stay there all the time and if a thief did have designs on some of our possessions, sooner or later an opportunity would present itself for the theft.

Here I am—half way around the globe giving you advice as to how to manage our place when you are right there to see the problems involved. Your arguments nevertheless, have not convinced me that we should rent the place. Please let me hear more of what you think about the matter.

The severity of my cold did not live up to the first indications and I am now almost recovered. For two days I thought I had the worst one of my long and varied career with the varmints but now the only reminders of the cold are the inevitable sniffles which hang on. As I told you in my last letter, almost everyone on this ship has been victimized by the epidemic. I do hope that I can go so long before succumbing. It has been six or seven months since I had my last one.

What a surprise meeting Fort Land[152] was. I don't believe that I have seen him since I was a Freshman or Sophomore at Tech. As you may remember, he went to Annapolis and is a regular Navy man. To be a member of the United States Navy used

---

152. Fort Elmo Land, Jr. (1920-1945) was the son of the Georgia superintendent of schools from Macon who died in 1927. He attended Georgia Tech before he secured an appointment to the Naval Academy in Annapolis, graduating in 1942. He served aboard the USS *Idaho* before transferring to the Navy Air Corps, receiving his pilot wings at Pensacola on December 26, 1944. As executive officer of a Naval fighter squadron, Lieutenant Commander Land died in November 1945 when his Hellcat crashed into the ocean some 15 miles southwest of San Diego. His body was never recovered.

After the war is over

to be something at which I marveled. I am talking about the regular Navy now so don't misunderstand me. Now one of our most frequent jibes at each other here on this ship is to call one another "regular Navy." It is considered the worst kind of insult that one can make. Of course, it is all in a jocular vein and we really don't have anything against the regular Navy except that we are afraid that they may try to keep us in longer than the present emergency. So you see I am in the United States Naval Reserve and not the United States Navy.

Well, Dad, if Talmadge[153] can come out for the abolition of the poll tax, he must be fairly certain that the change will not encourage the negroes to vote. He is well known all over the country as the most rabid advocate of white supremacy. After reading some of the clippings which you sent me on the subject, I am particularly convinced that the elimination of the poll tax might be a good change. You see the rest of the country looks down on Georgia because we still require the payment of the tax and the trend even among our Southern states is the gradual repeal of the poll tax witness Texas. I would like to hear more of what you think of the matter so let me know where you stand on this question.

It would be rather impractical to send me one of Dad's pictures because everything that we receive has been mauled unmercifully and I fear that his print would suffer in the mail. The proof that you sent me is enough to satisfy my wants and I'll let you know later whether to send the big picture. Hope you all are well. Thank Belle for the letter.

Bud

Typed Letter Signed (TLS), stamped envelope.

---

153. Former Georgia Governor Eugene Talmadge (1884-1946), who recently had called for repealing the $1-a-year poll tax which he believed disfranchised poor white voters. The white primary still in place, Talmadge argued, would be an effective-enough check on black voters. Georgia abolished the poll tax on February 5, 1945, by vote of the General Assembly and signed into law by Governor Ellis Arnall.

After the war is over

Chapter 10

"I would certainly welcome any change."

Ban Cools Gas-Fired Furnaces

Eastern Curtailment Denies Theaters Fuel; 200 War Plants Are Hit

WASHINGTON, Feb. 2.—(AP)— Winter conditions and rail traffic snarls, already cutting into industry through coal shortages, combined today to cool gas-fired war furnaces and force drastic curtailment of the use of that fuel.

The War Production Board announced that some 200 vital war plants already have suffered cuts of 10 to 90 per cent in gas delivery. WPB ordered use of natural and "mixed" gas cut off completely in amusement places in seven states and Washington, D. C., at 6 p. m. (Atlanta time) tonight. It accompanied the order with a plea to householders, schools and institutions to conserve the fuel.

The order is effective until 6 p. m. (Atlanta time) Monday or "until further notice."

PRESSURE LOWERED

Officials explained the ban this way:

Cold citizens with gas furnaces have turned them up.

Gas ovens in coal-short homes have been turned on to take off the chill.

The result, combined with ever-mounting use of gas fuel in war industry has dangerously lowered gas pressures in systems over a wide area.

Wherever natural gas is used in the prohibition area, even mixed with artificial gas, such places as theaters, moving picture houses, night clubs, bars, bowling alleys and other amusement spots were ordered to turn off all jets for the weekend and perhaps until further notice.

Affected are New York, Pennsylvania, Ohio, West Virginia, Kentucky, parts of Maryland and Virginia and the District of Columbia.

EMBARGO LAID

Winter-wrought conditions led to two other government actions:

1. A civilian freight embargo, except on coal, was ordered for four days beginning tomorrow in eight states of the same general area, following up a similar order last weekend to help clear clogged and winter-bound rail lines.

2. The Solid Fuels Administration requested Pennsylvania anthracite miners to work a full day tomorrow, even though under their contract the Saturday shift may not bring them overtime pay. Appalachian area soft coal miners have agreed to work Sunday.

WPB officials said the gas situation was so critical it would be impossible to consider appeals from any affected consumer.

Feb. 8, 1945

Dear Mom & Dad,

No word from you has arrived in the last few days— guess the excellent service we have been having is due for a change. Maybe the cause is the bad weather and transportation shortage there at home. We have been hearing quite a bit about the coal shortage and transportation difficulties. Are the Southeastern states affected at all by the tie-up? I do hope that you-all don't have trouble getting coal for our voracious furnace.

This article discusses an order issued by the War Production Board for all Atlantans to conserve fuel, owing to coal shortages, winter weather, and "rail traffic snarls." Atlanta Constitution, 2/3/1945, p. 1.

After the war is over

The captain of this ship[154] received his orders back to the United States yesterday and the executive officer[155] is succeeding to the command of the vessel. We all hate to see the old captain go away because he was such a prince. It does make a tremendous difference who the skipper is; however, the new captain, a young fellow about 24 is every bit as nice and congenial and I expect to get along with him just as I did the other skipper. Martin, the fellow who is going home, is quite deserving of some shore duty since he has been on sea duty for three years even though he has been in the U.S. some of that time.

I have received another letter from Cliff who is at the Naval Supply Depot in Spokane, Wash., as I told you previously. He is getting set in his job and seems to be well satisfied in the new position. He has written to many of the men in the flotilla and tells everybody about the same thing.

Ship's company had the rare opportunity of getting ashore two days ago for recreation. In company with other intrepid spirits, I attempted a desultory basket-ball game which has left me extremely sore and amazed at how badly we are out of shape. I suppose a week or so of such exercise would bring everyone back to normal. Little chance, though, of our having such luck again. One of my friends,[156] a skipper of a sister LCI, has procured a sailboat from some obscure source and has taken me sailing twice in the past few days. It is a sport which I had always wanted to try, and I find it exciting particularly when the wind is strong and steady. He has promised to take me sailing again soon and I am looking forward to it with pleasure.

My cold is fast disappearing after two or three death struggles and I will be most happy to see it depart. How are all the colds there at home? Has everyone had their quota?

---
154. Lt. Byrne Fowler Martin.
155. Ens. Max Henry Fischer.
156. Lt. John W. Peil. (See letter of March 10, 1945.)

After the war is over

The news is coming on in three minutes and it is too heartening to miss so goodbye for now.

Your loving son,

Bud

Autograph Letter Signed (ALS), no envelope.

Feb. 13, 1945

Dear Mom and Dad,

The last letter of your's [*sic*] that has arrived here was dated Jan. 31, and indicates that there are several letters in between which are missing. I understand that the mail service, that is, the air mail service has been interrupted so I guess that the missing letters will turn up sooner or later. It is a little hard to understand why my letters seem to arrive there in two's or three's. I imagine that you have learned by this time not to worry when no mail arrives for some protracted periods.

I am just as happy as you are to hear that Imogene has gotten settled so well there in Brazil— I am all the more anxious to visit her whenever the occasion permits. With all those servants her house must look something like a feudal estate. However, with the boys at the destructive age, she will need all the help that is available and three servants will prove to be the minimum that she needs.

The details about the canned fried chicken are gratifying—until I received your last letter telling me that Mrs. Ethier[157] had canned the meat[.] I was under the impression that you and Belle

157. Possibly Florence Achatz Ethier (1897-1966) from Michigan, whose son Lenard Charles Ethier attended Georgia Tech for two years before joining the Army in 1942.

After the war is over

must have done the job and I was wondering why you didn't put in more of the white meat. As you say the contents [were] composed mostly of drumsticks. I say mostly— I should say completely. Please thank her for me and tell her that it reminded me of home very much. But just between us, I don't think that these Yankees know how to cook fried chicken at all and they somehow have the impression that it should be baked. At least that is the prevailing idea on the ship. But, of course, I should hate to judge any sectional cooking by the stuff that is served in the name of food on this bucket.

The microfilms of the pay records have arrived now making my trip to the other island that I told you about worthwhile from a business angle as well as a recreational standpoint. I won't try to tell you why these microfilms prove helpful but suffice it to say that they have already proved their work. I still haven't written Bobby to tell him how much I appreciated his hospitality while I was with him. He helped me out a great deal and I must tell him soon.

How are things at the "Hitching Post?" Does that name apply to the whole farm or to only the big house. If it applies to the house, I should think that you will have to install a hitching post in front of the porch. Are your plans to screen the house now or to wait until I get home to do the work? I wish I were there now to help you clean up the mess the tenant or should I say Dad's tenant left behind him. I have meant to ask you before but it slipped my mind. Would it be possible to move the house by sections down to the location of the shack? When and if it is possible I wish that you would send me some pictures of the inside of the house. By opening all of the windows you should be able to obtain enough light to make fair pictures. What kind of furniture of sorts do you expect to take out to the house? Eventually, we must obtain some kind of a long sofa that will accom[m]odate my elongated form without drawing my knees up into a knot the way I used to have to do when reclining on

After the war is over

the sofa in our living room. I expect Dad will have the same request to make even though he never experienced any difficulty in going to sleep on the sofa that I recall.

Whenever you get time, I wouldn't mind if you could give me the latest statement of our financial position. I know that you told me only about two months back, but if you don't find it too much trouble, I should like to hear another recap listing the amount that we have paid and the amount that we owe on both the farm and on the shop and of course the amount we now have in the bank. Also, tell me the date my last allotment check arrived. You see we don't have much to think about and one of the things I look forward to is enjoying the money I am saving out here.

As to news, that which is worth telling isn't permitted and the rest is hardly worth repeating: we got ashore the other day on an island which we had not been on before. On a very rude basketball court, we attempted to play a game, but I am afraid that everyone was to[o] much out of shape to enjoy the exercise very much. Knowing very little of [t]he sport, however, I wasn't disappointed at all. Afterwards, I went sailing again in my friend's boat of which I told you in a previous letter. Since this all too brief recreational period, we have done nothing exciting but the same old thing — picket duty and patrol duty. Some of the skippers of these ships and my very good friends including the captain of the 729 have received orders back to the United States for further assignment. Unfortunately, there is no correlation between the personnel of the individual ships and the staff so I can draw no inference as to going home. Moreover, these fellows all have had more sea duty than I. The Navy has a policy of sending officers home for leave or shore duty after eighteen months overseas, but their policy must bow to the necessities of the war and our best hope is the end of the war might be sooner than expected the way things are moving along now.

After the war is over

Thank Belle again for the lengthy letter. Oh, yes, I don't know the exact day but Happy Valentine to all.

Your boy,

Bud

Typed Letter Signed (TLS), stamped envelope.

Feb. 17, 1945

Dear Mom & Dad,

Just to give a little relief, I'll write a letter for a change. It is somewhat late in the evening and I am afraid that there might be some objections to my spasmodic typing. A steady r[h]ythm would cause no alarm but my typing proceeds by jerks.

My last letter from home was Dad's dated Feb. 1, 1945, so you see we are still a little behind our usual elapsed time of delivery.

Your quandary over what to do with the house has given me an idea probably worthless but perhaps worthy of consideration. I will state it very briefly as follows: What do you think of the possibilities of selling the house and the section of land that is on the same side of the road as it is? Of course, I don't know too much about the topography despite your helpful maps, but from what I remember, there are about ten to twenty acres on the same side of the road as the house. It is possible that we could advertise the sale for some handsome figure, say $1500. And have buyers in little time. The figure I set is merely a wild guess and you are much better placed to decide on the maximum value of which the plot might be sold. Then with the money obtained from this sale, we might be able to purchase the better house of which you have written me. I don't know whether it (the $3000. house) is on the large or small side of the acreage so my ideas are a little hampered for want of definite information. It does not seem to me that the sum of $1500. Would be exorbitant for our house. Of course, I know little concerning our farm and the land around the house may be the most attractive spot on the farm. In that case, it would be foolish to sell off the beautiful section and retain the rest. The idea of purchasing that other house (the $3000. one) was an afterthought and is no doubt unfeasible but that would not necessarily prevent our making the sale and building our house in the best location when material becomes available. If we were to make the sale, we would then have acquired 80 acres for $700. which would be a bargain.

Folks, this is only an idea— give it a little thought and tell me what your opinions are.

Tell the rest of the family "hello" and write soon.

Your ever-loving son,

Bud

Autograph Letter Signed (ALS), stamped envelope.

Feb. 22, 1945

Dear Mom and Dad,

I have received a letter from each of you recently, but it is obvious that several intervening letters are missing because there is an interval of ten days when no letters are dated Feb. 1 to Feb. 10. I guess that they will all arrive sooner or later.

After the war is over

FACTS ABOUT THE COAL SITUATION IN ATLANTA

The wide publicity given to the fuel shortage in the North and to the nation-wide "brown-out" to save coal-generated electricity has created the impression among many that there is a severe shortage of coal in Atlanta.

This is NOT true.

There will be enough coal to supply every real need of every coal consumer in Atlanta for the rest of the winter, if each person is content with his fair share.

It is only natural that the widely-publicized national situation has caused some Atlantians to be concerned about coal, even when they have on hand an ample supply for four, five or six weeks. As a result, there has been an unprecedented number of orders which has severely handicapped local distributors, who are primarily and sincerely interested in seeing that no individual or business suffers hardships from lack of fuel.

This tremendous demand for "immediate delivery" of thousands of tons of coal would tax the yard and delivery facilities of Atlanta's coal merchants even in normal times. Under present wartime conditions, with a shortage of manpower and with rationing of trucks, tires and gasoline, such a situation is much harder to control.

To relieve the congestion brought about by this sudden avalanche of orders, the Solid Fuels Administration for War, with the co-operation of the Community Advisory Committee, has set up an office to receive coal applications at the Municipal Auditorium. The office is operated by volunteers from the Office of Civilian Defense, with the aid of salaried personnel supplied by the coal merchants themselves.

The purpose of this temporary office is to serve anyone whose supply of coal is critically low—less than a five days' supply. Atlanta coal merchants are co-operating fully by giving orders placed through this office priority over all others.

This situation is only a temporary one.

With only a few weeks of winter left, we urge you to help us make a fair distribution of the supply. Unless your supply of coal is critically low, please do not place an order now. Some people have an immediate, real need for coal, and we are sure you will agree with us that their requirements should come first.

COAL MERCHANTS
OF GREATER ATLANTA

Atlanta Constitution, 2/15/1945, p. 8.

My "Time" magazine devotes much space to the coal and fuel shortage in the United States this winter. Have we had too much difficulty getting coal for our voracious furnace? You haven't said anything about the local conditions although you did tell me that things were bad up in the North. The magazine further states that this is the worst winter so far in the war. None of the clippings that you all have sent to me have mentioned the possibility of snow in Atlanta. I suppose that we have had the usual amou[n]t of cold days but no prolonged cold spells. Even I would welcome some chilly weather for a change — as I told you in previous letters, our climate isn't too bad, yet it becomes extremely monotonous after so long a time in the place. On the nearby islands, the temperature becomes excruciatingly hot in the middle of the day but does cool down at night.

Yes, it is almost inconceivable that Hal Jr. could be old enough to be a second lieutenant in the army and I am even surprised to hear that he is overseas. I assume that he is in the European

After the war is over

theater of war. It seems only a few months ago that he was at our house for a visit and then he looked just like a gangling kid of fifteen or sixteen. How can he be old enough to be in the Army?

Well, I just returned from an island which I had never visited before and I will take up on this letter again. While on the island, I mooched a couple of cans of beer from the shore party of another ship who was having a beach party. The parties are almost the only diversion that the ships are able to provide and they occur but infrequently. The frolic consists of carrying several cases of beer ashore and then making one's own amusement. Of course, there are no facilities and the recreation consists of playing ball and exploring the island.

One of my fellow officers on the staff and I went exploring on the island and discovered (after a tip) a grove of Papayas. I don't believe that I have ever eaten these [*sic*] fruit before. Our instructor informs us that it is necessary to let them ripen before eating. We gathered a beer case each full of attractive-looking fruit and I will tell you how it tastes after they ripen. On this island there [are] trees which look just like our South Georgia Pine except for the miniature size. But when one grabs a handful of the needles and crushes them, the old familiar smell is missing— quite a disappointment.

As is usually the case, after the unusual exercise, I became exceedingly sleepy and had to take a nap after supper. My fellow officers would like to tell you that I am somewhat prone to take little naps after all meals, but I hope that you don't give credence to their stories; it does happen that I am occasionally found in the "sack" though I must admit.

You must stop sending me packages— when and if they ever reach here, they are pretty well wrecked, especially the candy and it makes me sad to think of all the trouble that you all went

After the war is over

to in packaging and mailing the stuff. The last one I received was the one containing the Yardley's shaving bowl and other welcome gifts. Nevertheless, thanks very much for sending me a Valentine. I won't give up hope that it reaches here until next Valentine's. I'm only kidding.

Everyone here is excited about the Iwo Jima invasion.[158] The men that planned it must have expected the stiffest opposition in the Pacific and apparently, they are receiving it. The radio tells us tonight that they have landed another division of Marines on the island. This makes a total of three divisions of Marines on the one invasion telling us something of the character of the expected resistance. Evidently we have complete control of the air because no Jap planes have appeared over the island as yet. Ther[e] is little doubt, however, that with Japan only 660 nautical miles away that we can look for intense air opposition soon.

I am still looking forward to hearing what you think of my suggestion of selling part of the farm which includes the house. Do let me know soon.

Your loving son,

Bud

Typed Letter Signed (TLS), no envelope.

---

158. The battle began on February 19.

After the war is over

February 25, 1945

Dear Mom and Dad,

Your missing letters arrived yesterday bringing us up to date pretty well except for the packages which I have grave doubts of ever receiving. I will try to answer a few of the questions that you asked in your letter of Feb. 4 and Feb. 16.

Maybe I didn't explain fully — Cliff was relieved by another supply officer by the name of George Buck. He is a full lieutenant and is originally from Connecticut and attended Amherst college near New York. The flotilla commander ordered him to move to another ship so he would be able to get around more. You see, our ship is a gunboat and he moved to regular LCI (L) which has the mail run and enables him to get on these islands and pick up supplies. He also gained more room by the splitting up of the office. The flotilla commander has suggested that I move to a different ship, but I prefer to remain on this one as long as I get along well with the officers and they provide me with [as] much room as I have now. The time may come, however, when he will suggest more strongly than he has to date, and then I expect that I will have to get on another LCI (L).

George C. Buck

After the war is over

I believe that I told you in a previous letter that the pictures sent [to] you by Cliff arrived here in good shape. I sent one of them to a friend o[f] mine; to be more definite, I sent one to the girl that I saw quite a bit in San Diego. She derived much pleasure from the one showing how hard I work on the ship. You remember, the snapshot of me sitting in the lawn chair in a semi-reclining position. If you really want the others, I will send them home, but I can't imagine why anyone would want those left.

None of the papers or news broadcasts that I have heard recently have mentioned the gasoline shortage which you [told] me of in the last letter—are we able to buy enough to take Dad to work or is even that much unobtainable? I hope that the situation is alleviated soon so you are able to go out to the farm. Which reminds me—please tell me sometime how much trouble it would be to get out there if one didn't have an automobile. In other words, what are the transportation facilities to the area and how far would one have to walk if he had no car?

It is very possible that we may want to go out there sometime when the car is not running or if I lived there, I would have to get into town without you all coming after me. It may even happen that we will not always have a car who knows?

How good are the chances of getting this new operator? From what you tell me, you certainly need one that will work steadily and not just when she pleases. You didn't answer my query as to what you thought about raising prices. It really is absurd for me even to talk much less suggest how you run your business that you know so much better than I [do]. My point [is] only brought up by the fact that if your prices were elevated, the smaller clie[n]tele would be just about what your organization could accom[m]odate during wartime. Of course, the plans would change radically after the war.

After the war is over

Thanks tremendously for the information as to our new worth. From your figures I gather that we have paid $2700. so far and are still indebted for $2500. With the $800. that we have in the bank we are now worth about $3300 more than we were at the start of the war. At the present rate, we will have the remainder of the debt paid off in a little over two years. We always have the privilege of paying it off sooner if we so desire, however. It is certainly gratifying to have even this little amount of security to fall back on in an emergency. We have much to be thankful for in these awful times.

After some thought, I have decided that the snapshot mentioned on the other side was sent directly to me by Cliff. At any rate, I am sending all that I possess to you. If you want my advice, destroy all of them immediately before my friend sees them.

Yes, I did receive Belle's letter some time back. Tell her how much I appreciate it and will fix her up with a big watermelon when I get home. I know she can eat a whole one.

Well, my cold has been gone [for] at least a month. Hope that you all aren't having too bad a time with the usual winter colds that always attack our family.

Thanks for taking care of me on Valentine's and hope that I can do the giving myself next year.

Your loving son,

Bud

Typed Letter Signed (TLS), stamped envelope.

After the war is over

March 6, 1945

Dear Mom and Dad,

It is quite apparent that I have run out of stationery again— the stationery you sent me incidentally. Please don't bother to send me anymore because I have only to walk up the ladder and buy some from the ship's service. The difficulty arises in that I never think to buy any until I sit down to write a letter.

Well, as usual, the news is at a premium which is one way of saying that there isn't any news at all. Yesterday I went swimming and got my nose sunburnt as is usually the case. The sun here is so intense that only an hour or so of exposure is sufficient to parboil any uncovered part of the anatomy. The members of the crew don't wear any shirts and most of them are the color of old mahogany. I have become addicted to the wearing of shorts— no beautiful sight I am quick to admit yet so very cool that I cannot resist.

Mom tells me in her last letter that she has approached the county commissioner on improving Nickajack Road. His reply is somewhat deflating is it not? Seriously, I do not regret the fact of his not knowing the location of our road. It means to me that our place is far away from the everyday traffic of the world and that is precisely what I crave. The farther away it is from everybody the better I will like it. I have meant to ask you before— is there any place on the farm which is invisible from the road, the neighbors, and everything else but God? If there is such a place on the farm, that is the location where I intend to build me a living spot. The pictures of the shack which you have sent me indicate that it may be the location I am seeking. Let me know in your next letter whether it is the thing I am looking for.

Mom also informs me that she has asked the Power Co. to investigate the possibilities of running a line out to our place. I

After the war is over

do hope that she has convinced them that such an improvement would be profitable from their viewpoint. There are so many contributions that electricity will make available such as a radio for Dad, to listen to the "soap operas," and a refrigerator for me to keep my pitiful little sandwich ingredients cool as well as a tray of ice cream for any visitors who might arrive unexpectedly. Of course, I don't care for the ice cream myself.

Some of your recent clippings and an article in "Time" have prompted me to inquire what you all think about the planting of this new soil-enriching Kudsu. It's [sic] exponents have made fabulous claims for this plant and Georgia appears to be the most receptive climate for its production. The main use of the crop is to prevent erosion and to enrich the soil. The crop can also be used for feed and has even been used for food experimentally. I understand that a Kudsu club has been formed in Georgia.[159] You might write to them for us and inquire if our soil is suited to the production of their namesake and whether it would [be] profitable to plant it unless one had a large stock farm. One of the advantages of this plant which appeals to me particularly is that no great amou[n]t of labor is required to maintain the crop. It is only necessary to plant it and forget about it. Sounds almost too good to be true, doesn't it? You must find out if I have been misinformed.

We are moving to a new location about a mile away where our mail will be picked up so I guess I had better finish this note.

Your boy,

Bud

Typed Letter Signed (TLS), stamped envelope.

159. Channing Cope, a public relations man for Georgia Power Company, popular radio host, and columnist for the *Atlanta Constitution*, organized the Kudzu Club of America in 1943 to promote the benefits of the invasive "miracle vine." At its peak, the club boasted more than 20,000 members in Georgia by 1949.

After the war is over

March 10, 1945

Dear Mom and Dad,

I often wonder how I will ever get used to working again— my daily schedule goes something like this: get up at about eight o'clock and stagger back to the wardroom to gulp down a glass of fruit juice (I don't get up when we don't have the juice on the menu). After drinking the juice and before fully waking up, I hurry back to the sack before I become too wide awake. On rising the second time about ten or ten-thirty I leisurely proceed to shave, clean up, dress, and take my vitamins all of which [consume] enough time to have me ready just in time for lunch. The afternoon is whiled away by reading and maybe even a bit of occasional work if available until approximately five o'clock when I start waiting around again for supper which usually comes off about five-thirty. Supper concluded, we play some in[n]ocuous card game for a slight wager until eight or nine in the evening when I again return to my reading which continues until slightly before midnight. After such a hard day, I have no trouble in falling asleep thus completing the cycle. Of course, on some days (three or four a month) we have quite a bit of work to do and it really isn't always as quiet as I have indicated above. You may laugh at me, particularly Dad, when I say that the above schedule is not of my choosing but rather forced on me by the lack of work to do. Honestly, I would certainly welcome any change which involved tasks consuming great amounts of time for that is the major problem out here. However, there is no job that the flotilla commander could give me which would not involve a drastic change in my living habits and maybe even require me to move to another ship. So I am remaining quiet and hoping that something will occur to change things soon. There is an old saying in the Navy "Never volunteer for anything" which I have always followed religiously and profited thereby. I cannot believe that any good could come from violating this ancient adage.

After the war is over

A few days back I received a letter from Hugh whom I had not heard from in quite some time. His news was startling: one of the ships he had been riding on had been damaged and only through a lucky accident had he escaped injury. He did not tell me the name of the ship and I suppose that he was not allowed to give any of the details. Nevertheless, it was apparent that he had been very fortunate to still be in one piece. His other information was that he expected to return to the States sometime in the near future and marry his girl, Fay, who, I believe, came to see you several months ago. A third morsel of news was that he wanted me there to perform as best man. What a joke! A suggestion, with as much possibility, would be for him to come out here to get married. However, my friend was never complimented on his practicality in normal times.

Bobby writes me that he is seriously considering my offer to live out on the farm with me. He is in somewhat the same predicament as I [am]: too little work and too much time to kill. However, a great difference is that while I want to work, I have grave doubts whether my friend, Bobby, has the same inclination. Or maybe I am deluding myself in the first place.

Some of the crew have been working furiously for the last few days to install an old pump motor in a boat we captured from the Japs. The boat is approximately fifteen feet long [and] made of heavy wood; obviously homemade, it is very thin and of shallow draft. If it runs it will surprise me, but nothing can depress the enthusiasm of the builders. I shall let you know in the next letter if the trial spin of the craft proved to be successful. I personally hope that it does because it will provide a method of transportation where we now have none.

To combat the boredom I went over to the ship of my friend who owns the sailboat and spent the night. He took me sailing in some relatively windy weather offering much fun. We took along sandwiches of peanut butter and cheese which tasted as well as they always do on a picnic. My knowledge of sailing is, as you know, limited to the distinguishing of the front and back of the boat or as they say in the Navy, fore and aft so Piel, my companion, took a somewhat malicious pleasure in instructing me in the intr[ic]acies of how to handle the jib sail and the fore sail and making caustic remarks about my experience all the time. I must confess that I have much to learn about this sport. You see, the difficulty appears when one wants to go in the direction in which the wind is <u>not</u> blowing. The solution is to tack, i.e., by successive courses at an angle to the course to eventually arrive at the required destination. You see, I can't even explain the procedure much less perform it.

Give my love to the whole family,

Your boy,

Bud

Typed Letter Signed (TLS), stamped envelope.

March 13, 1945

Dear Mom and Dad,

Letters from both of you have arrived recently dated as late as February 28 which brings us up to date pretty well. Your delightful fruit cake came yesterday—you remember, the one with a surrounding cover of marshmellows [*sic*]. The marshmellows [*sic*] were pretty far gone, but evidently, they had acted as a preservative for the cake for it is in perfect condition or was until the storekeepers and I started [to] work on it last night. I believe

After the war is over

that this cake is the best one which you have sent me.

In a letter I received yesterday, Cliff complained almost bitterly about the lack of work in his new assignment. I guess that no one in the Navy is ever satisfied with what he has and the fields always look greener on the other side of the fence. He had little else to say except that he was working on the swing shift from three in the afternoon to midnight thereby cutting down on his night-life.

Can you imagine the emotions evoked by your mention of fresh milk and butter from the neighbor's cow? I think if I were to be offered my choice of anything from home, it would be a long icy glass of milk. We used to prepare the powdered variety, but everyone became so disgusted with the preparation that it was all thrown away after each meal. Our closest substitute now in use is the familiar canned milk, and you know what an unsatisfying effect this produces. How much milk does the use of the pasture earn us? It appears that someone in our family will have to learn how to milk a cow or do you already lay claim to this valuable bit of knowledge?

Georgia Farmers' Market Bulletin, September 20, 1944.

After the war is over

While speaking of rural delights, I want to thank you for the copy of the Farmer's Bulletin[160] which you mailed the other day. As you may know, the paper is more of a political organ of Tom Linder's than it is a source for farm news, but even so, it may provide us with some useful hints or suggestions. By the way, what, if anything, did you all ever decide about buying some heifers for the season and selling them next fall? I asked Hugh for his opinion on this venture and he heartily recommended that we attempt such a proposition. Of course, I don't place too high a value on his rural sagacity yet it does seem to be a feasible idea. Let me hear what you think of the possibilities.

Apparently, Ada doesn't think so much of the selling of the parcel of land which contains the house. That is perfectly all right with me because I want some kind of a house for some time after the war. What did come as a surprise was the mentioning of purchasing another section in [the] back of our house. That too, is agreeable with me since the price couldn't be very high for land which has no front on the road. You may encounter some difficulty in locating the owner of this little piece, however. You didn't answer my query as to whether it would be feasible to move the house to a more favorable location. I admit that it is an outlandish suggestion and yet it might be possible. Give me your opinion in the next letter.

While at lunch this noon, I could not resist taking up the wager of the captain of this ship that the war in Europe would be over by the same date next m[o]nth. I did not encourage him in this statement, but when he continued to offer it, I had to accept it for a bet of ten dollars. As I see it, I win either way that things go, but it seems almost certain to me that I shall win the money rather than the shortening of the war. We have been here for six months lacking a few days and everyone is inevitably

---

160. Known as the *Georgia Farmers' Market Bulletin*, which criticized New Deal farm policies, the *Bulletin* was an official weekly publication of Thomas Mercer Linder (1887-1978), who served as Georgia commissioner of agriculture from January 1, 1935, through January 2, 1937, and again from January 1, 1941, to 1954.

discouraged and praying for a change in location. I see no hope for our moving anytime soon and have made quite an unpopular person of myself by insisting on this logical view of the situation. It is human nature to be optimistic I guess.

Don't forget to give me the recap of our finances in your next letter including the date of my last allotment check.

Your loving son,

———————

Typed Letter (TL), no signature, stamped envelope.

March 18, 1945

Dear Mom and Dad,

I have spent the last couple of days on the nearby island and consequently have been unable to write you. We won't be able to get any mail off until tomorrow and so there may be quite a gap between this letter and my last one. You must have become reconciled by this time to the long periods between letters that occasionally arise.

Likewise, we have received no mail recently and I am somewhat at a loss for conversation. You see, I depend very much on your letters for inspiration as to subjects to write upon and also for comment on your doings there at home.

My sojourn on the beach provided something of a vacation—I borrowed a jeep and toured the island seeing much of the place that I had not had the opportunity of observing before. In the evening in company with another officer from this ship, I attended a movie at the local base. The movie, "Woman in the

After the war is over

Door"[161] or some similar title, was most restful and I believe was a fairly recent production. However, a period on the beach always exhausts me because I am not used to the walking and heat, and we were very happy to return to the ship and rest up. It is odd how out of shape one can become in a few months of shipboard life. There are few opportunities for physical exercise and I must confess that when they do arise, I do not always avail myself of them.

Strangely enough, our summer is arriving and the weather is becoming warmer. In a couple of months, the rainy season begins and maybe that will cool off the hot days. We are supposed to have one of the greatest rainfalls of any location on the globe, but as yet, our showers have been most infrequent. We are fortunate to be located on the ship in this climate for the heat on these islands is as much as ten degrees hotter than that [on] the ocean.

By dint of perseverance and ingenuity (I cannot resist complimenting myself) we have obtained a movie projector for the ship and are planning to show our first movie tonight. The obtaining of the projector was something of an accomplishment since only one other of the ships of the flotilla has been so fortunate. I will have to postpone telling you [about] our success until we actually show a film which we should do tonight. As yet, we don't know what the title of our "premiere" will be. I positively refuse to be pessimistic and assume that it will be one of those superannuated Westerns or Grade "B" selections that plague the advanced bases. I will let you know in my next letter whether such optimism was justified.

I don't recall whether I informed you before that our commanding officer, Captain Morrill, is being relieved and given a change of duty. His relief[162] has not arrived yet and he is waiting for him

---

161. Perhaps Bud meant instead *The Woman in the Window*, a 1944 American film noir starring Edward G. Robinson and Joan Bennett.
162. Commander M. B. Brown of Fargo, North Dakota.

to take over the job of flotilla commander. Two members of his staff, line officers, are going back also under a program of new construction. Unfortunately, there is no provision for staff officers to get a change of duty under the new construction program and I will have to wait [for] the Bureau of Supplies and Accounts of the Navy to transfer me. I would not be human if I did not have a tiny hope that my transfer is not too far off in the future—of course, I have no grounds for believing this and can do nothing but store up disappointment for myself when no change occurs, yet it is human nature to hope and I am certainly no exception to the rule. My only justification for this hope is the fact that I have been on the same duty for nearly a year and a half. Sometimes the Navy relieves one after that length of time in the same assignment. As I told you previously, I believe that the flotilla commander must have asked to have Cliff transferred because he didn't care for him. It is unnecessary for me to remind you that Cliff must not be told of this if you happen to write to him. It is useless to discuss whether I would get an assignment in the United States upon a change of duty though, of course, I have hope. Such speculation is as futile as that of trying to guess when I will get out of the Navy. You must realize by this time that I am in the Navy for several years yet and the country does not intend to demobilize the Navy for some time after war. How long I will be in it is impossible to predict and I am reconciled to a few years. The duty won't be so bad if I am stationed in the U.S. after the war, however.

Hope to hear from you-all soon.

Your boy,

Typed Letter (TL), no signature, stamped envelope.

After the war is over

Mar. 23, 1945

Dear Mom & Dad,

I received a letter from Mom today dated Mar. 5, so you see we are quite a bit behind in our mail service; rumor has it that the interruption is due to weather conditions and the situation will be corrected in the next day or so. Let us hope so fervently.

I have been away from the ship for two days and consequently unable to write you. My mission on this trip was to get our movie projector repaired. You remember I told you in my last letter that I had acquired a projector for the 729, my ship. We were able to show two films with results not too satisfactory. It appears that there is some defect in the sound mechanism. I think that we will have it back in shape in a few days. The boys here on the ship were ecstatic over the rather poor [fare?] we were able to show so I know they will really appreciate some good movies when we manage to secure them. As I informed you, there are absolutely no recreational facilities here and the movies would prove to be a gift from heaven.

Yes, I must admit that the frequency of my letters to you has dropped off. It isn't that I don't want to write, but that our existence is almost completely devoid of newsworthy events. I promise you that I shall write more often in the future. By the way, if this scribbling appears even more indecipherable than usual, it is due to the rolling and pitching of our "packet cruiser" as we call this bucket. A recent assignment is one which [has] us underway all day and night, but never gets us anywhere.

Words are inadequate to express my feeling upon learning that Hal Jr. has been seriously wounded. As I told you earlier, it seems that he is hardly old enough to be in the Army, much less an officer overseas. I prefer not to comment until you [are] able

After the war is over

to relay more details of this tragic blow. You can appreciate my interest in learning the latest news from him.

Perhaps we aren't so far apart as the map would indicate. Your mentioning that you have had rain for the past few weeks is an exact description of our weather here. Our rainy season is not due to start for a month yet so we are unable to account for so much rainfall recently. When our rainy season does begin, we can expect showers every day and frequently many times daily for many months. This area is supposed to have one of the heaviest rainfalls on the globe.

Please tell Buie that I did receive his interesting letter and have been delaying a reply until I had some noteworthy news that I could relate. He will accept this excuse with his usual good humor, I trust.

No, your Valentine's package has not arrived yet, but I have gotten nearly all the rest of your lovely gifts and expect this one to arrive soon.

Thanks very much for the most competent statement of our financial conditions. From your figures, I see that we are still $2400. in debt on our ventures. Although our notes call for payments for two more years, we can breathe easily now with the knowledge that we are over the middle-way mark and could pay off the notes on [the] farm immediately if we so desired. I choose to disregard your ridiculous statement about retaining my allotment money separate from our other funds and obligations. Surely you realize that <u>we</u> are all together and all of our savings in a common pool. Please banish immediately from your loving minds any idea of paying for the farm without contribution and spend any or all of it on whatever you deem necessary. As regards, the survey and title guarantee, I confess an alarming ignorance and leave the matter to your judgment. I do not see how we

After the war is over

could go wrong, however, with the expenditure of only $100.

<u>Dear Mom</u> and <u>Dad</u> — occasionally, one is found to recall the ones at home who are waiting for him, and when I think of you-all, I become humble with the knowledge of how much you have done for me and how much you love me. I hope that I can sometime justify your faith in me.

Your <u>son</u>

Bud

Autograph Letter Signed (ALS), stamped envelope.

Monday, March 26 [1945]

Dear Mom & Dad,

Your letter dated Mar. 12th arrived today after quite a period during which I didn't hear from you.

Your description of Spring is most alluring particularly when I know that the trees and flowers so glowingly painted are our very own. You didn't mention whether or not you had planted tomatoes, but I assume that you have. I imagine Dad planted some of that huge ox-heart species which are so beautiful in a lettuce and tomatoe [*sic*] sandwich. I have promised myself that when I get home, I am going to eat <u>nothing</u> that comes from a can or jar. My sense of taste rebels at canned fruit and vegetables particularly.

Have you heard any more about the possibility of the Power Co. putting in electricity in our neighborhood? It seems that with the

After the war is over

number of petitionists [*sic*] you have captured, you should have them convinced that Nickajack Road is a growing community, fully deserving of their development. No, I don't believe my letter would exert enough influence on the County Commission to get our road repaired since I am unable to describe to them at this distance the particular spots which require filling and packing. Nevertheless, thanks for the address and don't forget that I'll do my best when I get home. Anyway, the coming of Spring should have a beneficent effect on the dirt roads eliminating the chances of getting stuck. How about the little road on the farm itself — is it passable in rainy weather?

I can appreciate the anxiety with which Halbert is awaiting a report from Hal Jr.[163] The strain of waiting must be almost too much to bear. I do hope that he hears something soon.

The 729 acquired a new boatswain mate some time back and with him came his dog — a big, black, clumsy dog with coal-black hair except for the tips of his paws and tail. His ears are the largest I have ever seen on any dog which stand up erect. He bears a startling resemblance to a mule because of these ears. Of course, the crew has taken "Mule" to its heart and he really is a good-natured dog and fairly intelligent. He is very solicitous of [the] ship's company and welcomes overwhelmingly anyone who returns to the ship from a sojourn ashore.

Everything is fine here,

Your boy,

Bud

Autograph Letter Signed (ALS), no envelope.

---

163. Big Halbert and Hal, Jr. (See letter of December 8, 1944.)

After the war is over

March 30, 1945

Dear Mom,

For some reason or another, the mail service here is nil. Probably it is due to the fact that we have been having bad weather recently or a combination of causes. The last letter that I received from you is dated the twel[f]th of March.

If this note seems a little incoherent, blame it on the paint chippers right above my head who are banging the deck like someone possessed. Every time I go up to see what they are doing to make so much noise, they quit, but just as soon as I climb back down the hatch to my office they begin again with renewed vigor. For some reason they have stopped right now—it can't last, however.

This started out to be a note of congratulation on your birthday but due to the interference mentioned above, I am not sure that I have succe[e]ded. I can only hope that you understand the spirit of the letter and not the roughness of the speech or the defects of the typing. You will remember that I was home just about this time last year for a hurried visit and I wish that I were home this April 11th to felicitate you on this occasion. Unfortunately, I am not one of those who can by an apt phrase or happy combination of words make their feelings known to their loved ones so you must be content with my prosaic but heartfelt "Happy Birthday Mom" and the knowledge of my ever-growing love for you. Certainly, the lack of words does not blind you to the magnitude of my affection for my mother.

A big "reefer ship"[164] has just arrived today and we are due to get filled up with fresh food soon. This type of ship is nothing but a floating refrigerator and carries fresh meat, fruit, vegetables,

---

164. A refrigerated cargo ship.

After the war is over

and a few fancies occasionally. [The] last time we received our allotment, the fruit was nearly rotten— we are hoping that the apples and oranges are still fresh today.

There has been a short intermission between this paragraph and the previous one. A small boat from the refrigerator ship arrived and I took time out to consume three apples and three oranges. You see my capacity hasn't diminished since you knew me rather it has increased. It is my intention to eat only fresh food when I get home. Today we received fresh celery, cabbage, [and] potatoes, in addition to the aforementioned fruit so we will indulge in an orgy of cabbage and potatoes until the stocks are exhausted.

One of the small boats just alongside had a tiny monkey perched up on the upperworks, but we were unable to make our dog see him. Reminds me of our futile attempts to make old Susie look at a horse or mule. I don't believe he actually wanted to see the monkey.

It appears that I shall have to stop this letter now if I intend to get [it] into the out-going mail; so until next time.

Your loving son,

Bud

Typed Letter Signed (TLS), stamped envelope.

After the war is over

April 3, 1945

Dear Mom & Dad,

My only communiqué from home today was the "Farmer's Bulletin" so I don't have too much to write about.

The past three days have been rather strenuous — we have been trying to get all the ships paid so that we won't be bothered the rest of the month by their frenzied calls for "pay." So successful have been our efforts that we have but two ships left on our list to be paid and after taking care of those, we can look forward to an undisturbed remainder of the month to read and see our nightly movie. You must know by now that we are the proud owners of a 16mm projector, and our only grievance now is the caliber of films which we have been able to obtain. To date, all of our presentations have been almost antediluvian. For example "Waikiki Wedding"[165] with Bing Crosby was made in or around 1938 and it has been our best so far. However, the future is promising for tonight we are showing a comparatively new one called "Laura"[166] or something similar. I am going to see the second showing which begins in a few minutes. It is necessary to hold two showings of the films so that everybody doesn't have to crowd into the little mess-hall and also to accommodate the fellows who are on watch during the first showing. Despite the poor sound effects which we have been unable to have repaired, we have had 100% attendance at the movies and I expect that will be the rule for some time to come.

I cannot tell you how I enjoyed the snapshots you sent me which you-all made out at the farm. I had almost forgotten what a fruit time in bloom looks like and even our house seems to

---

165. The American musical romance comedy film by Paramount Pictures was released on March 23, 1937.
166. A 1944 American film noir produced and directed by Otto Preminger, starring Gene Tierney and Dana Andrews, *Laura* received five nominations for Academy awards, including for Best Director, winning for Best Black and White Cinematography.

have taken on an air of Spring. Every time I show the picture of Mom to some of the fellows aboard this ship they take you for my girlfriend and refuse to believe me when I insist that it is a picture of my mother. You know that I am quite prepared for that reaction upon showing your picture because the inevitable disbelief is always exhibited.

Well, this is just a note until more news is forthcoming— I shall write again in a day or so.

Your loving son,

Bud

Autograph Letter Signed (ALS), stamped envelope.

April 9, 1945

Dear Mom and Dad,

Three of your letters arrived in the last few days bringing us up to date pretty well, I think.

I'm so sorry to hear that Mom has a form of rheumatism in the legs; perhaps it is only a temporary condition and will pass on soon. It seems that one member of the family is nearly always under the weather for one reason or another. I hope the coming of summer will clear up this latest trouble so that you will be able to enjoy the farm and not be hindered by pain from walking.

After the war is over

A faithful portrait of farm life in the Great Depression.

I am reading a book at the present time by the title of "RFD" by a fellow named Smart.[167] He retreats to a little farm he inherited in Ohio and trys [sic] to make a living out of it. He is a little more fortunate than many of his fellows however because he has an additional income of a few hundred dollars a year to help him along. He too started out [with] many of the same difficulties that we are going to encounter. His house, though more capacious and livable, did not boast electricity or plumbing and when the book was written three years after the original moving into the house, he was still doing without plumbing though he had secured electricity. Our farm is also similar to his in that the land was not too fertile and he was restricted in the selection of crops. For a money crop he resorted to sheep raising which, I confess, holds no charm for me. Remarkable in it's [sic] candor the story admits that the farm lost money each year of the operation, but seemed to be holding it's [sic] own last year. After some thought, I believe that our best bet is some form of an orchard or vin[e]yard. I imagine that the soil is [unfit] for a crop without a good deal of fertilization and care which we are not equipped to provide. However, there are many possibilities on our place and we can't lose too much on the venture since the land is so near Atlanta that we should be able to sell at a reasonable figure at our leisure.

---

167. Born in Cleveland and a 1926 graduate of Harvard, Charles Allen Smart (1904-1967) published this memoir that became a bestseller in 1938. Four years later, he enlisted in the Navy and served on a LST in the Pacific and also in the Normandy invasion of 1944, winning a promotion to lieutenant.

After the war is over

None of your letters mentioned whether you had heard from Hal Jr. so I assume that you have not. The suspense must be almost unbearable for Halbert and Lillian[168] and I do hope that they hear something soon. Was the letter they received from him written in his handwriting or was the letter written by someone else at his direction?

The big news here is that we may move out to another location. It is certain that the ships are leaving but very uncertain whether the staff will also leave with the ships or stay with another lot of new arrivals. If we stay, it will necessitate my moving the office to another ship and there is absolutely nothing that I hate worse than moving. You remember I have so much equipment and supplies that it is almost like moving a whole family to another house on Sept. 1st every year at home. The analogy can be continued by telling you that it is also necessary to move three storekeepers and myself. Though far from developing any affection for this bucket, I do get along with the officers very well and like the way the ship is managed. Then too, it is not pleasant to anticipate leaving all my friend[s] among the flotilla. As I said, the situation is still undecided and I'll let you know as soon as I find out what we are going to do.

A recent letter from Cliff indicates that he is not too happy in his present location, but I can feel little sympathy for him as long as I remain out here.

Oh yes, while I think of it, let me remind Mom not to write on both sides of the thin paper. After the ink settles in the paper, it is very difficult to read the script. But don't regard this as an excuse to write less.

---

168. Lillian Naomi Cook (1900-1986), originally from Duluth, Georgia, who married Halbert Hudson, Sr., on June 4, 1920.

After the war is over

Our latest movie shown last night was "Winged Victory"[169] [which] has pretty well convinced me that I should stay away from the things. That was the poorest, the least inexcusable of all the ones we have suffered through lately. Rumor has it that we are going to get "Wilson"[170] for tonight so I guess that I'll give them one more chance. Of course, I am only kidding myself and probably [will] attend anything that we are able to get aboard this ship, but even so, I don't have to admit that I like them.

Well, as Dad says "that's about all for now, will write more next time."

Your boy,

Bud

Typed Letter Signed (TLS), stamped envelope.

April 13, 1945

Dear Mom and Dad,

Dad's letter of March 29th arrived yesterday but I have an idea that some of our mail is going astray somewhere. It may be because this ship is supposed to leave this particular locality and our mail is already being directed to the new spot.

Probably the most newsworthy thing that has occur[r]ed recently has been our unprecedented luck in obtaining two exceptionally good movies. Night before last we showed "Wilson" which, I understand, has been acclaimed at home as one of the best

---

169. Released by 20th Century Fox on December 22, 1944, the American drama film deals with an Army Air Force crew stationed in the South Pacific.
170. A critically acclaimed 1944 biopic of the American President shot in Technicolor, and winner of two Academy awards.

After the war is over

productions of the year. It certainly merits this award; many of the hopeless Republicans on the ship do not agree with me that the picture is an unbiased record of the events of immediately preceding the First World War, but I think that the movie was too gentlemanly in the treatment of Senator Lodge[171] and the others of his tribe. No doubt you all have seen this fine show and I would like to hear what you think of it. If you have not seen it, I heartily recommend that you do so at the next opportunity. Our presentation of last night was almost as good. "Mrs. Parkington"[172] though not so serious was quite as entertaining and should also rank among the year's highest selections.

One of the officers just came down and informed me that Roosevelt has died.[173] No other details are available yet, but I assume that Truman has been appointed president. Just how great a tragedy this really is it is impossible to say at this time. I'm terribly afraid that our new president is not the caliber of man that is required at these momentous times. We need a genius and I'm fearful that we have only a good politician. However, maybe Truman can rise to the occasion and perform as good a job as his predecessor. I can imagine what the newspapers at home are saying: "He is not big enough for the job." ["] He got his start from a corrupt political machine" and many other portentuous [sic] remarks. Well, all we can do is to hope that he will surround himself with competent men and take their advice.

It would be almost an understatement to say that the next few weeks will be among the most important in the world's history. The spirit with which we enter the peace conference and the fidelity to our previously announced principles will be the only hope for p[e]rpetual peace.

---

171. Republican Senator Henry Cabot Lodge of Massachusetts opposed President Woodrow Wilson's Fourteen Points peace plan and led efforts in the Senate to reject ratification of the Treaty of Versailles and thus U.S. entry into the League of Nations.
172. A 1944 American drama film that tells the story of a woman's life via flashbacks, starring Greer Garson who was nominated for an Oscar for Best Actress and Agnes Moorehead for Best Supporting Actress.
173. FDR died of a cerebral hemorrhage at Warm Springs, Georgia, on April 12.

After the war is over

The latest news places us fifty-seven miles from Berlin— the end can not be far away. I suppose the people at home are almost mad with joy at the imminent collapse of German armed might and rightly so. Strange enough, the boys here accept the news of our prodigious advances with something approaching indifference. You see, it has been made so apparent that the Japs intend to fight to the last man that the war out here still seems almost interminable. The Japanese can retreat to the China coast and thence to India and drag the war out for many many [sic] months. Too, we have no assurance that they will ever stop fighting. All over the Pacific, there are small forces of Japs which have been cut off and isolated but not defeated. We all wonder if they will surrender when the rest of the Japanese fold up and capitulate.

Another late bulletin tells us that the president died in Georgia. This brings home the tragedy even more. Please send me some clippings of the local papers on the death so that I may get the true sense of how our people feel on this sad occasion.

Well, any other news would seem strangely incongr[u]ous in company with the earth-shaking events so I will conclude this letter until we hear more news.

Don't forget to let me hear how Hal Jr. is making out.

Your boy

Bud

Typed Letter Signed (TLS), stamped envelope.

After the war is over

Monday
April 16, 1945

Dear Mom and Dad,

I believe I mentioned in my last letter[174] that the paint chippers were pounding like people possessed right above my head. Well, they haven't stopped; they are still at it with renewed vigor if possible. You see, I must have some excuse for the mistakes made in this typing.

Thank you so much for enclosing the letter from Imogene from Sao Paulo. She seems to be very well satisfied with the conditions down there and who wouldn't be under those conditions.

From the sketchy information which you give me, I can see that Hal Jr. is in a most serious condition and has grave wounds. I am so happy to hear that he [is] improving—do you know whether the wounds will leave any permanent impairment of his arm or hand? You mu[s]t let me know just as soon as you receive any more letters from Halbert.

It appears that you are again disappointed in your expectations of securing a new operator. You didn't say why she failed to come to work for you as you had planned, but I assume that it was because she found a better-paying job. One consolation is that this is not a permanent condition and after the war you should have no trouble in finding girls to work in the shop. It will be something of a pleasure to have your choice of operators again instead of having to beg people to work for you at a salary which would be most inviting in the past. Once labor again becomes available, I suppose that you shall try to open up another booth. Actually the time shouldn't be too far off when labor will be in excess of the need. I think that if we can make a reasonable profit

---
174. Rather, see his letter of March 30, 1945.

After the war is over

[from] the shop, then we should have no trouble at all when the war is over.

Our movie fare since the excellent pictures I mentioned in the last letter [has] not been too good and that is a very polite understatement. Last night we showed "Hollywood Canteen"[175] which is enough to disgust one so thoroughly as to keep him away from the movies for several nights. The night before we showed "Torrid Zone"[176] of vintage 1940 which you must admit is slightly out of date.

In one of your recet letters you tell me that you all are planting watermelons out at the farm. I cannot resist imploring you to also plant some cantoloupes [sic] and or some honeydew melons. I can think of nothing that would taste better right [now] at the present time than an ice-cold watermelon or cantoloupe [sic]. Oh yes, you must plant some Brussels sprouts and broccoli on the chance that I might return unexpectedly. I have already told you that I intend to eat no canned food or preserved fruit when I get home. I have quit eating the vegetables we serve on board here and trust that my vitamin pills will suffice for the time being. What kind of apples do we grow on the place? I do hope they are of the hard variety and not particularly inviting to the worms. Don't forget to tell me [about] the peaches and the grapes that we planted recently.

I'll have to quit— the chipping is driving me mad.

Your loving son,

Bud

Typed Letter Signed (TLS), stamped envelope.

---

175. Warner Bros. produced this 1944 American musical romantic comedy about two soldiers on leave who spend three nights at a free entertainment club before returning to active duty in the South Pacific.
176. An adventure film starring James Cagney about a tropical fruit company's Central American banana plantation.

After the war is over

April 24, 1945

Dear Mom and Dad,

We are going to take a little trip tomorrow so I had better write tonight if I don't want there to be too long a gap between my letters. I can hear you saying now that there already is a long enough gap.

LCI(L)-737

This new ship that I am on, the LCI (L) 737,[177] takes the trip two or three times a month and the officers speak very highly of the recreation obtainable there in the form of exercise and fishing. I should have mentioned that the object of the journey is to transport supplies to a little island garrison quite a few miles away from the group where we are now located. The boys and I have gotten out our football and inflated it hopefully. My yet unused fishing tackle is also anxiously awaiting the fray and the engineering officer has promised to instruct me in the secrets

---

177. Laid down in January 1944 at the Commercial Iron Works of Portland, Oregon, launched on February 13, 1944, and commissioned on February 28, 1944, LCI(L)-737 had participated in the battles of Angaur and Peleliu. In 1948, it was transferred to the government of Argentina, disposed of by the Argentine Navy in 1951, fate unknown.

After the war is over

of landing the big ones. The captain[178] of this ship who is from Florida was a professional fisherman before entering the Navy. He too promises lessons.

Our new office is still only temporarily laid out and we are waiting for the ship to move some of its equipment so that we may move into the same space that we occupied on the 729. Although we hated leaving the 729, this new ship is much more comfortable since there are only about one-third the number of men on the LCI (L) as distinguished from the LGI(G). You can see that we are able to have more space and less noise than before. The chow (a most important consideration) is probably a little better than what we were used to, but there is still room for improvement. As I told you, I was able to bring the movie projector with me so all in all, I think we were quite a welcome aggregation aboard the new ship.

I have a whole compartment for my quarters which I share with no small quantity of boxes and stored items of supplies and spares, yet the quarters are much better than those which I had.

The ship's officers are all fine fellows and my storekeepers inform me that the enlisted men are nice shipmates so I guess we are really better off than we were before, yet I certainly do miss the friends that I had made on the other ship. It is impossible to be intimately associated with men as long as I was without cultivating either a strong friendship or a definite dislike. I am glad to say that I had very few of the latter.

The movie now showing up in the crew's mess is "Girl Crazy"[179] with Mickey Rooney and Judy Garland. I saw the show once

---

178. Lieutenant (j.g.) Donald Charles Brockway (1917-1993) was born in Billings, Montana, but had moved to West Palm Beach, Florida before 1930. He enlisted in the Navy on June 20, 1941. In June 1943 he was on the minesweeper YMS-65 before commanding the USS LCI(L)-737 from February 28, 1944, to October 17, 1945. After his discharge in January 1946, he worked as a painting contractor in West Palm Beach.
179. The 1943 film with songs by George Gershwin (music) and Ira Gershwin (lyrics) was one of the top box office hits for that year.

After the war is over

back in the States and once [in] Guam so I declined to suffer through it again. Because of the men on watch, we have to hold two showings of the movie despite the fact that there are only seven or eight men at the second showing.

The war news almost takes one's breath doesn't it? The last newscast that I heard placed the Russians in the center of Berlin and predicted a junction between the two forces imminently. Perhaps by the time that you receive this letter, the war in Europe will be over except for cleaning up isolated pockets of fighting Germans. The news of the Okinawa operation is still a little obscure and I can't tell just how we are doing there. The overwhelming question in my mind is "will Russia join the war against Japan?" I would like to hear what you there at home think of this possibility. I suppose that every paper in the country published a eulogy on the death of Ernie Pyle[180] and I understand that he has been awarded the Congressional Medal of Honor. He deserved it.

If anybody should ask, don't forget to give them my new address on the LCI(L) 737.

Please write soon and give me the report on the progress of our watermelon patch.

Your grateful son,

Bud

Autograph Letter Signed (ALS), no envelope.

---

180. Ernest ("Ernie") Taylor Pyle (1900-1945) was a Pulitzer Prize-winning American journalist and war correspondent who is best known for his stories about ordinary American servicemen during World War II. Pyle was covering the invasion of Okinawa when he was killed by a sniper on April 18, 1945. Although several bills were introduced to grant Pyle a Congressional Medal of Honor, he was instead awarded by President Truman the Medal for Merit, the nation's highest award for civilians, on July 4, 1945.

After the war is over

April 29, 1945

Dear Mom and Dad,

It is a little difficult to get used to the idea that I will receive no letters from you all for quite a while until the 729 is able to forward my mail to the new ship which I am riding on now, the 737. The location to which they are proceeding is some distance away and I expect it will be an exasperating length of time before they are able to send me my mail. You see, as soon as the post office receives word that the address of a ship has changed, they start sending their mail to the new location and the mail accum[ula]tes there until the ship arrives there and calls for their mail. Until they do arrive at their new location and pick up the mail then forward mine to me, I shall have to go without any. I expect that you have received my new address[181] by this time so it shouldn't be too long until I hear from you.

We have returned from our little trip to a small island some distance away and I enjoyed the trip exceedingly except for a stretch of rough weather which threatened my equilibrium somewhat. An army officer who was bunking in the same compartment with me was not quite so fortunate and I have teased him relentlessly since. We spent the night on the island and played poker so the trip was not only fortunate but profitable as well. A sightseeing trip around the tiny island the next day was made miserable by the presence of hosts of mosquitos and small gnats and I find now that there were even chiggers there — a pest which I did not think existed in the Pacific islands. This tiny spot in the ocean is so small that less than a hundred men are stationed there and they must become quite lonely at times. Luckily they do have a movie projector and we brought back eight films that they had finished with. The boys on the ship could not resist showing one of them even if it meant seeing four

---

181. Return address on envelope for this letter reads: "Lt. (jg) W. H. Pullen USS (LCI) L 737 c/o FPC San Fran., Calif."

After the war is over

or five of them in one day. That is not an exaggeration and I do believe that they would see eight in one day if there were enough time. As I have told you, the boys here are starved for any kind of diversion, and eight movies in two days was som[e]thing akin to manna from heaven.

My storekeepers tried their hands tonight at making doughnuts and the result was gratifying or should I say satisfying? The food on this ship is (I would not say this to the other ship) as bad as it was on the other and everyone appreciates it when the fellows pitch in and bake doughnuts just to break the monotony.

Our movie tonight is "Gaslight" with Ingrid Bergman and Charles Boyer. I had already seen[182] the picture in Pearl Harbor, but it was so good that I enjoyed it almost as much the second time. Did you ever see it there at home?

The life here on the ship tends to get out of shape in no time at all due to lack of exercise and (in my case) a lot of sleep so lately I have been taking long walks whenever we are on the island for any reason. It is surprising how easy it is to get tired and when I return to the ship it is impossible to resist the lure of a little nap. This sensation is not peculiar to me. I notice the same symptoms in everyone who returns to the ship after some unaccustomed work on the beach. The walk is not too pleasant because of the heat and the bright reflection from the coral roads. The whole landscape is one of dazzling whiteness and my eyes water even when I wear sunglasses. Nearly all the vegetation has been removed for one reason or another and the effect is almost as white as a snow-covered land at home. The islands here are not beautiful and they hold no charm for me. I cannot see why the natives or even the Japs should want them and I think the worst punishment that we could inflict on them would be for us to give them back to the enemy when the war is over.

---

182. See letter of July 26, 1944.

After the war is over

The little island newspaper informs me that the Russian and American forces have made a junction on the Elbe River.[183] It appears that the war is just about over except for cleaning up pockets of resistance throughout Germany and Austria. We don't get much national news so I don't know how the people at home are taking this wonderful bit of news. I'll have to wait for my "Time" to give me the picture there at home. I don't suppose that they are having the long-awaited V-E celebration, but there must be some sort of festivities to commemorate the occasion.

Well, folks as you see, it is hard to write when I don't hear from you and you will have to accept this patten for now.

Your loving son,

Bud

Typed Letter Signed (TLS), stamped envelope.

May 3, 1945

Dear Mom & Dad,

Though I really can't expect to hear from you all until approximately the middle of the month, I confess that I am becoming a little impatient at receiving no mail at all except the usual voluminous official correspondence. According to my calculations you should have gotten my new address by this time, and judging by past service, a letter from you should arrive here about the middle of May.

The other night right in the middle of a movie I received a message informing me that the movie projector would have to be

---

183. Elbe Day, April 25, 1945, is the day Soviet and American troops met at the Elbe River, near Torgau, Germany.

After the war is over

returned to its owner the next day because that ship was leaving the area. We certainly hated to part with it. The ship (737) was lucky enough to purchase a secondhand electric phonograph from another LCI ameliorating to a small degree the loss of the projector. The Navy will send any ship upon request a set of V-discs[184] which are records of all the latest and perennial favorites back home in the States so we are well supplied with records.

We are due to make another trip to the little island about which I told you in previous letters in a day or so, and I find that these trips provide something of a diversion unless the weather gets rough then. I swear again for the hundredth time that I shall never make a sailor and should give up trying (all I have to do is convince Uncle Sam). Our food today was unusually good— I stuffed myself [with] ice cream, Pepsi Cola, and Coca-Cola so you know that I am happy at least momentarily.

Atlanta Constitution, January 7, 1945, p. 66.

---

184. V-Disc ("V" for Victory) was a morale-boosting initiative involving the production of several series of recordings during World War II by special arrangement between the United States government and various private U.S. record companies. The records were produced for the use of United States military personnel overseas. Many popular singers, big bands and orchestras of the era recorded special V-Disc records. These 12-inch, vinyl 78 rpm gramophone recordings were created for the Navy between July 1944 and September 1945.

After the war is over

It doesn't seem possible that the war in Europe can continue longer than one week more. What do the people at home think of the announcement of Hitler's death?[185] Probably you all say "let us see the body" as we do out here. That would be satisfying wouldn't it? Every day's news brings more encouragement that the war will be over maybe earlier than we think. I would enjoy some clippings on the San Francisco Conference[186] if you can send them. Our news is somewhat sketchy and I enjoy the commentators' version which we do not receive at all.

Hope to hear from you soon,

Your loving son,

Bud

Autograph Letter Signed (ALS), stamped envelope.

---

185. Adolf Hitler, chancellor and dictator of Germany from 1933 to 1945, died by suicide on April 30, 1945, in Berlin. Although his death could not be confirmed at the time, the *Atlanta Constitution* editorial of May 2 read: "If Hitler is dead, good riddance."
186. The San Francisco Conference took place from April 25 to June 26, 1945, resulting in the creation of the United Nations.

After the war is over

[Monday]
May 8 [7], 1945

Dear Mom & Dad,

We are on the way back to our "home" from the little trip that we make several times a month. The sea is smooth— hardly a wrinkle and the sun is intense. I have just finished taking a sun bath in my desk chair that I brought with me from the other ship. One of the officers took the opportunity to pour a bucket of water on me, but it really didn't matter because the hot sun will dry anything out in a few minutes. [The] last time we went to the island I stayed ashore the whole time. This time I was taken up on my offer to stand a watch for one of the other officers (a consideration I had not anticipated), and found myself in the position of a deck officer for some six hours. Next time I shall not be so hasty in proffering my services.

For the past three or four days the storekeepers had been busy renovating our new office space on the 737. They have painted it all — bulkheads, overhead, and deck; refinished desks, moved our abundant furniture, and have greatly improved the whole appearance. The real reason for their activity is that we are completely out of work and they are consuming the time on their hands in this way.

We have just received the first sparse reports of Germany's surrender— few details are available yet, but it was said that tomorrow—Tuesday— will be declared V-E day and made the occasion of a national holiday.[187] Everyone here received the news problematically because it really doesn't mean too much to them for a while yet. That is not to say that the news is not cheering and inspiring but merely that people are really excited by the

---

187. Victory in Europe Day celebrates the formal acceptance by the Allies of World War II of Germany's unconditional surrender of its armed forces on Tuesday, May 8, 1945, marking the official end of World War II in Europe.

After the war is over

things that happen to them directly and the war out here seems almost interminable at times. We shall be able to obtain more details of the victory as soon as we get the island newspaper so I'll save my comments until then.

Tell Belle not to forget her recipe for ice cream—any kind.

Your loving son,

Bud

Autograph Letter Signed (ALS), stamped envelope.

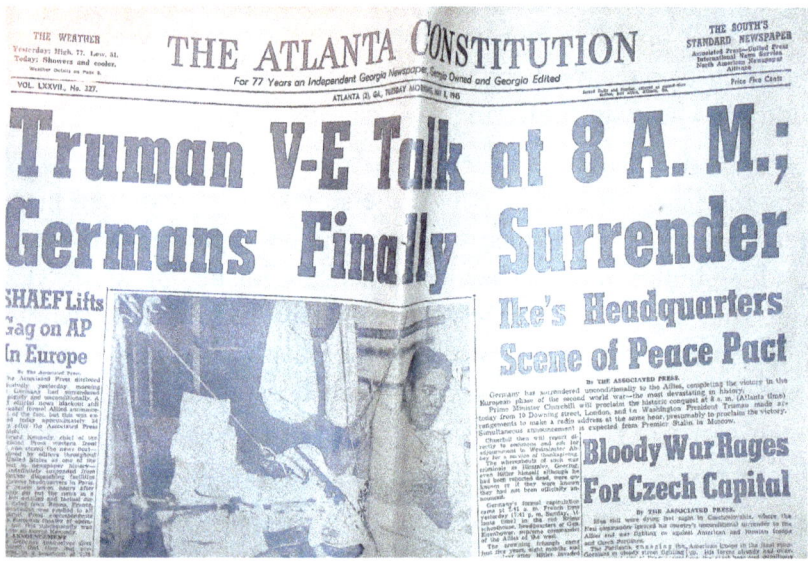

One of the newspapers among Walter Hudson Pullen's correspondence.

After the war is over

May 12, 1945

Dear Mom & Dad,

Still I have to utter those dismal words "No mail"; I have been expecting to receive some the last couple of days because according to my calculations, you should have received my address by this time, but our mail service is still erratic and varies from extremely good to "none." The storekeepers, however, are already receiving mail at their new address so I have hope of hearing something today or tomorrow.

Some friend of mine has just started pounding a sledgehammer on the deck directly over my head so this letter may seem a little incoherent at times because of the inescapable distraction. It appears that every time I sit down at my desk to do some work or more likely some reading, some maniac starts pounding relentlessly on the ceiling of my office.

Last night we heard that the ship which owns the movie projector has returned to this area so I immediately sent him a radio message to request the loan of the machine. A reply came in this morning saying that he was undecided and would advise us later. It seems fairly obvious to me that some other LCI is working on the same project as we are. I do hope we are successful.

About a week ago we received a load of fresh provisions; consequently, I have been stuffing myself with dozens of apples and oranges every day. At meals, we are blessed with fresh slaw and also another salad made of cabbage, celery, onions, and mayonnaise which is prepared by the pharmacist's mate.[188] You can imagine our gratitude for his truly delectable concoctions.

---

188. Probably Arthur Lloyd Budd (1922-1992), a former cabinet maker from Big Rapids, Michigan, who served as the only pharmacist's mate first-class aboard the LCI(L)-737 at this time.

After the war is over

I wonder if Hugh has gotten home yet. If he has I suppose that he is already married and living out at his new country place if it is fixed up yet for living.

It looks as though I may have to make a trip in the next few days[189] so I will forewarn you, perhaps unnecessarily, that there will be a period of time when you won't hear from me. Don't worry (if you did you would already be a nervous wreck) if you don't get a letter from me for a week maybe two.

Tell Belle not to forget that ice cream recipe.

Your loving son,

Bud

Autograph Letter Signed (ALS), stamped envelope.

---

189. Bud had received orders sending him back to the States.

Chapter 11

"I should have gone into the Army."

Sunday
June 17, 1945

Dear Mom and Dad,

I want to apologize for not sending Dad a gift for Father's Day, but I have been pretty busy, and although I did have some time, I was unable to determine a suitable gift. Please don't think that I forgot, however. I shall vindicate myself in the immediate future.

This new job is certainly different from the last one in many respects. Although there are only about two thousand people to pay, the volume of work is tremendous because of several things such as: civil pay rolls, discharges and the accompanying mustering out pay, post office receipts, and most of all, transportation. Transportation alone is enough to keep one or two people busy all the time. Fortunately, one of the civilian girls has quite a bit of experience in this line of work and takes care of the job now. If she were to leave, I shall really have to go to work.

I don't remember whether I told you or not that I have a private office as big as my bedroom there at home and in many aspects, the job is not too bad. However, one extremely disagreeable factor is that it is necessary for me to go out in the hospital and pay all the bed patients who are unable to get in the regular pay line. I have not performed this job as yet, and certainly look forward to it with misgivings.

After the war is over

My quarters at the BOQ are very good. I am bunking with a doctor (Lt. Comdr.) in a large room. The only criticism I have to make is that the hospital bed gives me the impression that I am sick every night.

Well, I just couldn't resist the impulse to buy an automobile. After making the long walk from our barracks to the office several times I broke down and bought myself a Chevrolet coupe with the seats in the back so it really can carry as many people as a sedan. The body and upholstery are not too good, but the motor and mechanical parts appear to be in good shape. I shall let you know later how correct my original estimate of the car was. The hospital will not permit one to drive a car on the grounds without liability insurance so I guess I shall have to take out the insurance. Will let you know later how the car performs.

Your loving son,

Bud

Lt. (j g) W. H. Pullen
Disbursing Officer
US Naval Hospital
Memphis, 15, Tenn.

Autograph Letter Signed (ALS), stamped envelope.

After the war is over

U.S. Naval Hospital, Millington, Tennessee, just north of Memphis.

U.S. Naval Hospital
Memphis 15, Tenn.
Sunday, June 24, 1945

Dear Mom & Dad,

I am aware that it has been quite some time since I wrote you all, but I have been so busy here that it was next to impossible to find time to write a letter.

Well, first I'll tell you about my "transportation." The first car I had, a 1940 Chevrolet coupe was really a junker and after driving it a couple of days I was very unhappy with the deal so luckily I was able to persuade the dealer to take the car back with only a small loss which I shall charge to experience. Now I have a 1935 Chevrolet Coach which appears to be a much better car and what is better not nearly so expensive. In fact, I think that whenever I get ready to sell it, it will bring me something very close to what it cost me. The tires have all been recapped recently and the whole car appears to be in pretty good condition considering the vintage and the "times." I really don't see how I can lose much on the deal since the car cost me only $305. And I could find

After the war is over

hundreds of buyers at $250. It may be just what we need out at the farm when I do get home.

You asked me in your last letter what I thought of the Ferguson's proposition as follows: they pay $500. of our outstanding notes and we assume their loan on their place [for] $2300. As I see it (correct me if I am wrong) we would be paying exactly $4000. for their house and 30 acres. That isn't a bad proposition at all, but on the other hand, it does give us quite a loan to pay off — $2300. You didn't tell me just how the 30 acres were located so I can't make any decision, but I think that they would be making a good deal more on their original investment than we would. Of course that doesn't disqualify us, yet I think that the deal might be more acceptable if we made it much simpler as follows: We assume their loan of $2300. and they assume our loan of $760. with the same swap of property that you mentioned in the original proposition. Please let me know where the proposed acreage that they intend to sell us is located and how much road frontage is on the place. Frankly, the proposal does interest me, and I would like to hear more details.

Let me allay your fears [about] my baggage— it arrived OK, and also your package of clothes and raincoat arrived here in good shape. About the only thing that I could use would be the little radio in my room if it isn't being used at all there at home. Don't worry about the clothes that are still in the laundry because I have plenty now and I was lucky enough to find some more khaki in a store in Memphis.

Yesterday I received a telegram from Hugh asking me to come down for the wedding which is to occur on July 2nd or 3rd. Unfortunately, that is on payday and it is completely out of the realm of possibility. I called him on the phone and so informed him, but the whole thing still appears to be up in the air.

After the war is over

One more thing before I close— my bed has been changed and I now sleep restfully on a very comfortable twin bed.

Well, I must save some for next time so please let me hear more about the farm deal.

Your loving son,

Bud

Autograph Letter Signed (ALS), stamped envelope.

Constitution Staff Photo—Bill Mason
THE PERFECT HOMECOMING—Lt. Hugh Howell Jr., of 40 Park Lane, lost no time in putting a ring on the finger of Miss Fay Moffett, of 1605 Utoy road, S. W. He arrived home a few days ago from the Pacific, where he served two and a half years. They will wed July 3.

Wedding announcement for Hugh and Fay. Atlanta Constitution, 6/25/1945, p. 2.

After the war is over

U. S. NAVAL HOSPITAL

Memphis, Tenn.

June 28, 1945

Dear Mom and Dad,

Your letter just arrived asking me what to do about a wedding gift for Hugh and Fay. I suggest that we send one present for the whole family even though I did receive a separate invitation. You know much better what kind of gift to get than I, but I think it would be nice if we could send them something for their silver service costing around $15.00. Anything that you can get will suit me very well so just use your usual good taste and send it from " the Pullens".

My automobile is still running though it has a tendency to skip occasionally. I must confess that I had a little tire trouble also, but I am still glad that I bought the car. Maybe after a little more tire trouble I shall change my mind.

Don't worry about my pants being lost. I don't think that I am missing two pair, but if they insist on paying for the ones that they have lost, tell them that the pants cost about $3.50 new. If the reimbursement causes you any trouble at all, it would be far easier to forget the whole thing. I bought myself a set of dress grey uniforms the other day which will prove very handy on the occasions when khaki uniforms are just a little out of place.

If you are sure that the loss of the radio won't bother you, I should like to have it here to listen to in the mornings and evenings. You know how I like to hear it in the mornings when I am dressing. I recall that it is a little out of repair, but why don't you send it on the way that it is now and if it is too bad, I'll have it fixed here.

Well, I just wanted to write you a note to tell you what to do about Hugh's wedding gift. (Are you any better off?) I've got to quit now and balance the cash for today. You know--- the bane of a disbursing officer.

Your loveing son,

Bud

Typed Letter Signed (TLS), stamped envelope.

After the war is over

July 5, 1945

Dear Mom & Dad,

My radio arrived yesterday— I don't think it has been turned off since it got here. Thank you so much for getting it repaired. We were lucky that the charge was only $2.75. I had expected to be bled white as usual on radio repairs.

It seems that you did an excellent job finding a wedding gift for Hugh. I always wish those jobs off on you and you never fail to do just exactly as I wanted. Hugh told me on the phone that he & Fay might be able to come through Memphis on their way to the West Coast, but he hasn't written me any particulars yet. I suppose that he will let me know.

Perhaps it is just as well that the Fergusons didn't care to make such a deal. I would love to have their house, but it is quite a bit of an investment when we could not live there. However, if they do broach another offer, let me hear it, because I am like you all, really attracted by their place and get excited over the thought of how we could fix it up to suit ourselves.

As far as I am concerned, however, we should go ahead [with] the arrangements to sell the house and the small acreage. The more thought I give it, the more it seems that we should be able to ask at least $1500 for the place. Of course, if electricity is due to arrive during July, it would be much easier to sell afterwards.

Yes, we have had watermelon several times at our mess and I am getting all the tomatoes that I can eat. Our meals here are about average for shore stations — that means infinitely superior to ships' cooking. My appetite has returned all right so don't worry. Any worry should be for fear that I get too fat.

After the war is over

Oh yes, I received the picture that John made of us when I was home. I showed it to the officer that I was relieving and he said, "Is that your wife or sweetheart?" He wouldn't believe that it was my mother.

My automobile is doing fine except for a little tire trouble occasionally. Please write soon.

Your loving son,

Bud

Autograph Letter Signed (ALS), no envelope.

U.S. Naval Hospital
July 12, 1945

Dear Mom & Dad

Probably the best way for me to write this letter is to answer some of the questions you asked in your last letter. I shall try to get to most of them.

No, I don't believe that you need to mail the Journal; we get all of the southern news in the Memphis papers and they frequently carry items of interest from Atlanta. Thanks anyway.

My radio worked perfectly for a few days then blew a tube. I have a fellow in Memphis today to pick up a new tube for me and expect that to cure the ailment.

After the war is over

Lt. William K. (Bill) Anderson, Jr. Atlanta Constitution, 5/20/1945, p. 13.

The news that Bill Anderson is being discharged is certainly startling.[190] It looks as though I should have gone into the Army. Of course, I could be going from Europe to the Pacific, however. The fellows who are getting out of the services now have their pick of the jobs.

Your suggestion that I have my tires condemned by an inspector was fine but a little late. I had already done just that and my application for two new tires is now pending before the ration board.[191] I'm afraid that the tires will outlast the car now. I am considering trading this car off. If any of your friends or customers mention selling a car, please let me know. You see, it is impossible to buy a good one from a dealer because all of the good automobiles are sold on the black market over the ceiling

---
190. Lieutenant Anderson was discharged in early July 1945 under the point system after more than three years in the service.
191. Since early 1942 the sale of usable tires in the United States, whether new or old, had been placed under strict rationing control. The OPA regulations permitted a user to obtain a tire for replacement purposes, only upon application to and action by a local rationing board, after an inspection of the old tire by some authorized tire inspector and a certification of its condition indicative of the need for replacement. Such regulations ended by December 31, 1945.

After the war is over

price. It is quite possible that you might hear of someone who is planning to sell his car.

Glenn Putnam's letter[192] arrived here all right. Thanks for forwarding it.

No, I haven't heard from Hugh since he was married either. I suppose that he will call me before he returns to the West Coast. If you see him, make him promise to do so.

Payday this time occurs on Monday, the 16th so I'm afraid that I won't be able to come home this weekend. I just couldn't take the chance of arriving late Monday morning to find 2000 people standing in line waiting for me. In addition, I would be so exhausted that I might make some expensive mistakes. I'm going to plan tentatively to come home the next week-end which would be on Saturday, the 21st. Maybe then I shall be able to sample those grapes and apples that you describe so glowingly.

As far as selling the farm— yes, I think it would be a good idea if we could ask as much as $3500 for it. Otherwise, I still would rather sell off the price of the house and retain the other larger section. By all means, sell it for $3500. if you can, however.

Well, that takes care of most of your questions. Will answer the rest later.

Your loving son,

Bud

Watch out for the spiders.

Autograph Letter Signed (ALS), stamped envelope.

---

192. Lt. (j.g.) Glenn Putnam was writing from U.S. Naval Air Station, Whidbey Island, Washington. His letter was addressed to Stella Pullen. Only its envelope has been found.

After the war is over

July 14, 1945

Dear Mom,

This is just a note to ask you to do something for me—

Please look in the top little drawer on the right. Or maybe the left— I'm not sure in my dresser and find my cash book. It consists of several large sheets of ledger paper about two feet wide and 1 ½ feet high. Look on the first page and you will discover a certificate posted in. This certificate is from a bonding company, the name of which I have forgotten. Please write down all of the name and address of the company and also the no. of the bond. I have to have this information immediately in order to renew my bond. Thanks very much.

If you haven't used those extra gas rations that I received for the base, I could certainly find a use for them here. I might even accept a "B" ticket if you send me one.[193]

I am kinda busy this morning so I shall wait to write you a letter.

Your loving son,

Bud

Autograph Letter Signed (ALS), stamped envelope.

---

193. During World War II, the OPA issued stickers to determine how much gasoline a driver was entitled to. The stickers were placed on the windshield. The amount of gasoline a driver received depended on whether their job was essential to the war effort. The most common sticker was the "A" sticker, which entitled the holder to four gallons of gasoline per week; later reduced to two. The "B" sticker or "ticket" was for business owners and permitted eight gallons per week. The "C" card was issued to doctors, nurses, farm and construction workers, and mail employees, each of which allowed them to buy up to 8 gallons of gas per week.

After the war is over

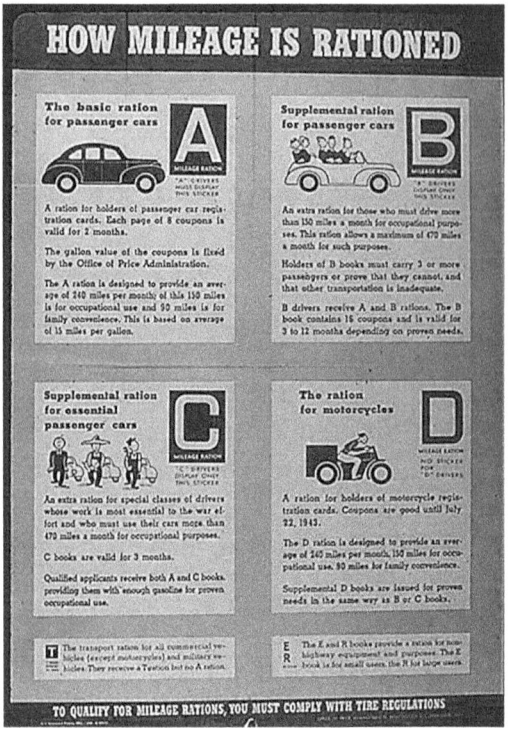

July 26, 1945

Dear Mom & Dad,

For some unaccountable reason, I find it more difficult to write a letter now that I am back in the States than I did when on the ship. No doubt this can easily be explained by the fact that I had much more available time while at sea.

It is quite unnecessary for me to tell you how much I enjoyed being home last week-end with my folks. My face must have shown my pleasure better than I could tell you.

My trip back to Memphis was uneventful except that upon arriving at the Naval Hospital I left my briefcase on the bus and

After the war is over

have been unable to have it located as yet. It is something of a loss since I had a new shirt and pair of pants in the briefcase. It is possible that I may recover it yet.

The assistant disbursing officer[194] arrived here yesterday and appears to be a very bright girl. I had not realized before that women could be so competent. Perhaps my experience in my younger days prejudiced me against women in business. The addition of the new <u>wave</u> is going to be a great deal of help permitting me to leave the office for more than a few minutes. Her arrival may make it possible for me to ask for a leave of a few days sometime soon.

I am still of the opinion that you all should make an effort to sell the house before the summer is over. If the fellow there at Mableton is unable to sell it, I believe we should give it to one of those eager agents who advertise in the newspapers.

I made a survey of the used car lots here today and returned home completely disgusted at the pitiful selection they have to offer. Don't forget to keep an eye out for a good car up to 1939 or 1940 with or without a trade; preferably without because I should have severe doubts about driving my "heap" to Atlanta. Some of the "women" at Mom's shop may decide to sell their automobiles.

WSB is on my radio and Dean De Ories[195] is talking about the teenage delinquency problem. It certainly is fine to listen to a radio broadcast from my hometown.

---

194. A blue-uniformed member of the Women Accepted for Volunteer Emergency Service, a division of the U.S. Navy commonly known as WAVES. Roughly one thousand WAVES were assigned to the Naval Hospital, Naval Air Station, and the Naval Air Technical Training Center at Millington north of Memphis in July 1945. See "WAVES? Millington has 1000 of 'em," *Memphis Commercial Appeal,* July 29, 1945.
195. Born in Liverpool, England, Raimundo de Ovies (1877-1962) was dean of the Cathedral of St. Philip, Atlanta from 1928 to his retirement in 1947, in addition to being a columnist for the *Atlanta Constitution* (1932-49), as well as host of a number of radio shows on WSB-Radio, and the author of four books, including *The Church and Her Children* (1941), *But, Maybe You're Not Crazy: An Introduction to Psychiatry* (1947), and *Dear Drunk* (1958), the latter dealing with alcoholism as a treatable disease.

After the war is over

Well, my ink is running out so I shall close until later.

Your loving son,

Bud

Autograph Letter Signed (ALS), stamped envelope.

Memphis Commercial Appeal, July 29, 1945.

After the war is over

Aug. 15, 1945

Dear Mom & Dad,

It doesn't seem that it has been three days since I left home. The news has had everyone in such a state of tension that time has been of little consequence. My trip back was quite uneventful and I did manage to retain my little traveling bag with me.

It is almost impossible to believe that we are at peace again. The news finally reached us last night[196] and the Commanding Officer of the hospital[197] gave everyone (that is, patients) two days leave. President Truman declared a two-day holiday[198] for all Federal workers.

The combination of these two happenings has disrupted my office completely. We held payday today amid great confusion and I am writing this letter while waiting for the girls to add up the payroll to see if I balanced the books. I will be agreeably surprised if we encounter no trouble in balancing.

Everyone here is overjoyed at the prospect of getting out of the Navy soon and almost any conversation is sure to contain speculation about the length of time required to demobilize the Navy. I do think it fortunate that I am getting away from the hospital here because it will necessarily be one of the last stations to be closed. Perhaps I will be [over] the needs there [in] New Orleans[199] and they may let me out sooner than some of my classmates.

---

196. At 7 p.m. on August 14, 1945, President Harry S. Truman announced the unconditional surrender of Japan to reporters gathered at the White House. Proclamation of V-J Day, however, waited upon the formal signing of the surrender terms by Japan, which occurred on September 2.
197. Captain (later Rear Admiral) Horace Ratcliffe Boone (1892-1964), former chief of surgical service at Bethesda Naval Hospital, Maryland.
198. August 15-16, 1945.
199. U.S. Naval Repair Base in New Orleans, his next assignment.

After the war is over

My radio blew another tube just at the crucial moment when we were awaiting the President's announcement of peace so I have to buy another tube on my next trip to town.

I called the HOLC[200] to ascertain the approximate amount of the monthly payments on a $12,000 home and they informed me that without taxes and insurance, on a 15-year plan, the payments would be $76.00 per month.

Let me hear what you find out from the Atlanta sources.

Your loving son,

Bud

Autograph Letter Signed (ALS), stamped envelope.

Aug. 20, 1945

Dear Mom & Dad,

You could never guess who I saw this week-end. When you read the following, don't be alarmed, just continue reading on through the letter very quickly.

About a month ago I received a letter here at my office and nearly fell out of my chair when I read the return address. It was from Marny Sampson Swift[201] who informed me that she had gotten my address from Hugh only a few days before and was just writing to find out how I was getting along. I was somewhat less surprised to discover that she is contemplating divorce from the

---

200. The Home Owners' Loan Corporation (HOLC), a government-sponsored corporation created as part of the New Deal.
201. Bud had taken Marney to a few K.D.K. dances in Atlanta years earlier. A native of Oak Park, Illinois, Margaret (Marney) Jane Sampson, born in 1922, was the only daughter of Harold Hubert Sampson (1898-1978), advertising manager for the *Atlanta Constitution*. A graduate of North Fulton High School, she attended Wesleyan College at Macon for one year before transferring to the University of Georgia, where she pledged to Phi Mu sorority.

After the war is over

fellow she married in 1942.[202] He went overseas a few months after their marriage and hasn't returned yet. Evidently, both of them want [a] divorce.[203] Marney was visiting her brother[204] in Arizona and was planning to return to her parents' home in Boston so I suggested that we meet in St. Louis on her way home. You see, I confess that I was still curious as to whether I was completely cured of the feeling I once had for her. Well, we met in St. Louis this past week-end. Today, I am still thanking the Gods [who] watch over me that I didn't marry her back in 1942. She hasn't changed perceptibly and is as helpless as ever. During the three years since I last saw her, she hasn't done any work of any consequence and hasn't even gone to school. My sense of relief was heightened when she described the "nervous breakdown" she almost had. A list of her ailments would compete with a first-aid handbook for variety and number. After spending a good part of two days with her, I was exhausted by the complaints she listed. I did enjoy the week end in St. Louis, however; we went to the Municipal Opera Saturday night to see "Bittersweet."[205] The operetta is held out of doors as is done in Memphis and we thoroughly enjoyed the music though our seats were too far back to see much of the acting. The next day, Sunday, we went to the movie that you were telling me [about] with Esther Williams and Van Johnson.[206] I liked the outdoor scenery and the singing of Lauritz Melchior exceedingly.

---

202. After their divorce, Swift married in March 1946 a former WAC captain from Anniston, Alabama, whom he had met in Cherbourg, France, where he was stationed with the 2nd Armor Division two years earlier.
203. After their divorce, Swift married in March 1946 a former WAC captain from Anniston, Alabama, whom he had met in Cherbourg, France when he was stationed there with the 2nd Armor Division two years earlier. In 1949, in Belmont, Massachusetts, Marney married John Kernachan Reddersen (1924-1982), an Army Signal Corps veteran and MIT graduate who worked as an architect in Chicago and later Maryland. The couple had two children.
204. Allen Theodore Sampson (1920-1992), a graduate of North Fulton High School, Gordon Military Academy, and the University of Georgia, was a career military officer of 28 years and veteran of World War II, Korea, and Vietnam, retiring in 1969 as a colonel in the Air Force.
205. "Bitter Sweet" is an operetta in three acts, with book, music and lyrics by Noël Coward. The story, set in 19th century and early 20th century England and Austria-Hungary, centers on a young woman's elopement with her music teacher.
206. *Thrill of a Romance*, an American Technicolor romance film released by Metro-Goldwyn-Mayer in May 1945, with musical performances by Tommy Dorsey & his Orchestra and Danish opera tenor Lauritz Melchior, which tells the story of Cynthia Glenn (Williams), who, after a whirlwind romance, marries a rich businessman. However, on the first day of their honeymoon, her new husband is called away to Washington, leaving her alone at a resort. During this time, she meets and falls in love with a war hero, Tommy Milvaine (Johnson).

After the war is over

MISS MARGARET JANE SAMPSON.

Miss Sampson and Lt. Swift To Be Married on October 17

The cordial and sincere interest of a host of admiring friends is centered in the announcement made today by Mr. and Mrs. Harold H. Sampson of the betrothal of their daughter, Miss Margaret Jane Sampson, to Lieutenant Thomas Madison Swift III, U. S. Army, formerly of Elberton, Ga. The marriage of the popular young couple is scheduled for Saturday, October 17, and will take place at a noon ceremony at St. Luke's Episcopal church, with Bishop John Moore Walker reading the marriage service.

The lovely bride-elect is the only daughter of Mr. and Mrs. Sampson, and the sister of Lieutenant Allan T. Sampson, U. S. Army, now stationed at Augusta, Ga. She is a graduate of North Fulton High school, where she was a member of the Pi Pi sorority, the Spinster Club, and the North Fulton Tallulah Falls Circle. Following her graduation, she attended Wesleyan College at Macon for one year, and was enrolled last year at the University of Georgia. At the university she was pledged to the Phi Mu national sorority.

The bride elect's parents, who reside at 3990 Club drive, came to Atlanta for residence 12 years ago, having moved here from Chicago, Ill. Mrs. Sampson, from whom the future bride inherits much of her beauty and charm, is the former Miss Ruth Rawson Allen, of Chicago.

Lieutenant Swift is the son of Mr. and Mrs. Thomas M. Swift Jr., prominent citizens of Elberton, and he is the brother of Miss Margaret Swift and Chris Swift, both of Elberton. Mr. and Mrs. P. W. Christian, of Atlanta, are his uncle and aunt.

Following his early education in the public schools of Elberton, the bridegroom-elect attended Tech High school in Atlanta, and graduated from the University of Southern California with the class of 1937. He is a member of the Sigma Chi fraternity. Prior to entering service with the United States Army, he was associated with the Atlanta branch of the Link Belt Company for two and a half years. He holds the rank of first lieutenant in the Field Artillery and is stationed at Southern Pines, N. C.

Atlanta Constitution, 10/9/1942, p. 17.

This description of our activities will indicate in some measure how little I cared to resume the old courtship. I told her that I didn't care to see her again. That was indeed putting it mildly. So we can all join in Thanksgiving that I avoided one mistake that could have so easily been made. I hope you find this letter interesting.

Your grateful son,

Bud

Autograph Letter Signed (ALS), stamped envelope.

Aug 27, 1945

Dear Mom & Dad,

The weather here has suddenly turned off cold and everyone is wearing coats and sweaters to work. However, the sun has just come out and all the extra clothes are rapidly coming off. This chilly weather is something new to me because I have seen very little chilly spells during the last year or so except for my brief stay in San Francisco on the way home.

Postcard of Sardis Dam and the lake and beach, near Batesville, Mississippi, about 85 miles south of Millington.

After the war is over

Yesterday, four of us rode down to Sardis Lake in Mississippi to go swimming. Don't be alarmed, the trip wasn't made in my car but in a fellow's from the hospital. The lake was a tremendous one and the whole edge along the dam was flanked by a wide beach very similar to those at the ocean. We enjoyed the outing immensely particularly since it was such an unusual favor to get in an automobile and take a trip of any distance.

What do you think of the 1937 Plymouth that your girl at the shop is desirous of selling? If it is a pretty good car I think that I would like to buy it, but if it isn't much better than the one I have, I think that it would be better to wait until the new ones come out and perhaps buy one of them. Let me know a little more about the condition of the car. Drive it, if necessary, and determine if it would be necessary to spend any money on repairs.

I tried to catch a plane home this past week-end, but the Navy planes leaving the Air Station were all filled. They have week-end hops which frequently go to Atlanta and I thought that I might be able to hitch a ride.

The news that Hal Jr. is getting married is quite a surprise.[207] Just how old is he?

Our business is a little slow and I am beginning to wish for my relief to arrive so that I can get a new job. I do hope that the spot there [in] New Orleans has a little more attraction than this one here.

Well, let me know if you have any news on the farm or on the house.

Your loving son,

Bud

---

207. Hal, Jr., married Dorothy Alma Keilholz (1925-1999) on August 25, 1945, in Cincinnati, Ohio. Included in Bud's correspondence is the wedding invitation.

Mr. and Mrs. Harry F. Keilholz

announce the marriage of their daughter

Dorothy Alma

to

Lieut. Hal A. Hudson, Jr.

U. S. Army

on Saturday evening, August twenty-fifth

nineteen hundred and forty-five

at seven-thirty o'clock

Hyde Park Baptist Church
Erie and Michigan Aves.
Cincinnati, Ohio

Autograph Letter Signed (ALS), stamped envelope.

After the war is over

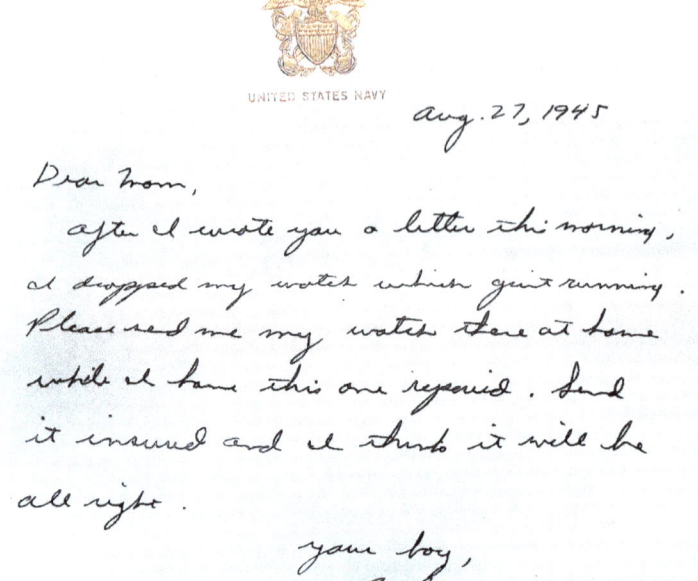

Autograph Letter Signed (ALS), stamped envelope.

Wednesday
Sept. 12, 1945

Dear Mom & Dad,

This has been a rather uneventful week so far except that we are quite busy getting ready for pay-day on Saturday and getting out the discharges.[208]

---

208. In late August 1945, the U.S. Naval Hospital at Millington had been designated as a Separation Center for Navy personnel, where they were given physical and dental exams, informed of their benefits under the G.I. bill, and issued their final Navy pay at the Disbursing Officer's window, prior to being discharged from active duty and transitioning to civilian life.

After the war is over

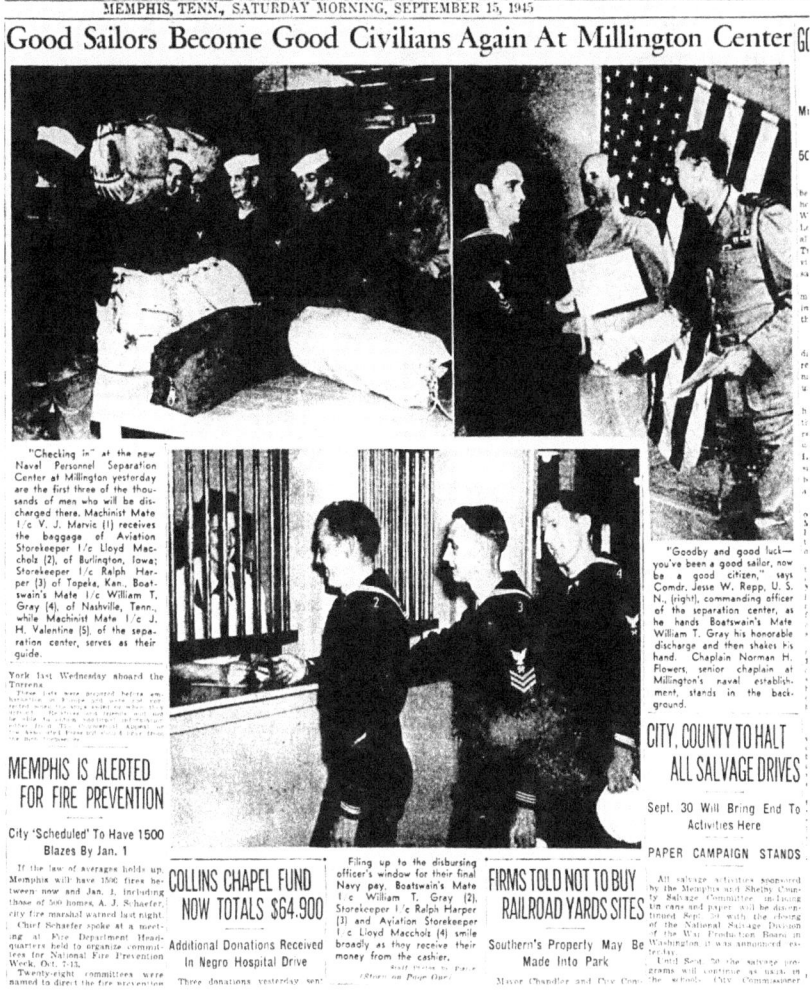

Memphis Commercial Appeal, 9/15/1945, p. 9.

I'm beginning to look for my relief pretty soon but it may be a week before she arrives. After she gets here, it will be approximately a week or ten days until I get away. I am still unable to plan definitely to get home but I do expect to do so.

The weather here has been very chilly the last few days and everyone has put on old sweaters and coats. I have been troubled by the blanket falling off in the middle of the night and waking up numb from [the] cold. I'll be glad to get to New Orleans if it is any warmer.

My automobile is crying for another tire— I have a certificate but hate to spend the money because I am planning on selling it before I leave here. Have you all ever heard of anybody desiring to sell their car?

Yesterday evening I saw the movie "The Strange Affair of Uncle Harry" which was reviewed in last week's copy of "Life" magazine.[209] The picture is good up until the last when the struggles to attain a happy ending leave everyone with a sense of disgust. However, I do recommend it when it gets to Atlanta.

Well, that's about all the news I have until I get a letter from home.

Your boy,

Bud

Autograph Letter Signed (ALS), stamped envelope.

Sept. 17, 1945

Dear Mom & Dad,

I'm so very sorry that Mom has had another attack of arthritis. I do hope that it isn't as painful or protracted as the other attack on the right knee. Don't try to do any work while it is painful because it simply isn't worth the agony.

[209]. An American film noir drama released by Universal Pictures on August 17, 1945, starring George Sanders as an aging bachelor who looks after his two sisters, one of whom tries to sabotage his romance with his co-worker. The *Life* reviewer wrote that the film "is a tautly paced and expertly acted psychological thriller" but the "trick ending muddles a murder."

After the war is over

It is quite fortunate that you were able to get a new girl to work in the shop even if only temporarily. It seems to me that the closing of the Bell Bomber plant[210] should make any number of workers available. I guess most of them are a little reluctant to go back to their pre-war jobs at lower salaries.

I expect my relief to appear sometime in the next ten days, but it is difficult to be definite. I just sent a telegram asking when she (a woman) was detached from Cornell University in New York.

Our cold spell is still lingering, but it is warming up and will doubtless be hot again by tomorrow. Many of the fellows notably sailors have gone into their blue uniforms because of the chilly season.

We didn't do much of anything this week-end but play volleyball and eat. Yesterday we had a bis steak for breakfast and fried chicken for dinner. After each meal, we come back to the BOQ [to] take a nap.

A fellow here, an Army officer, advertised a Ford for sale but had already sold it when I called. However, he offered me $300. for my wreck and I hope he doesn't change his mind. I am going to sell it in the next day or so unless he comes to and retracts his offer. Unless I find a good car I shall have to pack up the radio and books etc. that I have accumulated and send them to New Orleans. You know how I dislike packing so maybe I can persuade some of the girls here in the office to help me.

Will write again soon,

Bud

Yes, I received the $30.00 money order.

Autograph Letter Signed (ALS), stamped envelope.

210. On March 30, 1942, Bell Aircraft Corporation broke ground in Marietta, Georgia, for a new plant to B-29 bombers, and by March 1943, aircraft construction had begun. By the end of the war, the plant had supplied the U.S. Army Air Forces with 663 B-29s and reached its peak employment of 28,158 workers. The Bell Aircraft operation at this plant closed after V-J Day in 1945.

After the war is over

Thursday
Sept. 27, 1945

Dear Mom and Dad,

Well, my relief has arrived and it appears that [I] should be able to get away from Memphis on or about the 4th of October.

For a change, I am busy effecting the transfer of all of our records and equipment and expect to be busy right up to the moment of leaving.

My car is running fine, but I have discovered that it has a tendency to burn oil. When I get home or to New Orleans I hope to have it overhauled. Otherwise, everything seems to be all right.

It is with a real sense of pleasure that I contemplate walking by the pay line on the next payday and watch the WAVE officer who relieved me pay the rioting mob in the pay line.

We are going to hold another one of our little steak fries tonight and I plan to gorge myself to a new limit. At the last one I threw in a lot of olives, tomatoes, pickles, etc. while the steaks were cooking, but this time I'm going to save all the space for those delicious little filets.

Well, I'll save any more news (if any) until I get home next week.

Bud

Autograph Letter Signed (ALS), stamped envelope.

After the war is over

Chapter 12

"I need a little money."

Friday
Oct. 12, 1945

Dear Mom & Dad,

My trip down here to New Orleans was quite uneventful. The car performed admirably, but it was a little difficult to drive under forty all the way. I spent the night at Laurel, Miss., which is about 200 miles from New Orleans, and proceeded on the next day arriving about noon. The room assigned [to] me is by far the best that I have ever occupied while in the Navy. They have allotted me a private room which shares the bathroom with one other fellow in the adjoining room. He arises later than I do (can you believe it) so we have no trouble at all. In fact, I have only seen him a couple of times so far.

My job — well — it is just about what I expected. At my request, they placed me out in one of the warehouse offices where I can walk around and am not chained to a desk all day. From all the help I gather the news that the place used to be frantically busy, but now the work is almost non-existent. These big boys are afraid to cut the staff, however, because they anticipate a sudden increase in business due to the decommissioning of ships and other naval stations in this area.[211] So for the present, we are just marking time. After almost three years in the Navy I should be used to doing nothing, yet it is hard to get used to sitting in the office reading to pass the time. Actually, there are civilian

---

211. The U.S. Naval Repair Base in New Orleans was also an intake station and a temporary Separation Center as well. By mid-October 1945, thousands of men already had been processed.

After the war is over

supervisors who are quite capable of running the thing without the Navy Officers. Most of the other officers here in the supply department expect to be released by the end of the year so it looks as though I may be the only fellow left here.

> **New Orleans**—Discharge of men has started at the new Naval Personnel Separation Center here, newly established to enlarge the program first started at the Naval Repair Base.

The Daily Iberian, 9/25/1945, p. 1.

The more thought I give to that job that Mrs. McMillan suggested might be available, the better I like the idea. Do you think that there is anything I could do now to find out more about the work and make sure I will be the one they take into the outfit? If you think it advisable, I could go out to see the boss on my next trip home. Incidentally, the base here shuts down on Saturday and Sunday so I should be able to make it home about as easy as from Memphis. Please write me at the following address:

Lt. Walter H. Pullen, SC, USNR
B.O.Q.
U.S. Naval Repair Base
New Orleans, Algiers, La.

Your boy,

Bud

Autograph Letter Signed (ALS), stamped envelope.

After the war is over

Naval Station and Section Base, Algiers, Louisiana, 1945.

Oct. 19, 1945

Dear Mom & Dad,

Your nice letter arrived yesterday addressed to the B.O.G.. It should have been B.O.Q. for bachelor officers quarters, but the little error didn't matter.

I meant to tell you that the delightful lunch you fixed for me to eat on my trip proved quite a blessing. The sandwiches that one is able to buy on the highways are miserable so I thoroughly enjoyed the pimento cheese et cetera.

After the war is over

Bill Anderson, Preston Roddey,[212] an old friend of both of us whom we happened to bump into, and I had dinner the other evening at "La Lusianne"[213] one of the famous eating spots of New Orleans. I ordered Lobster Thermidor which was very good, but I confess that these exotic foods do not fascinate me. It seemed to me that the actual quantity of lobster which was edible was small compared with the tremendous plateful of stuff they served me. Last night some of the officers here who were recently promoted threw a party at a local sea-food house on this side of the river. In the middle of the table was a mammoth pile of shrimp with the shells still on. The procedure as explained to me is to peel of[f] the shell, dip the shrimp in a sauce and you know the rest. I found the shrimp more than palatable. Another new (for me) food was raw oysters. Everyone else appeared to be eating them with no ill effects so I mustered courage and bolted several finding them tasty. However, I'll still take my o[y]sters fried or made into a stew.

It's too bad that I can't be home to see Meddy and family. I don't recall how long it has been since I saw them, but it must be three or four years if not more. I'll bet the dogs are ecstatic at all the excitement. How long is the family planning to stay in Atlanta?

Hewitt Paul Theriot, Louisiana State University, 1937.

---

212. Born in Atlanta, Frederick Preston Roddey (1919-2010) worked for Southern Bell Telephone Company both before and after the war. Enlisting in the Army at Fort McPherson near Atlanta in June 1941, he was stationed beginning in July 1945 as a lieutenant at the U.S. Signal Corps school in Baltimore.
213. Located in the French Quarter at 725 Iberville, "La Louisiane" was established in 1881 but closed in 1996.

After the war is over

[The] day before yesterday while walking back to work from lunch I was startled by a shout from a passing automobile. My call proved to be Lt. Theriot[214] who was on the LCI Flotilla 13 Staff with me for the whole time. He had left the Palau islands only a month ago and had already been discharged from the Navy. He was visiting some old friends here at the Repair Base where he worked as an enlisted man. We were close friends always and it was truly a pleasure to hear all the latest news about my friends still in the Palaus. He lives about forty miles from New Orleans so I expect to drive down to see him some Sunday and participate in a shrimp dinner.

Well, I can't say just when I shall get home, but it will be fairly soon.

Your loving son,

Bud

Autograph Letter Signed (ALS), stamped envelope.

Wednesday
Oct. 24, 1945

Dear Mom & Dad,

Your <u>kind</u> money order arrived Sunday just in time to keep me from declaring bankruptcy. I don't know where my money goes down here, but the undeniable fact persists that I can't seem to stretch out my pay to cover the full two weeks. I think that I shall have to reduce my allotment from $125.00 to $100.00

---

214. A native of Chauvin, Terrebonne Parish, Louisiana, Hewitt Paul Theriot (1918-2006) enlisted in the Navy in New Orleans on June 26, 1941, following graduation from L.S.U. After two years at the Naval Repair Base in Algiers, he served as the communications officer on the staff of John H. Morrill, the commander of Flotilla 13.

After the war is over

sometime soon. You see my food here is more expensive than at Memphis and when one eats out in New Orleans, he can expect to contribute a goodly sum to restaurants.

My car is running fine, but I've found it necessary to have the battery charged and one of the tires recapped. It seems that it's always something when you own an automobile. Still, if I didn't have it, it would be quite a desolate existence here on this side (the wrong side) of the Mississippi.

I received the letter you forwarded from Cliff. He has startled me with the declaration that he has applied for the Regular Navy. I think I told you that my point score, 35, is the lowest of thirty supply officers here in our department.[215] This alarming discovery has convinced me that it will be at least late next summer before I can get out of the outfit. Although this isn't to my liking, maybe it's just as well because some of the fellows are encountering trouble in finding jobs.

My principal function here still is to sign my name about a hundred times a day and read books. The fellows who know insist that business is going to increase tremendously when the big Naval Supply Depot across the river closes down in a month or so, but for the present, everyone in the Repair Base is just coasting along. It is regrettable to see so much loafing but they are afraid to lay anyone off due to [the] anticipated increase of business soon.

Our weather here is perfect. The mornings are a little cool, but as the day progresses, the sun warms up everything and a coat is too much.

---

215. In order to qualify for demobilization post-WWII, the War Department required Naval personnel to meet or exceed points based on how long they had been in the service, how long they had been overseas, how many decorations they had received, how many campaigns they had taken part in, and how many children they had. Those with 85 points or more were first in line to be discharged. The number was later reduced to 50.

After the war is over

The people who know tell me that it is necessary to reserve a table at some of these famous restaurants weeks ahead for Mardi Gras so if you are coming down then please let me know in advance.

Your loving son,

Bud

Autograph Letter Signed (ALS), stamped envelope.

Nov 15, 1945

Dear Mom & Dad,

My trip back to New Orleans was completely uneventful and, as usual, quite exasperating. One consolation was that the train pulled into New Orleans exactly on time.

As you observed, my stay at home was most pleasant. I imagine there are few families who can get together for a trip to the country and have such a good time as we do, dogs and all. Everyone seems to enjoy walking through the fields and woods — even Belle.

The Thanksgiving dinner was superb, but I'm afraid you won't be able to make much turkey hash after my forays into the icebox. I can say that I appreciate your thoughtfulness in predating "Thanksgiving" but I guess if Roosevelt can change the date,[216] so can we.

---

216. At the beginning of FDR's presidency, Thanksgiving was not a fixed holiday; it was up to the President to issue a Thanksgiving Proclamation to announce what date the holiday would fall on. However, Thanksgiving was always the last Thursday in November because that was the day President Lincoln observed the holiday when he declared Thanksgiving a national holiday in 1863. In August 1939, Roosevelt announced that he was moving Thanksgiving up a week to November 23 at the urging of retailers to allow for more shopping days before Christmas. It was not until Congress passed a law on December 26, 1941, ensuring that Thanksgiving would be celebrated on the fourth Thursday of November every year.

After the war is over

There are literally hundreds of Navy planes roaring overhead right now in a salute to Admiral Halsey[217] who is visiting this city. I believe that in all something like 500 planes are supposed to participate in the ceremonies.

The Navy is staging a parade downtown[218] this afternoon in honor of Halsey, however, I was not called upon to march. A very fortunate decision of the bosses because I detest marching in parades— perhaps a hangover from my Boy Scout days.

NEW ORLEANS PULLS OUT NAVY FLAGS FOR HALSEY CELEBRATION

New Orleans, Nov. 14 (P).—New Orleans broke out all the nautical bunting it could find today in preperation for a triumphant visit tomorrow by the slugging hero of the Pacific, Admiral William F. "Bull" Halsey.

Prematurely but proudly, four-starred blue-and-white flags of a full admiral floated today from hundreds of flagpoles. Six members of the house naval affairs committee arrived to help welcome the third fleet commander.

They were Reps. F. Edward Hebert of Louisiana and Michael J. Bradley of Pennsylvania, Democrats; and W. Sterling Cole of New York, William E. Hess of Ohio, John Z. Anderson of California and Robert A. Grant of Indiana, Republicans.

Highlights of the celebration will be a parade in the afternoon and a dinner in the evening. Admiral Halsey will address a mass meeting in front of the city hall after the parade, and will be principal speaker at the dinner.

Shreveport Times, 11/15/1945, p. 6.

---

217. William Frederick "Bull" Halsey, Jr. (1882- 1959), Third Fleet commander in the South Pacific.
218. From Canal Street to St. Charles Avenue.

After the war is over

I made a trip over to the Army sales store this morning and bought you three sheets. I haven't examined them to determine what size they are. It doesn't really matter anyway, does it, since we can use them on the twin beds or large beds? I think I'll delay sending them until I get some more or some shorts for Dad.

Well, our weather here is very similar to that in Atlanta, chilly and invigorating, but warm in the middle of the day. I hope it doesn't become any colder.

Let me tell you again that I thoroughly enjoyed my week-end at home and look forward to Christmas eagerly.

Your loving son,

Bud

Autograph Letter Signed (ALS), stamped envelope.

Wednesday
Nov. 21, 1945

Dear Mom & Dad,

It was nice getting a letter from home yesterday, and I was delighted to hear that we have gas heat once again. I'm afraid we have lost the sources of endless disputes among the family as to whether the house is too hot or too cold. I suppose Belle is very happy now that she doesn't have to build a fire every day.

The only news in this area is that I am planning to go fishing with my friend Theriot early tomorrow morning if everything goes as originally planned. We are meeting down at his home near

After the war is over

Houma, La., <u>extremely</u> early in the morning. This little town is about forty or fifty miles from New Orleans so I shall have to pry myself out of the sack about five o'clock in the morning in order to meet his schedule. Theriot has promised me a boiled shrimp dinner (Louisiana style) even if we aren't so lucky with the lines so I haven't any worries as far as nourishment is concerned. As you know, my experience with fishing has been limited to dangling a line over the side of our LCI; a venture which [has] met with no success. So—even if I catch only one fish, I can say that the situation has improved.

The outstanding news in the paper this morning is the big General Motors strike.[219] Of course, I cannot but wonder what my position and future would be if I had returned to my job with the company, assuming that they had re-employed me. I imagine that everyone including management is laid off at least for a few days. Such strife only cements my desire to work for myself or a small company.

Our weather with the exception of a protracted shower yesterday has been well-nigh perfect. The weatherman is threatening us with a cold (44°) snap tonight, but such a drop appears improbable.

Thanks again for a lovely week-end.

Your loving son,

Bud

Autograph Letter Signed (ALS), stamped envelope.

---

219. From November 21, 1945, to March 13, 1946 (113 days), the United Automobile Workers (UAW) organized a nationwide strike.

After the war is over

Tuesday
Nov. 27, 1945

Dear Mom & Dad,

It is a little late to be relating the details of my fishing expedition last Thanksgiving day, yet I think you might be interested in hearing [about] my excursion to the Bayou country. My friend, Theriot, recommended that I come down to his house some eighty miles below New Orleans the night before we were going fishing so I arrived at his home about 9 o'clock in the evening and we started out early (5:00) the net morning. It was the coldest day we have had yet down here with the mercury hovering around 50°. We got a bucket of shrimp for bait and shoved off in our little boat for the fishing grounds some ten or fifteen miles further down the bayou which is about fifteen miles from the Gulf coast. Our guide, Theriot's brother,[220] decided that the day wasn't a good one for fishing after we had spent several hours in futile [*illegible*] so we hastily opened up our lunch at about nine o'clock in the morning and discovered that his mother had fixed us a roast duck, wild duck; I don't believe that I have eaten duck before, but I certainly hope to again. The flesh which is all dark meat has a decidedly pleasant taste somewhat like chicken, but different enough to distinguish the flavor. Well, about noon we gave up fishing and returned to Theriot's house for a shrimp dinner. The principal occupation of all the people in that section of the State is fishing for shrimp and oysters and trapping muskrats. Nearly all of the people are of French extraction and that language is spoken almost exclusively. The whole community is a tight little one where people are born, married, [and] die all within ten square miles. Everybody knows everybody else and his business.

Well, it is raining furiously here today but the sun may come out [at] a moment's notice. As I told you the weather here changes quite abruptly.

---

220. Theriot had four brothers.

After the war is over

If I am going to get this letter in the mail today I'll have to close.

Tell Bobby hello for me and tell him I hope we get together Christmas.

Your loving son,

Bud

Autograph Letter Signed (ALS), envelope stamped "FREE."

After the war is over

Monday
Dec. 3, 1945

Dear Mom & Dad,

This letter is being written under stress. The office maid is clamoring for me to abdicate my desk and let her sweep & mop. Well, I finally had to move to another desk — and then a third one which is too low, but maybe I can use it.

Yesterday I took a little trip that I'll bet you-all would certainly have enjoyed. I drove down to Buras, a little town about 50 or 60 miles below New Orleans, and the center of the citrus groves. As far as one can see there are groves of navel oranges, Valencias, grapefruit, tangerines, mandarins (a variation of a tangerine), cumquats, satsumas, lemons, and — I believe that is about all. The season is at its peak and all the trees are bending low with fruit. We stopped at one of the packing houses and a boy (age about 7) took us out to his father's grove in the rear of his house. As you can imagine we picked all we could carry of every variety at the same time stuffing ourselves with the delicious cumquats. All in all it, was a delightful experience and I am still eating oranges today.

It now appears that I shall be able to get home on the 22nd of December and stay until Christmas day when I'll have to leave to get back here by the 26th. That will give me a long week-end at home so I don't have any complaints about having to leave on Christmas day. I haven't decided yet whether to drive or not. It is a tough drive yet I hate riding the train so much that I may make the trip by car.

Oh yes, I almost forgot a most important item. I need a little money. If you don't mind please wire me $50.00 as soon as you receive this letter just as you did before.

After the war is over

That's about all the news— good & bad that we have here.

Your loving son

Bud

Autograph Letter Signed (ALS), stamped envelope.

After the war is over

EPILOGUE

Lieutenant Walter Hudson Pullen, service # 193550, finally earned enough points to be discharged from the Navy on July 2, 1946, after serving 3 years, 10 months, and 5 days. His replacement, Lieutenant Cyrus Lowell Brainerd, disbursing officer and paymaster, U.S. Naval Repair Base, New Orleans, originally from Wyoming, paid him $262.64 upon discharge.

Ribbon bar for Lieutenant Walter Hudson Pullen

According to his official U.S. Naval Service separation papers, Lieutenant Pullen had been awarded the American Theater of War Campaign medal, the Asiatic-Pacific Area (1 Star) medal, and the World War II Victory medal.

He returned home to Atlanta and moved back in with his parents at 224 Westminster Drive, where he had been writing letters for the past three and a half years. He soon joined his best friend, Bobby McGinty, in working for General Motors Acceptance Corporation in Atlanta, becoming a sales representative and later an adjuster in the Motors Insurance Company division.

After the war is over

Pullen (back row, 2nd from left), at M.I.C. sales representative school, Flint, Michigan, March 1949.

Walter and Louise, ca. 1949-50.

After the war is over

On January 28, 1949, at the Second-Ponce de Leon Baptist Church in Atlanta, where he was a member, Walter Hudson Pullen married 29-year-old Mary Louise Pugh, originally from Liberty, Tennessee. During the war, Louise had worked as a clerk stenographer at an Army Air Corps base outside Tullahoma, Tennessee, and then held a similar position at the German-Italian Prisoner of War (PW) facility at nearby Camp Forrest. Moving to Atlanta in 1948, she was working for the Federal Housing Administration when she met Walter.

MRS. WALTER H. PULLEN

Mrs. Pullen is the former Miss Mary Louise Pugh, daughter of Mr. and Mrs. John Floyd Pugh, of Bell Buckle, Tenn. Her marriage to Mr. Pullen, son of Mr. and Mrs. Walter S. Pullen, of Atlanta, took place recently at the Second-Ponce de Leon Baptist Church. Dr. Monroe Swilley officiated. The popular couple will reside in Birmingham, Ala., where Mr. Pullen is associated with General Motors.

Atlanta Constitution, 2/9/1949, p. 15.

Following their marriage, Walter and Louise then moved to Birmingham, Alabama, where they purchased a home in the suburbs and began raising a family, like millions of other veterans did after the war. He remained in the U.S. Navy Reserve for a few years, attending summer training in Charleston, South Carolina, though he was not called up to serve during the Korean War. In their spare time, Louise became president of a neighborhood garden club, while Walter entered local amateur golf tournaments. He would also give occasional talks to civic groups and organizations

After the war is over

about the need for auto insurance, the role of an insurance adjuster, and how claims are settled.

Tragically, Bud's life ended far too soon after the war was over. He died suddenly in Birmingham on August 16, 1962, at the age of 42. His funeral was held at the Second-Ponce de Leon Baptist Church, and he was buried in Westview Cemetery in Atlanta.

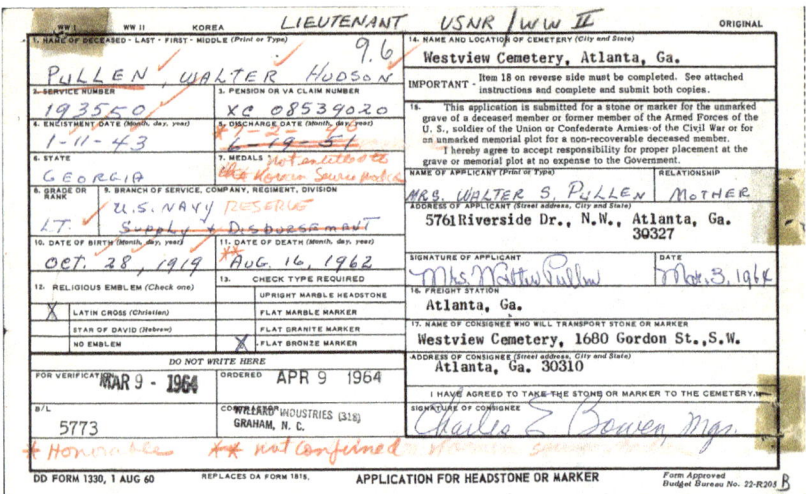

Headstone application for Walter Hudson Pullen, requested by his mother.

Westview Cemetery, Atlanta.

After the war is over

Packing a punch, the Black Cat USS LCI Flotilla 13 was bad luck for the Japanese.

About the Editor

R. B. Rosenburg received training in historical documentary editing at The University of Tennessee, Knoxville, where he earned a Ph.D. in history. Recently retired, he is now an independent scholar living in the Colorado Rockies. He plays tennis and pickleball, mostly indoors, while shoveling lots of snow in his driveway six months out of the year. He is married to Walter Hudson Pullen's only daughter and surviving heir, now a loving grandmother of four adorable children who call her "Nana."

After the war is over

INDEX

Acey Deucy (game), 190
Anderson, Elizabeth Louise (aunt), 69n, 245, 252
Anderson, William Knoll, 245, 252
Anderson, Jr., William ("Bill") Knoll (cousin), 70, 339, 360
Angaur Island, 34-35; battle for (STALEMATE II), 36-39, 204-5, 207n, 208n, 209n, 221, 259-60, 319n
Atlanta: Ansley Park, 11; Buckhead, 119; Candler Field, 70n, 178; Copenhill Avenue, 191; Fourth Ward, 10; Hemphill Avenue, 10; Inman Park, 10; Piedmont Park, 10, 13; Nickajack Road, 177, 294, 307; Stone Mountain, 23, 110, 133n, 137-38, 179

Babelthaup Island (Babeldaob), 34, 39, 228n
Bachler, Jr., Dudley Frances, 234n, 254
Baldwin, Jack LeRoy, 163
Barnum Bay, 40, 229n, 240n
Beall, Madison Lamar, 101
Beall, Jr., John Andrew (Boys' High School alum), 101
Bell Bomber plant (Atlanta), 355
Blackstock, Franklin Daniel (uncle), 124, 216, 237
Blackstock, Henry (Hank) Tucker ("Little Tuck") Ansley (cousin), 125, 128, 235
Blackstock, John Franklin (cousin), 125, 226
Blackstock, Mary Imogene Hudson (aunt), 69, 71, 99, 124-25, 127-28, 131, 197, 230, 235, 246, 250, 261, 263-64, 283, 317
Boone, Horace Ratcliffe, 345
Boys' High School, 12-17, 22, 66n, 70n, 101n, 222
Brockway, Donald Charles (LCI(L)-737), 320n
Buck, Frank Howard (big game hunter), 85
Buck, George Crawford (Cliff's replacement), 257, 271, 291
Budd, Arthur Lloyd (LCI(L)-737), 329
Buie, James Eston (uncle), 191, 305
Butzon, Hans Hermann (Boys' High School alum), 222-23

After the war is over

California: Borrego Desert, 109; Chula Vista, 30, 119, 123, 130; La Jolla, 143; Lake Cuyamaca, 30, 109, 131; Los Angeles, 29, 47, 94-96, 98-100, 110, 114, 128, 146; El Cajon, 30, 112, 126; Mount Wilson, 100; Salton Sea, 109; San Diego, 29-30, 87n, 93, 112, 114, 121, 124, 130, 140, 146; San Pedro, 30, 110; San Gabriel Valley, 100; Sierra Madres, 30, 99
Caravalla, Sue Gene (cousin), 111
Casa Marina Hotel, Key West, Florida, 79
Castleberry, Jr., Clinton (Clint) Dillard (Georgia Tech All-American), 66
Cate, Jr., Gustavus (Vassa) (UGA football star), 65-66
Censors (Navy): 19, 74, 99, 121, 174, 209n; rules, 28, 34, 180, 272, 285; complaints about, 41, 47, 78, 164, 167, 172, 180
Cornell, Francis Dell, 207n
Cornell, James Ardis (LCI(G)-729 engineer), 186-87, 214
Cornell, Josephine Ann Varin, 207-8n

D-Day (June 6, 1944), 34, 149
Dewey, Thomas E., 47, 168, 201, 211
Donahoo, Margaret (Maggie) Dolvin (Fulton County coroner), 167

Eil Malk Island (Mecherechar), 41, 43, 259-60
Elbe Day (April 25, 1945), 324
Equator line-crossing ceremony ("Rites of Neptune"), 34, 203-4
Ethier, Florence Achatz, 283

"Fred Waring Show" broadcast, 61
Fischer, Max Henry (LCI(G)-729), 187, 282

Galligan, George Thomas (Chula Vista resident), 123
Georgia: absentee ballots, 107, 168, 236; agriculture, 300; cigarette shortage, 248, 271; coal shortage, 281, 288; elections, 167-68, 191, 201; flu epidemic, 97, 102; gasoline rationing, 292, 341; hillbilly music, 144; Kudsu club, 295; mosquitoes, 177; poll tax, 279; synthetic tires, 183; tornados, 129; weather, 178

After the war is over

General Motors (UAW) strike, 366
Georgia Farmers' Market Bulletin, 299-300, 310
Georgia Institute of Technology (Georgia Tech), 10-11, 17-18, 21, 41, 66, 69n, 93n, 229, 244, 246, 253, 266, 283n; and Sigma Chi fraternity, 5, 17, 21, 52, 116n, 234n
Grand Canyon, 147-48, 151
Grand International Brotherhood of Locomotive Engineers, Division No. 368 (Atlanta), 9, 192, 194, 225
Guadalcanal, 24, 35, 188n, 190n, 203
Guam, 44, 194, 268n, 321

Halsey, Jr., William Frederick ("Bull"), 364
Hansard, Victor (Vic) Bond (LCI(L) captain), 223
Haynam, Arnold ("Arnie") Wayne (co-worker SSG), 235
Haynes, Emma Jean (grandmother), 10
Hitler, Adolf, death of, 47, 326
Howell, Ethleen Horne, 183
Howell, Jr., Hugh Hawkins, 21-23, 88, 97, 99, 111, 124, 135, 149, 160-62, 164, 166, 169, 174-75, 178, 181, 183, 199, 235, 257, 297, 300, 330, 334-35, 337, 340, 346
Howell, Sr., Hugh Hawkins, 23, 133-34, 137
Hudson, Etta Virginia (aunt), 191n
Hudson, Halbert Austin (Big Halbert) (uncle), 70, 249, 307, 313, 317
Hudson, Jr., Halbert (Hal, Jr.) Austin (cousin), 249, 288-89, 304-05, 307, 313, 316-17, 350-51
Hudson, James Lonnie (grandfather), 9
Hudson, John Wesley (uncle), 70, 245, 338
Hudson, Lillian Naomi Cook (aunt), 313
Hudson, Meldrin (Meddy) (aunt), 111, 360

Iwo Jima, 29, 290

Jimmye's Beauty Salon ("the shop"), 14, 41, 67, 78, 116, 125, 127, 143-44, 159, 176, 227, 239, 255, 285, 292, 317, 343, 350, 355
Jones, Clinton Story (LCI(G)-729), 187

379

After the war is over

Kappa Delta Kappa (K.D.K.) socials, 14, 21, 41, 101n, 234, 346
Keel, Louise, 116-17, 119
Kayangel Atoll, 41, 243n
Key West, Florida, 29, 47, 78-79, 84, 246
Kossol Passage, 38-40, 43, 211n, 228n, 237n, 240n, 259-60, 268n

Landing Craft Infantry (LCI): Flotilla 13 ("Black Cat"), 24, 26-27, 30-33, 35, 37, 39, 44-45, 74, 98, 102, 108, 117, 122, 155, 188n, 190n, 192n, 213, 216, 219, 231, 246, 258, 262, 266, 302, 313, 361; insignia of, 160-61, 375
Landing Craft Infantry (Gunboat): 29-31, 202, 291; LCI(G)-396, 43-44, 274; LCI(G)-472, 238; LCI(G)-729, 30-34, 36-41, 43-45, 155n, 168n, 182, 185-87, 192n, 202, 207n, 208n, 209n, 211n, 213, 217-18, 221n, 228n, 229n, 230, 233n, 237n, 240n, 246n, 262n, 264n, 267, 268n, 273, 285, 294, 304, 320, 322; mascot of, 307
Landing Craft Infantry (Large): 24, 26-27, 291; LCI(L)-474, 26-29, 31, 74, 76, 77, 81, 83, 87-88, 92, 97; LCI(L)-729, 31, 261; LCI(L)-732, 233n; LCI(L)-737, 44, 319-23, 325, 327, 329
Land, Jr., Fort Elmo (Navy fighter pilot), 278
Landing ship tank (LST), 24, 209, 235, 312n
Lang, Jr., Robert McDonald (Georgia Tech alum), 166
Lawlor, Jr., Edwin ("Eddy") Daniel (LCI(G)-729), 187
LeVee, Clifford Guy ("Cliff"), 27-29, 31, 33, 44, 74, 76, 80, 83-84, 88, 108, 112, 130, 142-43, 146, 155-56, 165, 174-75, 180-82, 186, 212, 216, 257-58, 261, 265, 271, 282, 291-93, 299, 303, 313, 362; writes to Stella Pullen, 259-60, 268, 273, 275-76
Linder, Thomas (Tom) Mercer (Georgia commissioner of agriculture), 300
Lindow, Donald August (Supply Corps School alum), 112

Martin, Byrne Fowler (LCI(G)-729 captain), 186, 282
McGinty, Mary Frances Gudger, 194, 271
McGinty, Robert Franklin ("Bobby"), 21-22, 44, 61, 63-64, 69, 74, 91, 160, 165, 171, 194, 201, 207, 227, 235, 243, 263-64, 267, 269, 271, 284, 297, 368, 371-72

After the war is over

Miller, Jr., Frank (LCI(G)-729), 186-87
Moffett, Anna Fay (girlfriend of Hugh Howell), 111, 162, 297, 335, 337
Morrill, II, John Henry (LCI Flotilla 13 commander), 25, 31, 44, 74, 92, 106, 114, 116, 132, 202, 203n, 291, 296, 302-03, 361n

O'Keefe Junior High School, 11
Okinawa, 321

Palau Islands, 34-35, 39-40, 196n, 361
Panama Canal Zone, 29, 84-85, 102, 114
Pearl Harbor, 32-34, 45, 92, 117-18, 143, 155n, 163, 166, 168n, 169, 172-73, 182, 203, 206, 215, 264, 270, 323
Peil, John William (LCI(G)-396), 146, 274, 282, 298
Peleliu Island, 35, 38-39, 43, 264n
Perry, Lynn Dennis (LCI(L)-474 crew member), 81
Prewitt, Joseph (Joe) Sidney (Supply Corps School alum), 244
Pugh, Mary Louise (wife), 372-73
Pullen, Earl Winfield (LCT Flotilla 6), 69
Pullen, Greenville (great-grandfather), 9
Pullen, Stella Marie Hudson (mother), 9-11, 14, 41-42, 45, 47, 54, 60, 67, 102; health issues, 105, 138, 226, 252, 254, 311; car accident, 191n
Pullen, Thomas Jefferson (grandfather), 9
Pullen, Walter Hudson: ancestors of, 9-10; as a Boy Scout, 10-12, 364; education of, 11-18; commissioned as Ensign, 23; training at Navy Supply Corps School, 23; assigned to U.S. Naval Amphibious Training Base, Solomons, Maryland, 23-26, 65-73; visits Key West, 78-79; passes through Canal Zone, 84-85; in San Diego, California, 29-30, 87-153; illnesses of, 101, 106, 134, 143, 145, 278, 282; bicycle stolen, 98, 102; on leave, 99, 114, 308; golfing, 30, 33, 130, 146, 150, 163, 180-81, 206, 274, 373; promotion to Lieutenant (junior grade), 30, 114; visits Grand Canyon, 30, 147-48; at Pearl Harbor, 32-33, 163-83, 206, 270; initiated into "Rites of Neptune", 34; during operations on Angaur Island, 34-39, 204-5; complains about Navy censors,

After the war is over

41, 78, 164, 167, 180; visits Guam, 44; at U.S. Naval Hospital, Memphis, Tennessee, 45, 331-56; at U.S. Naval Repair Base, New Orleans, Louisiana, 45, 345, 350, 357-70; discharge from Navy, 371; marriage, 373; death and burial, 374

Pullen, Walter Stanford (father), 9, 41, 45, 47, 55, 102, 128; injured on job, 192, 194, 200, 217, 225, 229, 242

Pullen, William James (LCI(G)-729 crew member), 151

Putnam, Glenn Richard (Supply Corps School alum), 58, 340

Pyle, Ernest ("Ernie") Taylor (war correspondent), 321

Roddey, Frederick Preston (lieutenant, U.S. Signal Corps), 360

Roosevelt, Eleanor, 169

Roosevelt, Franklin D., 134, 168-69, 193, 201, 211, 315-16, 363

Sampson, Allen Theodore (Marney's brother), 347

Saginaw Steering Gear (SSG) Division GM plant (Michigan), 18-19, 51-55; (Atlanta), 106

San Francisco (United Nations) Conference, 326

Schonian Harbor (Sebeseb), 40, 43-44, 259

Second-Ponce de Leon Baptist Church (Atlanta), 69n, 373-74

Sharp, Thomas Monterville (disbursing officer for Flotilla 3), 276

Sinkwich, Sr., Francis (Frank) (Heisman Trophy winner), 66

Skillman, John Henry (Naval Supply Depot at San Diego), 275

Smart, Atwood ("Woody") Ora (Supply Corps School alum), 211-12

Smart, Charles Allen (author of *RFD*), 312

Solomons Islands, 34, 203, 224

Southern Railway Company in Atlanta, 9-10

St. Mark United Methodist Church, 11

Stanford, Anna Azar (grandmother), 9

Swift, Margaret (Marney) Jane Sampson, 346-48

Swift, III, Thomas Madison (Marney's estranged husband), 347-48

Talmadge, Eugene, 279

Theriot, Hewitt Paul, 360-61, 365-67

After the war is over

Thweatt, Mary Jane (former K.D.K. fraternity date), 234
Tijuana, Mexico, 30, 102-5, 109
Tire rationing, 339
Tojo, Hideki (Japanese prime minister), 173
Truman, Harry S., 47, 271n, 315, 321n, 345
Tulagi Island, 188n, 190-92n, 196n, 203, 206, 214, 224

Ulithi Atoll, 38, 259
U.S. Naval Amphibious Training Base, Solomons, Maryland, 23-26, 65, 69, 73, 76-77, 88, 98, 116
U.S. Naval Hospital Memphis, Tennessee, 45, 331-56
U.S. Naval Repair Base, New Orleans, Louisiana, 45, 345, 350, 354, 356-70
U.S. Navy Morale, Welfare, and Recreation (MWR) program, 188
U.S. Repair Base, San Diego, California, 29, 31, 87-93
U.S. Navy Supply Corps School, Harvard University, 23, 27-28, 41, 57-64, 88, 149

V-E Day (May 8, 1945), 45-46, 324, 327-28
V-Disc records, 325
V-J Day, 345-46
V-Mail, 19-20, 155, 157, 166, 169, 248; microfilm records, 284

Women Accepted for Volunteer Emergency Service (WAVES), 343-44, 356
Wilkie, Lewis Wendell (Republican nominee for President), 214
Williams, Gladstone (Atlanta newspaper correspondent), 211
Willis, Ralph Holland (Georgia Tech alum), 92-93, 103, 112, 131
WSB-Radio (Atlanta), 144, 343

Yoo Passage, 41, 43, 246n

www.ingramcontent.com/pod-product-compliance
Lightning Source LLC
Chambersburg PA
CBHW050428240426
43661CB00055B/2313